Code Choice in the Language Classroom

Full details of all our publications can be found on http://www.multilingual-matters.com, or by writing to Multilingual Matters, St Nicholas House, 31-34 High Street, Bristol BS1 2AW, UK.

Code Choice in the Language Classroom

Glenn S. Levine

MULTILINGUAL MATTERS
Bristol • Buffalo • Toronto

Library of Congress Cataloging in Publication Data
A catalog record for this book is available from the Library of Congress.
Levine, Glenn S. (Glenn Scott), 1964-
Code Choice in the Language Classroom/Glenn S. Levine.
Includes bibliographical references and index.
1. Code switching (Linguistics) 2. Bilingualism. 3. Language and languages–Study and teaching. I. Title.
P115.3.L48 2010
306.44–dc222010041286

British Library Cataloguing in Publication Data
A catalogue entry for this book is available from the British Library.

ISBN-13: 978-1-84769-333-4 (hbk)
ISBN-13: 978-1-84769-332-7 (pbk)

Multilingual Matters
UK: St Nicholas House, 31-34 High Street, Bristol BS1 2AW, UK.
USA: UTP, 2250 Military Road, Tonawanda, NY 14150, USA.
Canada: UTP, 5201 Dufferin Street, North York, Ontario M3H 5T8, Canada.

Copyright © 2011 Glenn S. Levine.

All rights reserved. No part of this work may be reproduced in any form or by any means without permission in writing from the publisher.

Typeset by Datapage International Ltd.
Printed and bound in Great Britain by Short Run Press Ltd.

To my wife, Ursula

and to the memory of Frank Donahue, a great professor, mentor, and friend

That should have done it, that should have made the Camel pack a vessel of symbolic truth unprecedented in the last quarter of the twentieth century, a virtual lunar Bible, compact, accessible, and concise, as befitting a transistorized age. But the Red Beards, excited now, had a masterpiece by the tail and didn't want to turn it loose. They decided to take a further, daring step. They would try sending a *word* from their dimension into ours.

    How carefully that word was chosen!
    The word that allows *yes*, the word that makes *no* possible.
    The word that puts the free in freedom and takes obligation out of love.
    The word that throws a window open after the final door is closed.
    The word upon which all adventure, all exhilaration, all meaning, all honor depends.
    The word that fires evolution's motor of mud.
    The word that the cocoon whispers to the caterpillar.
    The word that molecules recite before bonding.
    The word that separates that which is dead from that which is living.
    The word no mirror can turn around.
    In the beginning there was the word and the word was

CHOICE

Tom Robbins, *Still Life with Woodpecker* (1980: 190)

Contents

Acknowledgments xi
Preface xiii

Part 1: Conceptual Framework
1 Monolingual Norms and Multilingual Realities. 3
    Code Choice in the Classroom, the Classroom in Society 3
    Code Choice and Language Pedagogy 5
    Five Myths about First Language Use in the Second
    Language Classroom. 9
    Summary and Conclusion. 17

2 The Conundrum of Babel: Toward a Theoretical Framework
    for a Multilingual Approach 19
    Striving for Monolingualism in a Multilingual World 19
    Why not a Psycholinguistic Approach to Classroom
    Code Choice? 22
    Sociocultural and Ecological Perspectives of Second
    Language Learning, Classroom Practice and Classroom
    Code Choice 23
    Tenets about Second Language Learning in Relation
    to Code Choice 43
    Summary and Conclusion. 44

3 What is a Code? What is Code-Switching? 47
    Language and Code 47
    Code-Switching. 49
    Summary and Conclusion. 65

Part 2: Empirical Support
4 The Code Choice Status Quo of the Language Classroom. 69
    The First Language Elephant in the Room. 69
    Empirical Research on Classroom Code Choice. 71
    A Case Study of Two Language Classes 84

Teasing out a Default Condition 98
Summary and Conclusion 100

5   Classroom Code Choice: Toward Becoming Bilingual 102
    Discourse Analysis as a Tool for Understanding
    Classroom Code Choice 102
    Example 5.1: An Activity in an Introductory
    German Class 107
    Example 5.2: A Discussion in an Intermediate
    German Class 115
    The Code Choice Status Quo 120
    Summary and Conclusion 121

Part 3: Curriculum

6   An Architecture of Classroom Code Choice 125
    Realizing the Multilingual Classroom Community
    of Practice 125
    Learner Training 130
    Co-Construction of Norms 144
    Multilingual Content Instruction 153
    Critical Reflection 156
    Summary and Conclusion 159

7   Getting from Marked to Unmarked and Back Again:
    Articulation of Multilingual Classroom Communities
    of Practice 160
    Principled Heterogeneity and Emerging Bilingualism 160
    Stage I: Co-Construction of Multilingual Norms 165
    Stage II: Emerging Multilingual Classroom 165
    Stage III: Multilingual Classroom Community
    of Practice 167
    Summary and Conclusion 168

Epilogue: Blessings of Babel 169
References 173
Index 182

Acknowledgments

I would like to thank many people for their contributions to this book. I have learned so much from the graduate student instructors in the Department of German at the University of California, Irvine; thank you for the many classroom visits, for the countless conversations about all aspects of language teaching and learning, and for your inspired and inspiring teaching. In particular, I am especially grateful to Natalie Eppelsheimer, Simona Moti, Magdalena Tarnawska and Jason Wilby for their helpful insights during the early stages of this project. Thank you to the UCI Department of German and the UCI Humanities Center for their support of parts of this research. My thanks to Carlee Arnett, Robert Blake, David Brenner, Claire Kramsch, James Lee, Ernesto Macaro and Hiram Maxim for their feedback and encouragement at key points in the work on this book. I am profoundly grateful to Alison Phipps for her wise comments, and for helping bring the manuscript to the attention of Multilingual Matters. Thank you as well to Anna Roderick at Multilingual Matters for her patience and encouragement throughout, and to Catherine Hogan for her excellent copyediting. Thank you to the anonymous reviewers for their helpful comments and revision suggestions. I am very grateful to Kurt Buhanan for his phenomenal editing work, and to Grit Liebscher for her reading of and comments on the manuscript. Finally, I am grateful every day for my wife, Ursula; you have given me the strength and inspiration to keep working, and you have been both patient and prodding when I needed these the most.

Preface

Sins of the Dogma

The idea for this book originated, like many other scholarly projects related to adult instructed second language acquisition (SLA), in observations and experiences in the language classroom. Having been trained in Krashen/Terrell-style communicative approaches to the teaching of German (Krashen & Terrell, 1983/2000), over many years I diligently pursued a satisfactory approach to target language use. Although I became adept at producing interactionally modified learner input – thereby keeping almost all of my teacher-talk in German – I was often frustrated by many students' apparent unwillingness or inability to join me in the 'exclusive target-language use' endeavor, especially during pair or group activities. Complicating the matter was my increasing shift to a more task-based, learner-centered approach to classroom activities, because the more control I gave students over the content and direction of classroom communication, the greater their tendency to unabashedly employ English rather than German! I noticed that in order to keep students in the second language (L2), I often held the reins of communication tightly under control. Of course, this also was not satisfactory. So, at one point, I began integrating explicit 'strategies instruction' into my lessons, involving, for the most part, discussion (usually in English) on the importance of exclusive L2 use and ways to 'stay in the L2'. I sought to involve students in the process of creating a 'simulated L2 environment', as I sometimes called it. In short, at the very least, I succeeded in stigmatizing the use of English to such an extent that learners were oftentimes more enthusiastic to keep all communication in German than I was. In the long run, while many students demonstrated greater 'fluency' than those in my earlier classes, their 'accuracy' in verbal interactions remained as much of a problem as ever. But, for the time being, I was content with greater fluency and was not so concerned with (or aware of) other issues, such as language socialization or L2 literacy.

With this canned approach to classroom L2 use, I began working as a German language program director. I encouraged, and at times attempted to require, graduate student instructors to adopt the approach. The attempt understandably, and in hindsight fortunately, failed. For into the mix came not only different levels and types of pedagogical training in and perspectives of second-language (L2) acquisition among the instructors, but also diverse teaching styles and personalities that did not connect with what I had to say about exclusive L2 use. It took some time for me to realize that this diversity of attitudes and personalities among the instructors was not only *not* a hindrance to providing undergraduates with effective, dynamic language instruction, it was, in fact, the key to it. For if the group of learners in a given language class is anything, it is a messy (for the researcher, anyway), complicated gathering that defies most attempts we make to fit square pegs into round holes. This became especially apparent in the occasional, candid remarks made by some students on course evaluations and elsewhere about the L2 use 'policies' in their classes. Some people expressed that they felt not only frustration about it, but even anxiety. These comments, along with many conversations with graduate student instructors and undergraduate students in the language classes, led me to rethink my position on exclusive L2 use, fueled also by my observations during classroom visits that even in the most stringent exclusive-L2-use classes, many learners *still* made frequent use of that forbidden code: English! Thus, over the last several years – guided in part by the pursuit to integrate sociocultural theory and ecological approaches into language teaching and program direction – my leitmotif in language teacher training has become the acknowledgment and encouragement of instructors to find their own groove in all pedagogical matters, including in their approach to L2 and English use, and to actively seek their individual classes' and students' groove in similar ways.

Now that I have unburdened myself of my earlier sin of dogmatic devotion to a rigid methodology of exclusive L2 use, we arrive at the central question that this book seeks to answer: how do we manage L2 and first language (L1) use in the language classroom, if it is to be managed at all? I believe that communication in the classroom is 'manageable' in many, but not all, regards, as I will show. In any case, the ambiguous verb 'manage' will be supplanted later on with the notions of affordances for learning through multiple code use, and curricular architectures as part of a multilingual classroom community of practice. Despite abandoning the 'exclusive' position, the process I went through to arrive at my post-exclusive-L2-use approach was instructive, and many aspects of the pedagogical model described here derive from the classroom practices I developed during that period of my career.

The question also arises of whether my own espousal of linguistic diversity implies a free-for-all of code use in the classroom. While it will be shown here that multiple codes are always at work in any language classroom regardless of explicit interventions, a theoretically motivated, principled approach to code choice can help teachers and students have what they need to regard the language classroom as a multilingual environment and as part of the 'real world'. For unlike language contact situations in the real world, language teachers have a good deal of control over the code choice conventions of the classroom, but primarily (or only) if the students are made partners in the co-construction and negotiation of those conventions. This book is about ways to think about and implement instruction that gives learners this important role.

This book is intended for adult L2 language teachers (secondary and university level), language program directors and coordinators, language curriculum designers and planners, and researchers in classroom SLA. As such, it would be useful as a coursebook on pedagogical methods and approaches for teachers in training. While I assume throughout some background knowledge of applied linguistics, I have attempted to define terms and discuss the key issues in this book in ways that are accessible and useful to language professionals not directly or frequently involved with the scholarly literature in linguistics, applied linguistics or theory. My first concern for all readers is that the ideas presented are not just well grounded in intellectual debates of the last few generations, but practicable in the classroom at the level of the curriculum, the lesson plan and the crucial moment-to-moment classroom interaction.

Organization of the Book

Developing a multilingual approach to classroom code choice requires our discussion to range into diverse directions, encompassing consideration of applied linguistics, sociocultural theory, bilingual studies and, of course, language pedagogy. It requires a coherent conceptual framework derived from theoretical approaches believed to facilitate successful L2 learning. To justify the multilingual approach proposed, we require empirical evidence of the imperative for it. And because, in my view, no scholarship on instructed L2 learning is worth much if it finds no application in the curriculum, we require a viable curricular framework that teachers can implement or adapt in their classrooms. Therefore, the book is divided into three parts. Part 1 consists of three chapters that establish a conceptual framework for a multilingual approach to language classroom communication. Chapter 1 offers a clarification of the goals of the book through a presentation of working assumptions about code choice and language pedagogy, and a critical look at some of the prevailing assumptions and what I hold to be myths about 'mainstream' language classroom practice as it pertains to code choice and the educated, monolingual, standard-language native speaker target. The purpose is to establish why the language classroom should be considered a multilingual rather than a monolingual environment.

In Chapter 2, a theoretical framework for a multilingual approach to classroom code choice is developed. Several models and approaches are outlined that come under the heading of sociocultural theory, ecological linguistics and the semiotics of language learning, with particular consideration of their relevance and usefulness to the issue of classroom code choice. These models share the perspective of language learning as a fundamentally social, dynamic, complex and politically marked undertaking.

In Chapter 3, I explore ways of thinking about *code* in relation to language as social semiotic, and I define and discuss the linguistic practice of code-switching. The two competing models of code-switching as social activity are presented, the interactional approach and Myers-Scotton's (1983, 1993, 2002) Markedness Model and the related Rational Choice Model. It is argued that both these models are useful for teachers in understanding code-switching as social activity, and both can be dealt with in the classroom in various ways. Thereafter, I describe a discourse-analytical approach to code-switching, suggesting that it is both useful for the empirical analysis of classroom code-switching and helpful in our rethinking of classroom code choice from an ecological perspective.

While Part 1 serves to provide a theoretical motivation for a multilingual approach to classroom communication, the purpose of Part 2, consisting of two chapters, is to offer empirical evidence of the pedagogical imperative for a multilingual approach. In Chapter 4, a sketch is presented of what I call the status quo or default condition of typical university-level language classrooms in the USA. The purpose is to demonstrate empirically why it would not be sufficient to simply 'allow' the L1 in the classroom without the sort of theoretically motivated approach proposed in this book. I will also show how the L1 and not the L2 appears to prevail in the group dynamics of 'typical' language classes, at least more often than would be desirable for the maximal or optimal use of L2 (Macaro, 2009). Along with a review of the pertinent empirical studies, my arguments are supported by evidence from a case study of two university-level language classes.

Moving beyond the descriptive portrait of the language classroom code choice default condition, in Chapter 5 I take the reader through a discourse analysis of learner code-switching. For this, I use Gee's (2005) method of analyzing discourse, which is compatible with an ecological perspective, in that it views the moment of code-switching to be a choice made by a speaker against the backdrop of multiple layers of context. Here, I seek to 'ferret out the unapparent import of things' (Geertz, 1973: 26) in L2 learner code-switching in order to establish a framework both for analyzing the sorts of code choices made in the classroom and as an empirical foundation for the curricular architecture presented in the last two chapters.

Part 3, which consists of the final two chapters, represents an implementation of the ideas presented to that point in approaching curriculum design, teaching and articulation. In Chapter 6, I formulate a specific curricular manifestation of a multilingual approach. I present ways of understanding the progression from the code choice status quo (Chapter 4), in which the L1 is effectively the unmarked code and the L2 is the marked code, toward the objective identified for the approach, that the L2 and the L1 serve dynamic and varied functions and can be either marked or unmarked depending on the wishes and inclinations of the speakers in situated interaction (students and instructor) to either follow or flout co-constructed code choice norms. In the process, a second goal is pursued, namely, to raise learner awareness of and ability to assess code choice practices and their implications in the classroom, and to place code choice in the larger context of L2 use and developing bilingualism. Examples are offered of the sorts of activities that I believe would facilitate learner awareness, critical reflection, co-construction and analysis of code choice norms, and affordances for learning in and about the L2.

Chapter 7 deals with the implications and issues of a multilingual approach to code choice for language program articulation. I first discuss horizontal articulation in terms of principled heterogeneity and vertical articulation in terms of emerging bilingualism. Thereafter, three stages in the development of a multilingual classroom community of practice are described.

The book closes with an Epilogue addressing a few large-scale questions and issues of code choice and language education.

Part 1
Conceptual Framework

Chapter 1
Monolingual Norms and Multilingual Realities

> *In our days of frequent border crossings, and of multilingual multicultural foreign language classrooms, it is appropriate to rethink the monolingual native speaker norms as the target of foreign language education. As we revisit the marked and unmarked forms of language usership, I propose that we make the intercultural speaker the unmarked form, the infinite of language use, and the monolingual monocultural speaker a slowly disappearing species or a nationalistic myth.*
> (Kramsch, 1998: 30)

> *We reach here the very principle of myth: it transforms history into nature.*
> (Barthes, 1972: 129)

Code Choice in the Classroom, the Classroom in Society

The purpose of this book is to provide language teachers, teachers in training and teacher trainers with a conceptual and curricular framework for rethinking what happens in the classroom in terms of multiple codes. Code choice in classroom communication is admittedly a frequent and central concern for teachers and students. For teachers, it usually has to do with preventing students from using their first language (L1); for students, it is often about how to use the L1 and still function and succeed in the language classroom. In scholarship on second language (L2) learning, code choice has remained, for the most part, a tangential concern. A second purpose of this book is, then, to move the issue of code choice to a more central place in our thinking about L2 theory, curriculum, practice and research.

It is no accident that the title of this book emphasizes *code choice* rather than code-switching, because much of what I will argue is based on learner choices in classroom interaction and teacher choices in curriculum design and teaching practice. For the typical high school or university student in the USA, whether or not to study an L2 is often not a matter of choice. But most other aspects of the endeavor are: which language to study, when to study, how much energy or effort to invest in it, whether and when to speak the language (except when called on by the teacher), and crucially, whether one should buy into using the L2 in the contexts in which the instructor and the curriculum mandate.[1] Unfortunately, many students are probably not aware of many of these choices as they make them. Our job as curriculum designers and teachers, then, is to find ways of raising learners' awareness of choice, of facilitating the management of code-switching in classroom conversation, which means raising awareness of which language to use, with whom, when and why. The larger purpose of this endeavor is to provide students with affordances for language learning through multiple code use in the classroom, and ultimately to help them become bilingual users of L1 and L2. It is also to help teachers and learners to recognize and realize the language classroom's potential, not just for learning a new language and culture, but to make critical intercultural connections about language, discourses and life.

To accomplish these goals, we must develop an approach to treating the language classroom as an authentic social environment in its own right, rather than as an artificial aberration from normal social life, and for promoting learner autonomy by allowing learners a say in the ways code choices are made. For language professionals, whether researchers or classroom teachers, this book seeks to call attention to an area of instructed L2 learning that has received relatively little attention, and actually no attention at all in some of the areas of inquiry in which it would be most needed.

In its current 'post-methods' form (Kumaravadivelu, 2003; Richards & Rodgers, 2001: 244), L2 teaching and learning is a varied and sophisticated contrivance, striving to be a virtual second-language and second-culture environment within four walls and against the clock of perpetually inadequate numbers of instructional contact hours. In recent years, numerous scholars have called our attention to many problematic aspects of the ways we understand this ostensibly artificial microcosm (Atkinson, 2002; Breen, 1985; Firth & Wagner, 1997; Kumaravadivelu, 2003, 2005; Lantolf & Appel, 1994; Reagan & Osborn, 2002; Savignon, 2002; Schulz, 2006; Tudor, 2001; van Lier, 1988). One of these aspects is that, by and large, a *monolingual* set of norms and ideals is assumed and applied to classroom practices (Blyth, 1995; Butzkamm, 2003; V.J. Cook, 2001;

Kramsch, 1997, 1998, 2009; Turnbull & Dailey-O'Cain, 2009). We proceed with the assumption that if the instructor teaches in the L2 and students carry out activities in the same code, then the lingua franca of the classroom *is* the L2. At worst, we stigmatize the use of the L1. At best, we often see little pedagogical value in its use (Macaro, 2001). Considering the limited number of contact hours of most university language courses, this is understandable; most instructors rightly seek to use every available minute for meaningful L2 communication. Yet, as observed and demonstrated empirically by some scholars, the language classroom is a *multilingual* environment (Antón & DiCamilla, 1999; Belz, 2002, 2003; Blyth, 1995; Chavez, 2003; V.J. Cook, 1999, 2001; Kramsch, 1997, 1998; Levine, 2003, 2005; Liebscher & Dailey-O'Cain, 2004). This means that for each learner, at least two languages are involved in the L2 learning process. For us to deny, in our pedagogy, a role for the cognitively and socially dominant language, is to ignore a large part of the L2 learning process and the individual learner's personal experience. With an increasing acceptance of eclectic and critical approaches to language teaching and learning and of pedagogical implementation of ecological and sociocultural approaches, the time is ripe for the development of a principled, *multilingual approach* to language classroom communication.

Code Choice and Language Pedagogy

The multilingual approach I propose proceeds from four working assumptions about code choice and language teaching and learning. First, the curricular proposals presented in this book do not mean that the classroom should seek to re-create the norms of societal multilingual environments (V.J. Cook, 2001).[2] Just as the assumption of a monolingual norm is naïve and insufficient on its own, so too is the assumption that it is equivalent to a multilingual environment outside the classroom. The contrived nature of communication in most language classrooms is ubiquitous (compared with non-instructional learning environments; see van Lier, 1988, 1996; Wenger, 1998), and any pedagogy considering code choice must balance the fact that it is a multilingual environment with the fact that it is, in many regards, an 'artificial' one, at least in terms of the settings and contexts that prevail in people's daily lives. Edmondson (1985: 162) points out that, 'we seek in the classroom to teach people how to talk when they are not being taught'. While this is certainly true, it is also crucial to note that this classroom artificiality of communication does not mean it is not also *authentic* human communication. Indeed, this very feature of classroom communication allows us – and, in fact, requires us – to develop a principled, theoretically motivated approach to the use of both L2 and L1. This book offers such an approach, to explore the ways in which language learners should acquire not only the idealized monolingual norms of communicative competence, but also those of *multilingual* and *intercultural* communicative competence (Byram, 1997; Kramsch, 1993).[3]

The second working assumption is that some sorts of classroom code choice practices can facilitate L2 use, and thus development, and some sorts can undermine or frustrate it. As yet, I don't believe anyone has been able to test this claim empirically, it is one of those aspects of teaching and learning that teachers just 'know'. It is also one of the red threads, whether expressed or not, in much of the literature dealing with code choice in the language classroom. Put another way, the question is: does L1 use foster or hinder L2 use and successful L2 learning? The problem with testing this empirically is that one would seek to control for myriad other factors. Yet, code choice is not the same as a morphosyntactic or phonological feature that can be identified, observed, counted and so forth (at Time 1 the feature X is absent and at Time 2 it is present). Code choice pervades all sorts of encounters between teacher and students and among students, from the first day of introductory instruction through the most advanced levels, and locating cause–effect relationships, or even significant associations, between particular code-switching practices and language gains would always lead back to a focus on other variables. This is perhaps also one reason why many scholars who have sought to account for classroom code choice have adopted constructivist or sociocultural approaches, rather than approaches rooted in psycholinguistics and cognitive science prevalent in much of the literature on second language acquisition (SLA). So, instead of pursuing a linear sort of cause and effect chain, in this book I will attempt to show some of the ways code choice practices constitute a set of discourses all their own, discourses that intersect with and influence certain of the numerous discourses at work in the language classroom.

Following from the second assumption, it is also assumed that maximal or optimal L2 use indeed contributes to successful L2 learning, and that maximal or optimal L2 use in the classroom is a desirable situation toward which to strive.[4] This may sound like a self-evident truth, but hundreds of classroom visits over the years have convinced me that teachers, even those who would agree with this basic claim, do not often keep the idea in mind as they plan lessons and manage what happens in the classroom. In Chapter 4, I will detail what I believe to be the code choice 'status quo' of many typical communicative-approach language classrooms, and here it will be evident that even when most of a class is conducted in the L2, we cannot say that the L2 was used optimally or maximally, in part (but not only) because teachers tend to do most of the talking!

A fourth working assumption in this book is that teaching and learning in the secondary and university-level language classroom takes place most effectively in the framework of a principled, meaning- and task-based approach, one that responds to diverse learning styles and strategies, promotes learner autonomy and acknowledges the classroom as a sociocultural environment in its own right (i.e. not separate from the 'real world' though it often mimics or simulates situations in the real world), one that embraces the inherent complexity of L2 teaching and learning rather than continually seeking to reduce that complexity.

Before delving into the sociocultural and ecological approaches in Chapter 2, it should also be made clear to the reader that the admittedly eclectic approach to code choice proposed here does not translate into a free-for-all of pedagogical practices, techniques and methods based on the teacher's or students' intuitive judgments (for eclecticism in the popular sense often means just this sort of anything-goes perspective). Rather, as asserted by Kumaravadivelu (2003: 30), we should proceed in a 'responsibly eclectic' manner (see also Larsen-Freeman, 2002), that is, tap into a range of methods and approaches, but in a principled way. Geertz (1973: 5) put it well when he wrote that 'eclecticism is self-defeating not because there is only one direction in which it is useful to move, but because there are so many: it is necessary to choose'. Thus, an appeal to principled pedagogical eclecticism with regard to code choice means that we must ourselves choose a path; to my mind, principled eclecticism means embracing the complexity of the issue based wholly on a rigorously defined theoretical framework. Too much of what language teachers practice – and I am guilty of this in my own courses – derives from often incommensurable theoretical approaches, approaches that many teachers are often unaware of when designing and carrying out lessons. In this book, I seek to make some of these theoretical approaches transparent and useful to the classroom teacher and language program director.

A further conceptual clarification is in order: the pedagogical model proposed in this book is not only about method or curriculum design. In line with the ecological perspective proposed by Kramsch (2002a) and van Lier (2004), methodology is just one aspect of the local, dynamic social environment of the classroom. Hence, I attempt to demonstrate the optimal conditions for a multilingual classroom community of practice, facilitated by a pedagogical or methodological framework, which I will call a 'curricular architecture'. As will be shown, an ecological perspective necessitates viewing language learning not as the linear acquisition of a set of linguistic features or objects, but rather as a complex, dynamic human activity (Larsen-Freeman & Cameron, 2008). Code choice practices are, of course, just one part of the ecology of L2 classroom language, but I offer a framework for 'designing' conditions likely to provide affordances for learning through code choice awareness and practices. Multilingual classroom norms thus serve as a starting point and a vehicle for different sorts of communication and learning.

As a combination of theoretical discussion, empirical research report and pedagogical model intended primarily for language teachers and language program directors, this book also represents a rejection of the ubiquitous theory/practice dichotomy, which I believe has been a millstone around the neck of language teachers for decades. Like van Lier (1996: 2–3), I regard theory, research and practice as 'an essential unity in the process of doing curriculum; theorizing, researching, and practicing are thus inseparable ingredients in the professional conduct of a language educator'. I offer here some new ways to think about a key feature of the language classroom environment that I believe deserves greater attention among language professionals: the way the students and teacher choose and negotiate their use of the L1 and the L2 to 'do curriculum' (van Lier, 1996: 2). Thus, the book is also about letting both teachers-in-training and language students in on aspects of language learning and use that have traditionally been the exclusive territory of the applied linguist, the theorist, the philosopher of language and the veteran language teacher (although often this latter group, too, has been excluded from debates about the nature of language, learning and activity). It is about moving away from considering language classroom communication as a bundle of discrete features and toward a view of the classroom as both a reflection of the world outside the classroom as well as a component of it, about exploring ways for learner and instructor reflection about code choice, and also, about politicizing that critical reflection (Gee, 2005), such that L2 learning itself becomes about much more than the acquisition of linguistic features or factual knowledge about culture(s).

There is also one thing that this book is *not* about. It is actually not about code-switching! Although the focus throughout is on dual or multiple code use among language class members, and Chapter 3 does deal directly with definitions and models of code-switching, no new model of code-switching is presented here. As will be seen in Chapter 3, I draw on those concepts and constructs in the code-switching literature that I regard as most useful and accessible and applicable in the classroom context. If anything new is offered to those who research code-switching, it is that some of the tools and methods of discourse analysis (Gee, 2005) can also be put to good use in understanding what students do with the L1 and L2 in classroom communication. In discussing code-switching, I proceed on two levels simultaneously: one is the level of theory that underpins the development of a multilingual pedagogical approach, and the other is the level to which learners and instructors may or should be exposed. Of course, this extended treatment of classroom code choice will hopefully serve to highlight what I see as a gap in the code-switching literature as it pertains to this interesting site of multiple code use.

Five Myths about First Language Use in the Second Language Classroom

The central position of this book is that the L1 has a productive and important role to play in successful L2 learning, and language teachers and learners can and should be aware of, reflect critically on, and in some ways, explicitly manage the ways in which the L1 and L2 are used in the classroom. This position does not appear to be in harmony with some widely held ideas about target language use in a mainstream communicative language teaching (CLT) framework. In fact, it is not: a multilingual approach can serve as a concrete tool for implementing many of the tenets of ecological and sociocultural theory (SCT) approaches proposed, as discussed by numerous scholars in recent years (Johnson, 2009; Kramsch, 1993; Lantolf, 2000; Lantolf & Thorne, 2006; van Lier, 1996, 2004) and perhaps affect a rethinking of CLT itself, to move the approach closer to its conceptual roots in Hymes's original notion of communicative competence (Breen & Candlin, 1980; Hymes, 1972; Kramsch, 2006). In these terms, some common and fairly robust assumptions about L1 use in L2 learning should be critically examined in order to foreground the imperative for a multilingual approach in ecological and SCT terms.[5] These include the following:

Myth 1. Monolingual L2 use is an intuitive mode of language classroom communication.
Myth 2. Monolingual native speaker norms represent an appropriate target for the language learner.
Myth 3. A monolingual approach reflects the reality of language classroom communication.
Myth 4. Use of the L1 in the language classroom could bring about fossilized errors or pidginization.
Myth 5. Use of the L1 minimizes time spent using the L2.

The purpose of this section is to lay the conceptual foundation for a multilingual approach to classroom code choice, to establish the parameters of the theoretical and pedagogical imperative for it. To accomplish this, I examine each of these five myths in turn.

Myth 1: Monolingual second language use is the most intuitive mode of communication in the language classroom

In this section, I consider the commonly held belief that monolingual L2 use is the most intuitive mode of communication in the classroom. Primarily, my aim is to show that the monolingual perspective has deep roots in American educational thought and policy, and as such cannot be regarded simply as a given in L2 language teaching.

In the US educational system, there are many things that we often regard as inevitable developments. Tudor (2001: 125) points out that 'all methodological choices rest on certain assumptions about the nature of language and of language learning', and that there are no unmarked pedagogical decisions. One assumption that has influenced myriad pedagogical choices is that a *monolingual approach* to L2 classroom communication is the most intuitive and natural, something to be taken for granted, the starting point for pedagogical choices that follow from it (e.g. about teacher-talk, the amount and nature of student participation). Horner and Trimbur (2002: 596), in calling into question the monolingual English principle underpinning modern university composition courses, describe in detail a 'chain of reifications that has settled into our current beliefs and practices' for teaching both composition and modern foreign languages. The authors describe the links in this chain as follows:

> First, the territorialization of languages according to national borders puts into place a reification of social identity in terms of language use: one's social identity is defined in terms of nationality, which itself is defined in terms of a *single language*. Next, language use itself

is reified and identified with a reification of language, located most commonly in writing, so that the variety, range, and shifting nature of language in use are reduced and restricted to the canons of "proper usage" embodied in standard written English. Finally, and of great relevance to writing teachers, these reifications are used to locate individual learners on a sequence of development fixed in its order, direction, and *sociopolitical significance*. (Horner & Trimbur, 2002: 596; my emphasis)

I understand this last point as a critique of the common practice of essentially pre-assigning within our curricula the sociopolitical significance of that which is learned. Horner and Trimbur proceed with the argument that our contemporary monolingual approach to both college-level composition and L2 teaching came to be hemmed in by a monolingual (or monolingualist) view rooted in the nationalistic, imperialist thinking of the 19th century, as well as by the primacy of the written over the spoken form of language. They trace the modernization of the university, a process whereby a multilingual approach to learning involving Latin, Greek and the student's vernacular was abandoned, supplanted by a curriculum in which English reigned supreme. Prior to these reforms, university students engaged (however loathingly) in discourse in Latin and Greek. Put another way, higher education had been embodied in earlier times by an inherent *multilingualism*, even though that multilingualism involved 'dead' rather than modern languages, an acceptance of a multiplicity of languages as part and parcel of the educational process. Through the subsequent reforms of teaching and learning (in the 19th century) in the USA, the modern 'foreign' languages were set up in service to English, the language in which most or all writing was then carried out. In relation to English, it came to be believed that 'the other modern languages are unnaturalized and alien, *foreign* languages territorialized outside the U.S. by the borders that map the nation-states as discrete geopolitical entities and the modern languages as separate departments in the university curriculum' (Horner & Trimbur, 2002: 607). Learning L2s also came to be 'viewed as a social attainment and a sign of good breeding rather than proper intellectual work' (Horner & Trimbur, 2002: 603). These factors contributed to what Horner and Trimbur (2002: 597) see as the problem of monolingualism, a 'limitation of U.S. culture', rooted in 'assumptions about language that were institutionalized around the turn of the century, at the high tide of imperialism, colonial adventure, and overseas missionary societies' that have 'become sedimented in the way we think about writing pedagogy and curriculum' (Horner & Trimbur, 2002: 608) and, relatedly, about language pedagogy and curriculum (see also Simon, 1980: Chapter 4).

The impact of this way of thinking on our approach to classroom code choice is twofold. First, we tend to take for granted the idea that in, say, a German class, only German should be used because, well, it's a *German* class, defined by the boundaries of a German department just as Germany is defined by its national boundaries. As such, there is little place for any other language(s). Second, this national-language view is itself based on a standardized version of German, basically reflecting the norms of *written* standard German, with little or no attention paid to social, regional, gender- or class-based variations of the spoken language (Valdman, 1989). And, of course, the issue of bilingual varieties of the German language (of which there are many, see, e.g. Dirim & Auer, 2004) are also not considered relevant to the L2 learning process. Third, the mainstream perspective described by Horner and Trimbur restricts the entire task of language learning to the acquisition of a skill – knowledge of a new grammatical and vocabulary system – rather than as a vehicle for humanistic inquiry and intellectual growth equal to those in other fields in the humanities. This narrow approach to code choice, while undoubtedly keeping things fairly simple for students linguistically, also restricts the possibilities of what learners could do with language and languages if the limitations of monolingualism were lifted. Learners would be free to engage in all sorts of language play, or in demonstrations of intellectual skill that move beyond the contextual functions laid out in most language textbooks (see Belz, 2002; G. Cook, 2000; Crystal, 2001). For while the logic that the classical languages 'provided students with cultural literacy, mental discipline, and the ability to write and speak well in English' (Horner & Trimbur, 2002: 599) is both outdated and logically flawed, the underlying premise is sound that a multilingual approach to education, whether in English composition or the foreign languages, can lead students to make crucial, intellectually stimulating comparisons among their languages and engage in more productive critical thinking than is currently the case in typical university-level L2 classes. This is also the premise put forth by Ortega (2010) in a plenary speech, in which she asserts a monolingual bias in most research of L2 acquisition, and criticizes the 'appearance of monolingualism as the norm', and the 'mirage of L2 acquisition as monolingual-like' (see also Cummins, 2007).

Myth 2: Monolingual native speaker norms represent an appropriate target for the language learner

In proposing a multilingual approach to classroom code choice, one crucial question to ask is, what do we expect L2 students to acquire? Kramsch (1998), who has probed this question in depth, puts the problem as follows:

> The question that has occupied linguists and language teachers alike, namely, "Can a non-native speaker *become* a native speaker?" loses much of its relevance if one looks at the problem not in a nativistic or educational perspective, but in a sociocultural one. The question has to be rephrased as: What prevents potentially bilingual outsiders from becoming integrated into a group? What is the authority of the speech community based on? (Kramsch, 1998: 23)

In questioning the authority of the native speaker, Kramsch's answer, also encapsulated in the epigraph of this chapter, is that not only does the native speaker target reflect a nationalistic myth, it also fails to acknowledge or make room for the diverse and interesting experiences and beliefs that learners bring to the task of language learning. Language teachers and SLA scholars have set up the elusive native speaker as the target, and not just the native speaker, but the *monolingual* native speaker. The problem can be compared to that of the fashion media and the public at large. The fashion media present us with images of ourselves as we (think we) would like to be, yet we know that most of us will never come close to hitting that attractive target (which, of course, does not stop us from spending billions trying!). In many of our language classes, we proceed with the (most often) unspoken understanding that most or even all learners will never achieve the native speaker norms (or even near-native speaker norms) that we demonstrate and carefully lay out for them. The dilemma is aggravated by the expertise of the instructor, whose language skills – while instructive – communicate to many learners that try as they might, they will probably never be as good as the instructor.

Therefore, Kramsch (1998: 24) proposes that language teachers, along with scholars of SLA, should seriously ask whether 'a pedagogy of the authentic should not better be replaced by a pedagogy of the appropriate'. A multilingual approach as the basis for language classroom communication can be viewed as an acknowledgment of the 'privilege of the intercultural speaker' and a foundation on which to integrate this speaker on her/his own terms into what we do in the classroom. In line with the functional goals of CLT, this sort of language training would also serve to prepare students more effectively for the realities of language use in the target country/culture(s), because no matter how far a learner may remain from 'near-native' proficiency in the L2, she/he will always be a multilingual, intercultural speaker. For this reason, principled training in the ways of communicating as such would be well placed in beginning and intermediate language instruction.

Myth 3: A monolingual approach reflects the reality of language classroom communication

The central argument of V.J. Cook's (2001: 405) case for allotting a formal role for the L1 in the language classroom is encapsulated in the metaphor *'naturam expelles furca, tamen usque recurret*. Like nature, the L1 creeps back in, however many times you throw it out with a pitchfork'. The often-quoted opening line of Romaine's (1995: 1) *Bilingualism* also rings true – 'it would certainly be odd to encounter a book with the title *Monolingualism*'. And yet, as Romaine (1995: 1) points out, 'it is precisely a monolingual perspective which modern linguistic theory takes as its starting point in dealing with basic analytical problems'. A generation later, Ortega (2010) lamented that the field of applied linguistics is still rooted in a monolingual bias. Not surprisingly, in studying and discussing the language classroom, many scholars and teachers also adopt the same sort of illusory perspective, buttressed by the proposals of organizations such as the American Council on the Teaching of Foreign Languages (ACTFL): 'ACTFL... recommends that language educators and their students use the target language as exclusively as possible (90% plus) during instructional time' (ACTFL, 2008). Proponents of what Tudor (2001) calls a 'hard' version of CLT might argue that the question of whether to 'allow' the L1 in the language classroom is irrelevant because there neither is, nor should there be, a formal pedagogical role for the L1 in the L2 classroom (see also Macaro, 2001). In Chapter 4, I offer a review of the literature in classroom L2 and L1 use along with a report of some of my own research on this topic, but the most important insight of much of this work can be revealed here: the question of whether to *allow* the L1 into the classroom is irrelevant, not because of the theoretical bedrock of presumed L2 interaction in the SLA literature, or because of a rejection of any pedagogical value of L1 use, but because of the basic reality of what Chavez (2003) labels classroom diglossia in the Fishman/Ferguson sense of the term. An increasingly vocal group of scholars has acknowledged this reality; indeed, part of the purpose of proposing a multilingual approach is to bring those voices into chorus with one another. These scholars have highlighted the ways in which the L1 plays a role, whether or not the instructor desires it or the pedagogical approach sanctions it. So, added to our earlier argument for the untenability of the monolingual native speaker as the target for language learners, is the observation that regardless of policy or instructor philosophy, the L1 does play a role in L2 classroom interaction (see Lucas & Katz, 1994). The task this situation sets before us is to respond appropriately in our architecture of instruction, our pedagogical approach (Chapter 6).

Myth 4: Use of the first language could bring about fossilized errors or pidginization

In my many conversations with colleagues and students on a multilingual approach one recurring objection to the sanctioned, systematic use of the L1 for pedagogical, discourse and scaffolding functions is that learners' multilingual patterns could become fossilized components of their speech in the form of a mixed or pidginized L1–L2 code. The main concern would be that these learners would carry those idiosyncratic – and presumably erroneous – speech patterns into societal use with speakers of that L2. Yet, if one accepts the widely held observation that code-switching is always a creative and socially dynamic behavior (Auer, 1998, 1999; Liebscher & Dailey-O'Cain, 2004; Li Wei, 1998), I contend that such a mixed code would not be a problem for adult L2 learners, in part because human beings as users of language, whether monolingual or multilingual, always possess not just one code but a repertoire of codes, over which they have sophisticated, if not always conscious, control (Gardner-Chloros, 2009; Myers-Scotton, 1993; Valdman, 1989). In addition, for a variety of reasons, users of language in convergent verbal interaction almost always seek to accommodate to their interlocutors (Giles & Smith, 1979; Le Page & Tabouret-Keller, 1985). Most crucially, if a bilingual speaker, even one adept at and accustomed to producing mixed codes, knows that a particular interlocutor is not bilingual, she/he will be disinclined to code-switch at all (Zentella, 1997). If a bilingual speaker of, say, English and Spanish, interacts with a Spanish monolingual speaker, the L2 speaker would be aware of the utter inappropriateness of using English in that situation. This heterogeneous understanding of codes, so long acknowledged in the sociolinguistics literature, begs the question of why language instructors have long assumed or expected the learner to acquire a repertoire of just one code, rather than assume him/her to be an emerging intercultural L2 speaker and, accordingly, acquire and possesses a creative, dynamic repertoire of codes. Therefore, like Valdman (1989), I do not propose that learners acquire a pidginized variety of L2. On the contrary, the goal in providing affordances for learners to make use of all their linguistic resources *in a systematic way* is to provide them, as 'potentially bilingual outsiders' (Kramsch, 1998: 23), with the tools for becoming integrated into the target culture(s) and society on their own terms, and not become just poor imitators of the mythical native speaker (Belz, 2002). Our job as language professionals is to provide the means for students to accomplish this.

Myth 5: Use of the first language minimizes time spent using the second language

The preceding arguments in favor of a multilingual approach to classroom code choice could be interpreted as standing in opposition to the ubiquitous principle of maximal L2 use, and more ominously, that the approach would actually curtail the amount of time that learners spend hearing and using the L2. This is a valid concern for teachers and students; I have observed many languages classes that 'devolved' into nothing more than discussions in English of aspects and issues of the L2, where L2 use was effectively absent. This concern is coupled with the powerful popular belief that code-switching, or the use of more than one language in a sentence or conversation, is an aberration from normal conversation, something to be avoided. Later on, I will show that this is far from the truth, that dual or multiple code use is both natural and the norm in many, or possibly all, societal bilingual situations. I will also show that the L1 can have many uses in the classroom that do not involve shifting entirely to the L1. Taking what some might consider a somewhat extreme stance, I propose that a multilingual approach instead both extends and enriches the amount of time the L2 is used by learners, for three reasons. First, when it comes down to it, even in the most communicative of language classes, learners typically talk a dismally low percentage of the time overall, with the instructor dominating the floor much of the time (Guthrie, 1984; see also Chapter 4). If a pedagogy were in place that would (1) allow learners to function as intercultural speakers, making use of all their linguistic resources, and (2) involve learners actively in the process of the co-construction and use of code choice norms through critical reflection and discussion, and overt strategies instruction (Chapters 6 and 7), then the amount of time that students spend talking overall would increase. While the absolute ratio of L2 to L1 communication might decrease – with more L1 being used overall than is typically 'allowed' in language classes, the absolute amount of time spent communicating in the L2 (or some variety of it) would increase because students would be talking more. And if the ultimate goal for all class participants, instructor *and* students, was to make some version(s) of the L2 the unmarked classroom code, I believe that many or most students would welcome the challenge.

Summary and Conclusion

Barthes (1972: 110) asserted that 'mythology can only have an historical foundation, for myth is a type of speech chosen by history: it cannot possibly evolve from the "nature" of things'. In this chapter, I have sought to show that the ways we think about the place of the L1 and code choice within our language pedagogy, even the eclectic approaches that come under the heading of CLT, are not 'natural', but derive from the particular historical trends and trajectories in language education of the last few hundred years, and perhaps from popular, intuitive beliefs, or beliefs based on anecdotal evidence (which themselves have historical roots that one could trace). Barthes also argued that the myths we make use of, while an important part of meaning making and getting things done in society, serve to reduce complexity, make the existence of the myths themselves transparent and distance us from the very history from which our myths spring. At the same time, the meaning and function of our myths are always specific to a particular time and place, and to the particular groups that can or should make sense of them. So it is with language pedagogy, and the crucial issue of code choice in the classroom: we assume certain things about classroom code choice are 'natural', but in fact even these assumptions are myths rooted in the history of how – and why – we teach language. In language teaching, our myths about code choice are linked to our eclectic CLT pedagogies, but here the very terms 'exclusive target-language use' and 'resorting to L1', so often heard in discussions of language teaching, point toward the existence and deep roots of our myths. Thus, the agenda of this book comes into focus: to establish a framework for classroom code choice that liberates us from the constraints of these myths, in order to facilitate communication and learning in a classroom community of practice.

Notes

1. In this book, the discussion of L2 learning and use refers primarily to *oral* production in the language classroom. Also, the terms L2 and, occasionally, target language (TL) will be used to refer to what students learn in university-level language classes. I have intentionally avoided using the term 'foreign

language', which is in line with the trend in the profession to move away from representing the languages we teach as 'foreign' from the outset (is Spanish a *foreign* language in the USA?). With regard to the use of the term L1, the term is used here in opposition to L2 or target language, but it is understood that in US language classes, L1 really means English. At the same time, no assumption is made that English is the L1 of all students in the classroom. The term L1 is thus employed for the sake of simplicity of expression.
2. In this book, I refer to 'societal' bilingualism as distinct from language classroom bilingualism. By societal, I mean all the manifestations of language contact in communities in the world, such as immigrant situations, indigenous language situations, pidgin and creole situations and so forth. I acknowledge that this is a gross oversimplification of bilingualism or multilingualism in society, but it is meant only to establish a working dichotomy with the language classroom as a multilingual social space.
3. While the term 'multilingual', meaning two *or more* codes, would be most appropriate throughout this book, I use the terms *bilingual* and *multilingual* interchangeably, in part because *bilingual* is the most widely used expression in the literature. Byram's concept of intercultural communicative competence is defined and addressed in Chapter 2.
4. I am indebted to Macaro (2009) for refining the 'how much L1?' question from the 'maximal' to the 'optimal'.
5. See also Cummins (2007) for a critical examination of similar issues of what he calls a monolingual approach.

Chapter 2

The Conundrum of Babel: Toward a Theoretical Framework for a Multilingual Approach

(1) And the whole earth was of one language, and of one speech.
(2) And it came to pass, as they journeyed from the east, that they found a plain in the land of Shinar; and they dwelt there.
(3) And they said one to another, Go to, let us make brick, and burn them thoroughly. And they had brick for stone, and slime had they for mortar.
(4) And they said, Go to, let us build us a city and a tower, whose top may reach unto heaven; and let us make us a name, lest we be scattered abroad upon the face of the whole earth.
(5) And the LORD came down to see the city and the tower, which the children of men built.
(6) And the LORD said, Behold, the people is one, and they have all one language; and this they begin to do: and now nothing will be restrained from them, which they have imagined to do.
(7) Go to, let us go down, and there confound their language, that they may not understand one another's speech.
(8) So the LORD scattered them abroad from thence upon the face of the earth: and they left off to build the city.
(9) Therefore is the name of it called Babel; because the LORD did there confound the language of all the earth: and from thence did the LORD scatter them abroad upon the face of the earth.

Genesis 11:1-9 (King James)

Striving for Monolingualism in a Multilingual World

In pursuing a theoretical and conceptual framework for a multilingual approach to classroom code choice, I felt it appropriate to go back to the source of the Western attitude to code choice, as it were, condensed in the Biblical account of the world's diversity of languages. The Tower of Babel story from the Book of Genesis is an important and useful starting point for rethinking code choice in the classroom, important because our predominant conceptualizations of languages, at least in political and social terms, can be traced back to this short passage, and useful because reflecting critically on the nature of God's curse may give us a basis for recasting what goes on in the language classroom. Just like Tom Robbins's irreverent explication of the origins of human choice cited in the epigraph of this book, in this Biblical passage it all boils down to choice, man's choice and God's, brought on by man's presumptuousness and arrogance, and derived, in some interpretations, from God's resentment of this striving (Derrida, 2002: 108). The crime was man's desire to be God-like, and God's punishment was to impose mutual unintelligibility, to ensure that the struggle to be like God or to touch God directly was supplanted by the perpetual struggle to overcome the barrier of Otherness. In his essay 'Des Tours de Babel', Derrida (2002) addresses the issue of translation using the Babel story as his vehicle. He suggests that no matter how much or how well we translate one language into another, it will always be difficult to know what the correct meaning is and how to interpret it. This, he concludes, is the 'legacy of confusion' that makes translation both a necessity and an impossibility. Derrida asks

> Can we not... speak of God's jealousy? Out of resentment against that unique name and lip of men, he imposes his name, his name of father; and with this violent imposition he opens the deconstruction of the tower, as of the universal language; he scatters the genealogical filiation. He breaks the lineage. He *at the same time* imposes and forbids translation. (Derrida, 2002: 108)

There are, presumably, many ways to interpret the Tower of Babel story, but it is generally agreed that the diversity of languages is to be regarded as a *curse*, something we must seek to overcome, which the very multiplicity of languages ultimately makes impossible. Nevertheless, we strive for mutual intelligibility, for access to the language and culture of others, through translation, through globalizing particular languages (e.g. Latin and French in earlier times, English nowadays) and, of course, through learning second languages. The same sort of striving that prompted the people to try to build the Tower is now spent trying just to get back to one another, and to a world 'of one language, and of one speech'. It is this very understanding of language and the multiplicity of languages that has had as profound an impact as any linguistic theory on the ways we think about and teach languages. I would even go as far as to suggest that *all* the theories and models used to design language curricula and teach in the classroom can be traced conceptually to this seminal tale. It begins with the premise that the existence of multiple languages is a barrier we must pierce, a hurdle we must scale. It ends with the deep-seated belief that success will always elude us, that non-native speakers of a language can never be natives, that speakers of other languages will always retain their Otherness. However, as discussed in Chapter 1, in teaching this Otherness to our students, we set up *native* Otherness as the unattainable target toward which they must strive. This is a key part of the problem. In our current conceptualization, the language class is a place where we strive to overcome the curse of Babel, but in fact perpetuate that curse in the ways that we go about teaching and learning the languages of others. We conspire with our students to overcome the confusion of Babel, we fill them with the promise that they might achieve this, and all the while we feel that few if any might move toward erasing the effects of that curse.

Yet, if we approach the issue from a different perspective, based on alternative assumptions about the nature of language, of meaning making, and particularly in how we conceive of the 'voice' that the nascent L2 user has or develops (Bakhtin, 1981; van Lier, 2004), then we may find a way, not to smash the Babel curse as if it were a literal barrier in our path to successful L2 learning – for it is ancient and deep-seated in Western culture and is likely to remain so in the popular imagination – rather to simply go around it by making principled use of the multiplicity of codes at the learner's disposal, including the new L2, to discover each learner's own multilingual voice. The framework, or frameworks, that I believe fit the bill come under various headings: sociocultural, constructivist and ecological models, among others. While I will try to limit my discussion of theory, it is crucial to lay the conceptual foundation for the analysis of code-switching in Chapter 5 and the curricular architecture I propose in Chapters 6 and 7. It is also important because at the heart of it, an ecological and sociocultural approach to code choice can serve as a useful starting point for rethinking other aspects of what happens in the classroom. What should crystallize out of this discussion is that the innatist or cognitive paradigms on which much CLT classroom activity is based, with the presumption of a language mechanism or endowment, and with an ideal, educated native speaker looming above as the elusive target for the L2 learner, in fact accords with the Babel-curse assumption of the impossibility of mutual intelligibility. In L1 development, according to innatist models, linguistic parameters are set during early childhood based on the input in the environment, practically ensuring that any re-setting from puberty onward will keep the L2 learner from becoming native in the L2 (parameter re-setting, while often researched, has remained controversial; see Birdsong, 1999). By contrast, an ecological perspective, which is also a theory of mind (Bronfenbrenner, 1979), views language as a dynamic, context-bound activity in the world, as 'relationships between and among individuals, groups and the world' (van Lier, 2004: 53) and effectively renders the Babel-curse conceptualization of language and language learning irrelevant. If we were to take an extreme stance, we might say that the principles of an ecological approach are at odds with the notion that it was not the linguistic scattering of people that prevented or prevents people from doing that 'which they have imagined to do', rather a host of many other social ills. Within a sociocultural and ecological framework, rethinking and designing a curricular architecture using learners' full linguistic repertoires – whatever these are at any given point in their language development – becomes not only feasible, but a logical imperative for successful learning. In this way, it is my hope that we might recast the curse of Babel in terms of a blessing (see also Haugen, 1987).

Why not a Psycholinguistic Approach to Classroom Code Choice?

In the face of such a rejection of innatist models, the reader may wonder at this point, in following the discussion of classroom code choice as it moves squarely into sociocultural and ecological perspectives, why psycholinguistic or 'mainstream' second language acquisition (SLA) approaches to classroom code choice are not given equal time in this volume. After all, much of the work in SLA since its beginnings in the 1960s and 1970s has concerned itself in large measure with the ways that the L2 develops in the individual learner. Research in this area has adopted the methodologies and oriented itself toward the tenets of developmental psychology and cognitive science, the latter based on innatist models of language and a language faculty. In this paradigm, concerned as it is primarily with the ways that L2 form and meaning are mapped, there has been little room for consideration of the role of the L1 in L2 learning. This is because psycholinguistic studies of L2 acquisition are, on the one hand, concerned primarily or solely with form-meaning connections and mappings *in the L2*, and second, the L1 is considered primarily in the ways it *interferes with* L2 comprehension and production. The L1 is viewed as an impediment to acquisition

(Cummins, 2007; Ortega, 2010). If language choice was considered within SLA research in ways not related to interference, then we might examine differences as a component of the oft-investigated rubric of 'individual difference' in L2 learning, together with motivation, aptitude and anxiety, all of which exist at the interface of personal traits and personal choice. Whether and how a learner, or a teacher, uses the L1 in the L2 learning situation could indeed be studied as an individual phenomenon. My own questionnaire study (Levine, 2003), which will be described and discussed in Chapter 5, was concerned in this way largely with the individual learner and teacher, not L2 learners as part of a dynamic classroom group.

The second reason that a psycholinguistic or innatist approach would be unproductive in our discussion of classroom code choice relates to the connection between research and pedagogy. In the SLA literature, most empirical research reports end with an 'implications for instruction' section, which addresses the ways the research findings can inform our thinking about curriculum and teaching. There is often a disconnect between the research findings regarding what happens – or might happen – within the mind of the individual learner, and what can or should happen in the social space of the language classroom. For the curriculum designer or language teacher it is always a bit of a leap to 'apply' such research findings to classroom activity. Often, the findings are not 'appliable' at all. While the research itself is valuable and crucial for our developing understandings of language, language acquisition and learning, for a comprehensive treatment of classroom code choice it is insufficient, because the theoretical framework and the business of creating curriculum and working with students in classrooms must be, if not seamless, then at least congruous. The model must jibe with the observed reality without continually considering what may be going on in the minds of individual learners. Which is what I feel must happen for psycholinguistic models of L2 acquisition to link up with the messy activity of language use in the classroom.

Sociocultural and Ecological Perspectives of Second Language Learning, Classroom Practice and Classroom Code Choice

In the remainder of this chapter, I will outline the key tenets of theories and models that support a multilingual approach to classroom code choice. These are Vygotskyan sociocultural theory (SCT), ecological perspectives of L2 learning, intercultural competence and learners' 'third places', and the concept of the legitimate peripheral participant and classroom community of practice. I close the chapter with several summarizing tenets related to classroom code choice.

Sociocultural theory and classroom code choice

Central to a sociocultural theory account of instructed L2 learning is the notion that cognitive development, including L2 development, is a mediated, collaborative process driven by social interaction. Stetsenko and Arievitch (1997: 161; cited in Swain & Lapkin, 2000: 254) write that 'psychological processes emerge first in collective behaviour, in cooperation with other people, and only subsequently become internalized as the individual's own "possessions"'. Ohta (2000) succinctly sums up how Vygotsky's theory is applied to L2 learning:

> For Vygotsky, learning is a socially situated activity. What a learner at first accomplishes only in a social setting, she or he will eventually be able to do independently... Through social interaction, L2 constructs (whether vocabulary, grammatical structures, etc.) appear on two psychologically real planes, first the interpsychological or "between people" plane, which is developmentally prior to the intrapsychological, or mental, plane. In other words, social processes allow the language to become a cognitive tool for the individual. These planes of functioning are dynamically interrelated, linked by language which mediates social interaction on the interpsychological plane, and mediates thought on the intrapsychological plane. (Ohta, 2000: 53–54)

In order to describe his understanding of how social action transfers into cognitive development in children, Vygotsky conceived of the Zone of Proximal Development (ZPD).[1] With regard to child development, the ZPD was defined as 'the distance between the actual developmental level as determined by independent problem solving at the level of potential development as determined through problem solving under adult guidance or in collaboration with more capable peers' (Vygotsky, 1978: 86). Vygotsky (1978, also discussed in de Guerrero & Villamil, 2000: 52; and Ohta, 2000: 52) conceptualized this guidance or collaboration as occurring through 'scaffolding' or 'assisted performance' (Tharp & Gallimore, 1991) and through *prolepsis* (I will discuss prolepsis shortly).

Though at first interpreted by SLA scholars as assistance to L2 learners provided by native or near-native speakers, reflecting Vygotsky's basic position that development occurs between a child and the more capable adult, more recently scaffolding has been reinterpreted to include assisted performance of not necessarily more capable peers (de Guerrero & Villamil, 2000; Ohta, 2000; Swain & Lapkin, 1998). The ZPD is comprised of two developmental levels: the 'actual developmental level' is determined by what the learner can do alone, without assistance, and the 'potential developmental level' by what the learner can do when assisted (de Guerrero & Villamil, 2000: 51; Vygotsky, 1978: 85). As will be shown in the coming chapters, code-switching in conversation can be especially helpful in situations when the learner pursues affordances for learning or simple maintenance of social position in conversation with the teacher, or when learners, as social equals, scaffold interactions toward intelligibility and learning.

According to Atkinson (2002), one aspect of Vygotskyan vis-à-vis neo-Vygotskyan SCT may be problematic in accounting for adult L2 development, namely, what he claims is the one-way nature of cognitive development from the external/social to the internal/cognitive in the Vygotskyan conception. Drawing from connectionist models of language processing and acquisition,[2] Atkinson asserts that '[n]either language acquisition nor language use—nor even cognized linguistic knowledge—can be properly understood without taking into account their fundamental *integration* into a socially-mediated world' (Atkinson, 2002: 534; my emphasis), that is, in a non-directional, non-linear fashion. For Atkinson (2002: 530), the cognitive and the social do not simply interact, they are mutually constituted; the use of language 'crucially assumes the preexistence and interactionally-achieved development of shared sociocognitive perspectives'. Although the author concurs with most of the Vygotskyan and the neo-Vygotskyan accounts of L2 acquisition, his interpretation derives from the assertion that acts of cognition

> do not start in the head, although the head is certainly involved, nor do they end in the head, because the output is social action. Nor do the social (signifying) practices involved simply take on their meaning once they arrive in the head; instead, they come with meaning already, in a sense, built in—just as language carries with it meaning that is only "borrowed" (Bakhtin, 1990) in specific instances of language use. The point here, then, is that cognition is not a private activity that occurs exclusively in the confines of an independent,

isolated cerebral space, but rather that it is at least a semipublic activity, produced as part of a substantially open system. Whenever we participate in social activity, we participate in conventional ways of acting and being that are already deeply saturated with significance. (Atkinson, 2002: 531)

Although these assertions by Atkinson, as an attempt to link SCT to what happens with language learners, have not really caught on compared with others' treatments of SCT (most notably Lantolf, 2000; Lantolf & Thorne, 2006; and, of course, van Lier, 2004), I have brought Atkinson into our discussion because it will be useful later on when we address the critical and politicizing function of classroom multiple code use, and also because it provides a bridge to consideration of van Lier's ecological perspective. At the heart of it, I think Atkinson's take on SCT remains somewhat limited compared with the ways that Lantolf and Thorne (2006) and van Lier (2004) have dealt with SCT, yet Atkinson's connectionist perspective does jibe with what van Lier has to say about the interpersonal, socially constructed nature of meaning, and especially the ways that van Lier regards the importance of context and how learners select what is relevant and important in a context.

The implications of SCT and Atkinson's connectionist spin on SCT for our consideration of classroom code choice are interesting and exciting: learners and the teacher co-construct bilingual norms appropriate and integral to the learning environment, and it holds a place for a multiplicity of code choice conventions already 'deeply saturated' with social and sociolinguistic significance. In keeping with Le Page and Tabouret-Keller's (1985) assertion that the social use of language constitutes 'acts of identity',[3] and Atkinson's ideas about the relationship between the 'cognizing individual and the socially-constructed and mediated world' (adapted from Gee, 1992: 530), a multilingual approach derives from the acknowledgment of explicit roles for language learners' linguistic multi-competence and of the intrinsic cultural value of the language class in its own right and as a component of the larger cultures of which it is a part.

Ecological linguistics, language learning and classroom code choice

A sophisticated, nuanced synthesis of a number of theories and models of language, meaning and learning is developed by van Lier (2004) in his book, *The Ecology and Semiotics of Language Learning: A Sociocultural Perspective*, a work that I expect will have an ongoing impact on how language is taught and learned in the coming years.

Drawing primarily on the ideas of Peirce, Halliday, Bakhtin and, of course, Vygotsky, van Lier establishes a framework for considering language teaching and learning in an ecological perspective. In this section, I will do my best to summarize those aspects of the work that are germane to our discussion of classroom code choice and that have contributed directly to both the theoretical underpinnings of the proposed approach as well as the curricular proposals I will present later on. The reader who has not yet read the work, however, is strongly encouraged to do so.

The basic premise of the book is that language learning – and here it should be mentioned that van Lier includes both first and second language learning in his discussion – is best understood, and the teaching of L2 framed, in an ecological perspective. Right up front, as in earlier works (e.g. 1994) the author makes clear that the ecology of language learning is not to be understood as a separate or new field of inquiry, rather as a *'transdisciplinary* endeavor' (2; author's emphasis). The study of language and language learning from an ecological perspective is presented as a means of informing the linguistics community about important educational issues that hold implications for linguistic theory and language learning and use (presumably to improve linguistic theory and empirical research), and for the educational community, in order to 'make the study of language more central, relevant, and interesting' (to improve teaching and learning; 2–3); in line with this goal, the present book also seeks to develop a means to make language learning and teaching more central, relevant and interesting for students and teachers than it currently tends to be in high schools and colleges.

Of course, van Lier is not the first to develop an approach to language learning based on SCT or even 'language ecology' (Haugen, 1972). Lantolf's (2000) volume, and of course Kramsch's (1993) seminal work, laid the foundation for what van Lier, to my mind, makes both theoretically accessible and directly applicable for curriculum design and teaching. New in van Lier (2004) is the way in which the author weaves together the ideas of numerous important scholars of the last century, from Saussure to Halliday, and from diverse fields in the social and natural sciences and philosophy, in terms of congruent assumptions about or treatments of, especially but not exclusively, language, meaning and learning. In particular, van Lier introduces the reader to scholars who have received little attention from the applied linguistics community in the USA, notably Peirce and Halliday.

In the following, I would like to focus on just four of the tenets that van Lier presents for an ecological perspective. The first is that, with regard to theories of language,

> language is always a meaning-making activity that takes place in a complex network of complex systems that are interwoven amongst themselves as well as with all aspects of physical, social, and symbolic worlds. It is not immune to social, political and economic factors, and it harbors misconceptions with the same ease as wisdoms. (van Lier, 2004: 53)

The implications for the ways we approach language teaching and learning of this social semiotic view of language cannot be understated. Essentially, considering language in these complex, dynamic and fundamentally social terms represents a rejection of what van Lier describes as a 'building block' approach to language, whereby language is analyzed and studied, both by linguists and language students, as a set of separate components: phonemes, morphemes, words, phrases, clauses, utterances and texts. The author arranges the traditional view of language graphically in a hierarchy, in line with much of structural linguistics, a pyramid with the phoneme at the top and the text at the bottom. The alternative, ecological graphic offered is likened to an onion (originally presented in van Lier, 1995; reproduced below), whereby 'there are many ways of interpreting linguistic action, and they cannot be limited to some inner formal core of words and sentence pattern' (van Lier, 2004: 43). This means that linguistic activity also includes non-verbal signs, including gesture, facial expressions and the like, allusions to the physical and social properties of the world (Figure 2.1). The idea behind the onion is that,

> one cannot peel away the layers of an onion and get to the "real" onion within. It's layers all the way down. Any utterance carries multiple sources of potential information that are present all at once. Arriving at an interpretation requires that we "scan" the utterance – and utterer – for particular meaning clues. It is as if we run our mental scanner across all the layers and "read" a plausible interpretation. At any of the layers something can go awry—causing ambiguities or surprises. The interesting thing is that – in general – any problem that occurs at a particular layer (say, clause) will be resolved by looking at the next layer(s) up. (van Lier, 2004: 43)

To illustrate, van Lier offers the following example: the meaning of 'She won't go out with anyone' is ambiguous, and the sound, word and

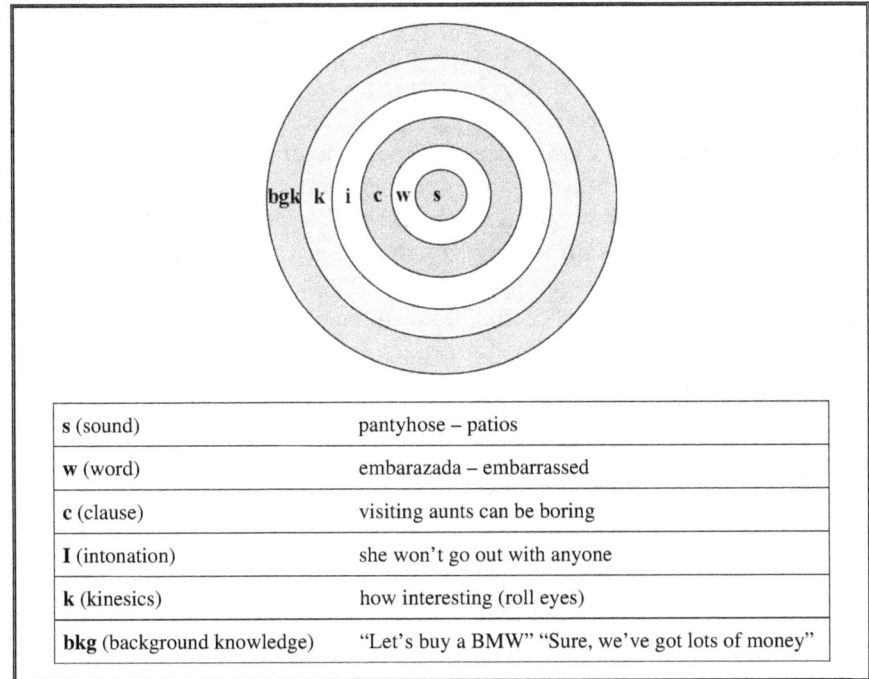

Figure 2.1 Layers of meaning, levels of interpretation (van Lier, 2004: 44)

clause levels do not help resolve the ambiguity. To resolve the ambiguity, we need to get information from the next level up, which is intonation. If the word 'anyone' carries a rise-fall intonation, then the utterance means that she will go out with someone, if that someone is special. If the word is pronounced with a sharp falling intonation, then she will just not go out with anyone, period (van Lier, 2004: 43n).

A second tenet of an ecological linguistic perspective, following from the rejection of a componential view of language, is a fundamental rejection of what could be called a cause and effect basis for explaining language learning. Applied linguistics research and, subsequently, much of our language pedagogy is based on the notion of cause and effect: the common research practice is to isolate a language feature, measure learners' demonstrated knowledge of that feature, intervene in some way (teaching), re-assess learners' demonstrated knowledge and then attempt to isolate the specific variables that led to learners' acquisition or non-acquisition of the feature. Like van Lier, I do not criticize here the value of this research; the gains the field has made through empirical research are immeasurable (see also Bronfenbrenner, 1979: 20). In an ecological perspective, what drives or brings about L2 learning cannot be reduced to a narrow set of variables, that context and the perspective of the observer, and the particular 'causes' one seeks to uncover will always vary. Our pedagogy must reflect this dynamic complexity. To illustrate this important distinction between a cause and effect approach and a complexity or dynamic-systems approach (which comes under the umbrella of an ecological perspective; see de Bot *et al.*, 2007; Larsen-Freeman, 2002; Larsen-Freeman & Cameron, 2008), van Lier offers a simple example of the problem with a reductionist approach: a rock hits a window and the window breaks. Here are several 'explanations' van Lier offers for the event:

(a) The glass broke because the rock hit it.
(b) The glass broke because it was fragile.
(c) The glass broke because Cody was fooling around throwing rocks.
(d) Cody is always fooling around because his mom lets him run wild. (van Lier, 2004: 201)

The idea is that knowing a cause does not provide a full explanation of the event. Only knowing all these factors together provides a rich description, and even here we cannot speak of A causing B. Rather, we can speak of a 'nexus' of factors all intersecting at the particular moment the window is broken (see also Scollon, 2001; Scollon & Scollon, 2004).

The reader may now be asking: what does this have to do with establishing a theoretical foundation for a multilingual approach to classroom code choice? van Lier offers parallel examples of L2 learning/acquisition 'causes' to the window example:

(a) The student learned because she received comprehensible input.
(b) The student learned because the affective filter was low.
(c) The student learned because there were lots of interesting activities she could participate in. (van Lier, 2004: 201)

Only by looking at all three 'causes' can we begin to get a complete picture of what happens with an individual learner. The same holds true for accounting for any instance of code-switching or L1 use in the language classroom. I will delve into greater detail about this in Chapter 5, but let us now examine a brief excerpt from a conversation in a second-year university German class between a teacher, who addresses the whole class, and a student, who responds to what the teacher has said:

1 TR ok so wir haben jetzt im prinzip um sieben ausstellungen eins zwei drei vier fünf
ok so we have now in principle about seven exhibits one two three four five

2   sechs sieben (.) das ist auch ok =
six seven (.) that is good too ok =

3 S1 = yeah (.) wir haben nur ein eine gemacht weil sie so (.) **comprehensive** (.)
=yeah (.) we only did one one because it so (.) comprehensive (.)
Please see Chapter 5, note 3 for transcription conventions.

There are indeed several possible explanations for S1's use of the word 'comprehensive' in this exchange. The first is obviously that she could not think of the German word for 'comprehensive' at that moment, or perhaps the word is not in her German vocabulary at all. In an ecological, dynamic systems-based perspective, however, we must consider setting and context. At the micro-level of interaction, the switch is likely motivated either by a gap in vocabulary or by lexical retrieval difficulties (we could not know which it is for sure without having tested the student on just this word beforehand). Yet, there are several additional, plausible explanations that we should consider:

(a) The student desires to keep the conversation moving and opts to insert the English word rather than negotiate the meaning of the word in German.
(b) The student is aware that the teacher is fully bilingual in German and English, that he will comprehend any English word she uses.
(c) The student is aware that in the setting of the classroom the purpose of communication is (also) language learning. Although the teacher did not follow her use of the word 'comprehensive' with its German equivalent in this case, this would have been an unmarked event if he had, and indeed S1 may have expected it.

Each of these accounts is possible, and in an ecological perspective we can only understand the use of the L1 in this otherwise L2 exchange if, in fact, all of them are taken together, as different components of a complex explanation. The key to understanding how this holds true is to consider this same person, S1, in a monolingual German situation. If this conversation had taken place in the company of interlocutors that S1 knew to be monolingual speakers of German, she also would have been aware that her use of 'comprehensive' would not have been understood. She would have either engaged in circumlocution to express herself, or she would have abandoned the attempt (both are common practices in bilingual language use). This is a crucial fact, one that compels us to consider any such use of the L1 in classroom interaction as integral to the classroom setting itself. The classroom setting in which this switch took place is itself governed by conventions and norms, of which both the teacher and the student are a part.

The reader should also note that the three additional explanations offered for the switch are based on different sorts of learner *awareness*. Awareness is not always the same as overt consciousness *in situ*, but it clearly plays a part in verbal behavior in any setting. Speakers always 'know' how they may and should use language based on who is talking to whom, where and in what context. Learner awareness is a central part of the curricular architecture developed in Chapters 6 and 7.

A third tenet of an ecological perspective is the close relationship between activity and learning, which van Lier describes as *affordances* for learning. van Lier writes:

> A learning context is constituted of physical, social and symbolic opportunities for meaning making, and the central notion that drives this meaning making is *activity*. Instead of instructional material (facts, skills, behaviors) that is inculcated through processes of presentation, practice and production, an ecological-semiotic approach envisages an active learner who is guided and stimulated to higher, more complex levels of activity... The directions in which the processes are taken by learners working together or alone cannot and should not be exactly predicted or controlled, a notion that must horrify many educational planners. (van Lier, 2004: 62)

No doubt, those of us involved in curriculum design and teacher training are, perhaps not horrified, but at least intimidated, by the notion of a curriculum that eschews predicting the exact nature of the activity in which students engage. In fact, we may be a long way off from an entire curriculum based on this principle. Yet, integrating a multilingual approach to classroom code use into what happens in the classroom provides us with a feasible first step, whereby we create affordances for learners to function as nascent bilinguals. To understand how this can occur, consider the Vygotskyan notion of *prolepsis*, which is related to the ZPD. van Lier explains prolepsis as follows:

> Vygotsky speaks of "good learning" as that which is in advance of development...we can note that the parents and the sociocultural community around the child project onto the child's actions a higher

level of maturation than is actually manifested in the actions. So, when the baby points to a dog and says "Goh!", the caregiver will say, "Yes, isn't that a nice doggie?" or something similar... caregivers act as if children can do and say things that they actually cannot yet do and say, and this provides a conceptual and experiential "space" for the child to grow into. Of course, the distance between what the child produces and what the caregiver pretends that the child produces must not be too great... For example, if in response to the baby's "Goh!"... the adult had responded: "Notice, small fellow, that this particular canine, which you have somewhat ambiguously referred to as 'Goh!,' – presumably your immature approximation of the word 'dog' – is of the sub-species 'mutt,' characterized by crooked paws and lopsided ears, found originally in the foothills of Neasden, and recently promoted to the status of domestic companion in the Bavarian hinterland," the baby might not have made much headway linguistically, cognitively or socially, in spite of the vastly superior level of information provided. (van Lier, 2004: 37)

This anecdote suggests what is possible with code-switching as a normal, creative aspect of bilingual speech in the language classroom. By developing a principled approach to code choice, we create a conceptual and experiential space – the space of the bilingual user – for the learner to grow into.

A last tenet I would like to highlight of an ecological perspective is the place it grants to the classroom as part of the 'real world'. In many social situations with people unconnected with the university or teaching, I have sometimes caught myself actually defending the language teaching and learning endeavor. Many regard what happens in the classroom – and this includes many students and language teachers – as unconnected to the real world, regardless of how useful some consider that which is learned (i.e. to use an L2 out there in the real world). Yet, the classroom is and always has been as much a part of the real world as any other social gathering. Tudor (2001) argues that the

distinction [between the classroom and the real world] relates to a functional view of the classroom as a place where knowledge and skills are developed for use at some stage in the future. With respect to language learning, this means that the language skills which are developed in the classroom are designed to facilitate language use in the communicative situations that students will or may encounter at some future stage in their professional, academic, or personal lives. This is, of course, a perfectly reasonable way of seeing the ultimate purpose of the classroom. *We should not, however, forget that the classroom itself is part of the real world of students in the here-and-now of their life as individuals and social actors. Communication, then, is not just something which happens "out there," but also a process which occurs within the social environment which we call the classroom.* (Tudor, 2001: 115; my emphasis)

The communication that goes on in the classroom, whether in the L1 or in the L2, is carried out by people in interaction, and this interaction varies just as much as in other spheres of life. There may be degrees of authenticity to classroom communication with regard to what happens in societal target language situations, but 'the authentic' is distinct from the social; and even the contrived interaction so common in language classrooms is still authentic human interaction, with its own functions, purposes, norms and outcomes. Tudor (2001: 19) states that 'the language classroom is certainly a pedagogical entity, but one which is embedded in the society and culture of which it is part'. This point follows van Lier (1988: 29–30, also cited in Tudor, 2001: 115), who argues that 'the transformation of "classroom communication" into a rather narrowly focused enterprise... is largely so because we have failed to consider the communication potential of the classroom *itself*, and the authentic resources for interaction it has to offer'. Both van Lier (1988) and Tudor advocate for regarding the classroom 'as a social reality in its own right with its own communicative dynamics' (Tudor, 2001: 115). Even in the contrived classroom context, learners and teacher continually assert their own sense of identity and cultural belonging in ways that can either support or frustrate L2 learning.

For van Lier, the classroom is a 'complex adaptive system' and the mind of the learner is 'the totality of relationships between a developing person and the surrounding world, and of learning as the result of meaningful activity in an accessible environment' (van Lier, 1988: 783; see also de Bot *et al.*, 2007; Larsen-Freeman, 2002; Larsen-Freeman & Cameron, 2008). Tudor (2001: 128) observed that the interactive dynamics of the classroom 'give rise to a social reality which is specific to that classroom' and 'each classroom develops its own rules and thus its own form of socialisation around which individual participants, including the teacher, have to negotiate their specific role and identity'. If one pursues a monolingualist approach to code choice, then an ecological perspective must be rejected, for a multilingual approach requires that code choice norms are continually co-constructed and negotiated by learners and instructor, validate learners' sense of ethnolinguistic identity *in situ*, and also respond to the specific social reality of each particular classroom. What this translates into, in pedagogical terms, is structure. As Tudor (2001: 208) expresses it, '... methodological choices need to be made not just on the basis of theoretical principle, but in terms of the meaning which these choices assume for the students and teachers present in a given setting'. I reiterate my point from the opening lines of this book: it's about choice. Everything else that happens in the classroom proceeds from the choices we make. Our job as language professionals is to take as many of those choices as possible out of the hands of the institution, the curriculum designers, the textbook authors and even the teachers, and place them in the hands of the learners (Dörnyei & Murphey, 2003). In order to do this successfully, though, all parties concerned, including the learners, need a principled, informed and critical set of tools at each stage. An ecological approach offers some concrete guidelines for 'exploring the dynamics of their own situations and in approaching decision-making in a locally meaningful and sustainable way' (Tudor, 2001: 209),[4] guidelines that are invaluable in approaching the issue of classroom code choice. Tudor (2001) proposes that we do the following:

- Acknowledge the complexity of language teaching in an open and constructive manner. In order to design and implement curricula we often sweep complexity under the carpet. This guideline asks instructors to develop a "willingness to look beyond the neat, elegant structures within which language teaching is often discussed and programme goals defined."
- Acknowledge diversity in an inclusive and constructive manner. "Effective teaching depends crucially on teachers' ability to help their students find a sense of personal meaningfulness in the teaching-learning process. This, in turn, depends on an inclusive and constructive acknowledgement of students' individuality, and thus of their diversity."
- Work with situations locally, in terms of their own inner logic and dynamics. "Language teaching as lived out in the classroom is always a local phenomenon. General principle can, of course, provide insights and open up potentially productive lines of reflection, but the value of general principle needs to be evaluated critically in the light of each situation in its own terms."
- Evaluate methodological choices from an ethnographic perspective. "No methodological choice is unmarked. ...The main point here is that it can be very easy to misunderstand or to react

judgementally to classroom behaviours that are different from those which we have been prepared to expect from our own educational socialization."
Tudor (2001: 209–212)

These guidelines will be applied in Chapters 6 and 7, where I offer one set of methodological choices for fostering a multilingual classroom community of practice in a dynamic framework based on regarding classroom communication simultaneously as a local phenomenon and the product of complex social and political factors, driven by a reflexive, critical approach to code choice norms.

Intercultural communicative competence, learners' 'third places' and classroom code choice

From the Vygotskyan focus on cognition as rooted in and driven by social interaction to Atkinson's claim that *all* human encounters are deeply saturated with meaning (including those in the language classroom), there is a clear link from these ideas to the conceptualization of language as social semiotic (Halliday, 1978). This means that language should always be viewed in terms of its functions, its roles in making meaning, for all language use involves meaning making. At all times, we are 'doing being' something, such as 'doing being bilingual' or 'doing being normal' (Cashman, 2001; Liddicoat, 2003), and at all times language is a primary vehicle we use to accomplish this. Further, the very essence of culture, according to Scollon (2001), is the ways in which individuals, groups or entire countries make and interpret meaning. In this view, language and culture are not separate constructs; language does not merely reflect culture, it constitutes it. So, just as the cognitive and the social are mutually constituted in sociocultural and sociocognitive terms, the linguistic and the cultural are also mutually constituted in social semiotic terms. For Byram (1997), Kramsch (1993, 1998, 2002b, 2006), Crozet and Liddicoat (1999) and others, the goal of adult L2 learning goes beyond the acquisition of what is generally understood under the rubric of communicative competence, the goal for learners is and should be to achieve *intercultural* communicative competence (ICC). ICC is defined by Byram (1997: 3) as the sum of 'qualities required of the [language learner as] sojourner', the soujourner distinguished from the tourist in that

> the experience of the sojourner is one of comparisons, of what is the same or different but compatible, but also of conflicts and

incompatible contrasts.... Where the tourist remains essentially unchanged, the sojourner has the opportunity to learn and be educated, acquiring the capacity to critique and improve their own and others' conditions. (Byram, 1997: 1–2)

From this goal – arguably loftier than that of communicative competence in the framework of conventional CLT – the use of language in interaction becomes inextricably linked to culture; communication is not merely about communicating in culturally appropriate ways, it is about who one is, about the establishment and maintenance of human relationships, about identity construction and actually playing a role in the cultural reification of the L2 language and culture (Byram, 1997: 32–33; see also Pennycook, 2001). This raises questions, such as, 'whose culture is acquired?' and of course, 'what is culture?' Liddicoat (2003) understands culture in relative and relativistic terms, allotting not only a place for the L2 learner in the culture construct, but for giving the learner a role in co-constructing the target culture as part of the learning process. Liddicoat argues that culture should be viewed as a dynamic set of practices rather than as a body of shared knowledge because this

> engages the idea of individual identity as a more central concept in understanding culture. Culture is a framework in which the individual achieves his/her identity using a cultural group's understandings of choices made by members as a resource for the presentation of the self. Language learning provides a challenge for identity in two key ways. First it raises the question "Who am I when I speak this language?" and secondly "How am I me when I speak this language?"
>
> When culture is viewed as dynamic practice it gives a way of dealing with culture as variable. We move away from the idea of the national culture and the idea of a monolithic "French culture" or "Japanese culture" and recognize that culture varies with time, place, and social category and for age, gender, religion, ethnicity, and sexuality. Different people participate in different groups and have multiple memberships within their cultural group each of which affects the presentation of the self within the cultural context. (Liddicoat, 2003: 9–10)

So, in asking learners to engage with the cultural practices of users of the L2 language and culture (called 'linguaculture' by Crozet & Liddicoat, 1999) on their own terms, issues of code choice become about striking a balance between the appropriation of new ways of meaning and the questioning, or even rejecting, of prescribed ways of meaning. For Byram (1997), the acquisition of ICC involves developing what he calls *savoirs*, a taxonomy representing the interrelationship between the knowledge, skills and attitudes of the intercultural speaker. Byram's taxonomy is presented in Figure 2.2. For the classroom language learner, engaging with multiple codes contributes to all five categories. First, in terms of skills, multiple code use contributes to a learner's ability to understand (*savoir comprendre*), manipulate and use (*savoir apprendre/faire*) L2 forms. It can contribute to the learner's understanding of the L2 (*savoirs*) in terms of her/his relationship as an individual, and an outsider, to the L2 culture and society, and in terms of her/his relative value as a bilingual L1/L2 speaker (*savoir être*). Finally, engaging in multilingual content instruction (see Chapter 6), learners can become critically aware of multilingual speakers and communities in the L2 country or countries (*savoir s'engager*).

In its 2007 MLA Ad Hoc committee report, a related construct was proposed for foreign language education, particularly at the collegiate level: 'translingual and transcultural competence' (MLA, 2007). Translingual/transcultural competence is defined as,

	Byram's (1997) "Savoirs" of the Intercultural Speaker		
	Skills interpret and relate (*savoir comprendre*)		
Knowledge of self and other; of interaction: individual and societal (*savoirs*)	**Education** political education critical cultural awareness (*savoir s'engager*)	**Attitudes** relativising self valuing other (*savoir être*)	
	Skills discover and/or interact (*savoir apprendre/faire*)		

Figure 2.2 Byram's (1997) 'savoirs' of the intercultural speaker

the ability to operate between languages. Students are educated to function as informed and capable interlocutors with educated native speakers in the target language. They are also trained to reflect on the world and themselves through the lens of another language and culture. They learn to comprehend speakers of the target language as members of foreign societies and to grasp themselves as Americans—that is, as members of a society that is foreign to others. They also learn to relate to fellow members of their own society who speak languages other than English. (MLA, 2007: 4)

In addition to functional language abilities, students should also develop 'critical language awareness, interpretation and translation, historical and political consciousness, social sensibility, and aesthetic perception' (MLA, 2007: 4). Language learning based on the development of either ICC and/or translingual/transcultural competence leaves no room for the separation of language and culture, and it allows L2 learners to explore the L2 culture on their own terms. It also helps language professionals to move away from solely skills-based and linear approaches, approaches that parse out language and culture learning as a matter of course, toward orienting the learner to operate within and move toward a 'third place' (Kramsch, 1993), a state of linguistic and cultural knowledge and awareness that is not represented by either the learners' original L1 knowledge and experience or the L2 language and culture (also described in terms of "symbolic competence"; Kramsch, 2006). Connected to this is the assertion, presented already in Chapter 1, that the sole curricular focus on the monolingual native speaker's L2 language and culture are, in fact, an inappropriate target for the adult learner.

With regard to a multilingual approach to code choice, this conceptualization of language and culture, and of the job of learners defined in terms of achieving ICC or translingual/transcultural competence, begs the question, as briefly addressed in Chapter 1: do L2 learners create and acquire some idiosyncratic, hybrid (or even pidgin) language that might be fine and appropriate in the confines of the classroom, but be useless, or worse, corrupt, when placed in a societal environment in which the L2 is used? I believe the answer can be found in Liddicoat's conceptualization of cultural repertoires (see also Bakhtin, 1986, on speech genres). While it is true that the learners in a multilingual classroom might develop linguistic or cultural norms that are peculiar to that classroom environment, verbal behavior as part of this group membership would serve as just one of a learner's competencies.

Despite the sanctioned use of the L1 in the classroom and the impact that may have on the nature of classroom verbal interaction, each learner is indeed exposed to authentic L2, from the instructor, from recordings, the internet, books and other texts and, of course, the learner also produces (hopefully copious amounts of) spoken and written language that does not involve code-switching or multiple code use. Adult L2 learners, just like proficient users of languages in societal bilingual situations, always use language appropriately, or at least they always strive to, depending on the situation, accommodating to their interlocutors as the situation demands. This does not mean, of course, that a language user could not opt to intentionally subvert socially or culturally appropriate language use norms in particular situations: people do it all the time outside the classroom, so, of course, they would as well inside the classroom! Part of the larger goal of a multilingual approach is to help learners become aware and take advantage of these sorts of linguistic, social and cultural choices.

Multilingual classroom communities of practice

Lave and Wenger's (1991) and Wenger's (1998) social theory of learning, itself derived from a range of intellectual sources in social psychology and sociology and manifested in the notion of communities of practice, is important and useful in framing code choice in the language classroom and developing tenets to 'design' instruction in which code choice plays a role in L2 learning; Lave and Wenger's model, though not a theory of language or language learning, helps us conceptualize how code choice practices interact with the L2 learning endeavor overall. The model is also valuable in its own right, for it lends support to the assertion that multiple code use, as part of normal practice in the language classroom, may facilitate learning, as learners and instructor engage as members of a community of practice.

Lave and Wenger's model is also appealing because it serves to link the priorities and claims of SCT and ICC perspectives of language learning in its basic premise that learning is a socially and locally constructed event, that learning happens when people get together to pursue some common goal. Lave and Wenger take it one step further, to propose that nearly all aspects of life involve learning, that it would be narrow-minded to think of learning as happening *only* in the classroom, and hence, that we should use what we know about learning outside the classroom to inform how we approach learning in the classroom.

I see this model as related to Byram's (1997) concept of 'enculturation' and the development of what an intercultural speaker should know in order to engage in meaningful intercultural communication. Wenger (1998) paints learning in the largest of strokes, with four central premises, points that I will use to motivate my own choices in designing instruction within a multilingual approach:

- We are social beings. Far from being trivially true, this fact is a central aspect of learning.
- Knowledge is a matter of competence with respect to valued enterprises – such as singing in tune, discovering scientific facts, fixing machines, writing poetry, being convivial, growing up as a boy or a girl and so forth.
- Knowing is a matter of participating in the pursuit of such enterprises, that is, of active engagement in the world.
- Meaning – our ability to experience the world and our engagement with it as meaningful – is ultimately what learning is to produce.

This last point, that learning is intended to produce meaning, is crucial for understanding the central role of code choice in the classroom: engaging critically and in a principled manner with code choice allows a large part of the language learning process to remain in the control of the learners, and further, to be or remain meaningful for them, especially as regards the development of 'third-place' identities as developing bilinguals.

Lave and Wenger also develop the notion of practice, derived in part from activity theory (Leont'ev, 1978) and social theories of power (Bourdieu, 1990, 1991; Foucault, 1980). Wenger (1998: 47) writes that 'the concept of practice connotes doing, but not just doing in and of itself. It is doing in a historical and social context that gives structure and meaning to what we do. In this sense, practice is always social practice'.

A community of practice is therefore a social institution, a way of getting things done, of sharing knowledge and information, a forum for achieving satisfaction in the many 'tasks' of life, of learning in many subtle ways that are both explicit and implicit. Communities of practice exist throughout our societies, inside and across organizations, schools and families, in both realized and unrealized forms,[5] they are also 'not a design fad, a new kind of organizational unit or pedagogical device to be implemented' (Wenger, 1998: 228). They are 'about content – about learning as a living experience of negotiating meaning—not about form. In this sense, they cannot be legislated into existence or defined by decree' as 'practice itself is not amenable to design' (Wenger, 1998: 229). This is an important concept toward grounding my critique of the code choice 'status quo' in Chapter 4, and toward approaching the pedagogical proposals offered in Chapters 6 and 7 in appropriate and meaningful ways. To the assertion that practice itself cannot be designed, Wenger writes

> One can articulate patterns or define procedures, but neither the patterns nor the procedures produce the practice as it unfolds. One can design systems of accountability and policies for communities of practice to live by, but *one cannot design the practices that will emerge in response to such institutional systems* [my emphasis]. One can design roles, but one cannot design the identities that will be constructed through these roles. One can design visions, but one cannot design the allegiance necessary to align energies behind those visions. One can produce affordances for the negotiation of meaning, but not meaning itself. One can design work processes but not work practices; one can design a curriculum but not learning. One can attempt to institutionalize a community of practice, but the community of practice itself will slip through the cracks and remain distinct from its institutionalization. (Wenger, 1998: 229)

This strongly worded litany begs the question, if a teacher as part of an institution cannot design that which we assume we design, namely, the structure of learning itself, then what can we do? Wenger's assertion is indeed that while learning as practice is not the result of design but rather a response to it, we cannot design learning as such. We can only create 'a conceptual architecture for learning', which I understand to mean that we can create the conditions by which learning can take place, within the classroom community of practice. We can 'make sure that some artifacts are in place – tools, plans, procedures, schedules, curriculums – so that the future will be organized around them' (Wenger, 1998: 231) and we can and should think about classroom teaching not as the totality of the learning event, but rather 'as a resource for the practice of learning communities that are in charge of their own learning' (Wenger, 1998: 250).

It is important to make clear why the social theory of learning put forth by Lave and Wenger is pertinent, and in fact indispensable, to developing a principled approach to classroom multiple code use. The model provides the final conceptual tools we need to take a crucial step in doing what must be done in order to pursue the goals of a multilingual language classroom: in order for learners to achieve ICC and an intercultural third place in part through code choice practices, their model helps us by eliminating, in symbolic terms, the very walls of the classroom. If we can reframe the entire L2 learning endeavor in terms of the following principles, then the development of a multilingual approach to classroom code choice with and for our learners takes on levels of significance that no prescriptive pedagogy could offer:

- The L2 classroom is one community of practice that is linked in a myriad of ways to many other communities of practice.
- The learning that goes on in the classroom is a *response to* rather than the *product of* the curricula we design, but nonetheless valuable and necessary on those terms.
- The specific sorts of communication and learning that students engage in as members of multiple communities of practice represent an important component of the diverse sorts of life-learning that all of us benefit from all the time.

Proceeding with Wenger's tenets, learning, practice and communities of practice make what happens in the classroom, as part of the real world, important and, for each individual learner, personally meaningful. It makes the code choice component of the language course a key vehicle for all sorts of other contexts and opportunities for learning; to view the development of a multilingual approach in terms any less magnificent would be to reduce the use of multiple codes to just another 'skill' to be acquired.

Tenets about Second Language Learning in Relation to Code Choice

The foregoing discussion of social, sociocultural and ecological perspectives of language learning and their relation to classroom code choice practices can be summarized with the following tenets:

- The language classroom should be viewed as a sort of 'ecosystem' (van Lier, 2004) in a sociocultural framework, in which learning does not just 'happen', rather it *emerges* from the social and pedagogical contexts and through interaction. Code choice practices, as an aspect of verbal interaction, are inherently part of the process of conversation and interaction.
- Learning is an emergent process, not a product to be received by learners. Our curricular architecture must therefore provide affordances for learning in these terms. Principled code choice

practices can act as catalysts to affordances for learning and rich, multilingual communication.
- All learning occurs in social interaction. Code choice practices serve multiple functions in social interaction, for the individual and the group.
- All language use carries social and cultural meaning. Multiple code use itself can carry its own social and cultural meaning, as well as facilitate the expression of other sorts of cultural and social meanings.
- Contrary to the ways in which most pedagogical approaches are designed and many teachers plan and execute instruction, the ways that learning proceeds in individuals or the ways that interaction can or will happen in the classroom cannot be exactly predicted or controlled. An ecological perspective also questions whether it is even advisable to ever try to do so (van Lier, 2004: 62). Following from this, the ways that code choice may contribute to learning for an individual or group also cannot be predicted. Therefore, a focus on awareness, norms and a critical, principled approach to code choice is appropriate.
- L2 learning is effective when it occurs in the learners' ZPD (Vygotsky, 1978) and is driven by prolepsis. The use of the L1 through principled code-switching can be useful in driving development: if the teacher or other interlocutor proceed with the assumption that the learner is a developing, functional bilingual with the ability to code-switch creatively as societal bilinguals do, then we can expect learners to move into that bilingual space through classroom communication.

Summary and Conclusion

While the discussion of these diverse theoretical models may come across as a sorely pared down primer in constructivist approaches to SLA, my objectives for bringing these into the discussion of code choice must be made clear. First, these models provide a framework that liberates us from the narrow constraints of the interlanguage construct, of the sentence level of analysis, as it were, and compels us to regard what goes on in the classroom at the level of the discourses at work in the classroom, of politics, power relationships and even the role that the language classroom plays in society. Second, the models provide a means of investigating and considering classroom code choice at the intersection of social science (at least certain strands of it) and humanistic inquiry, which I also think is necessary for a viable multilingual approach. The theoretical concerns of mainstream applied linguistics, which, broadly expressed, have often involved identifying universal constraints and tendencies and exploring learner variables in interaction with language performance, are useful in helping us reduce L2 learning to discrete sets of observable variables or quantifiable constructs. Yet, as is evident in the ongoing theory/practice debate, it is more problematic how they relate to pedagogical means of embracing the inherent complexity, creativity and dynamics of adult L2 learning. For this, we need sociocultural and ecological perspectives that also remain open to the important progress made in applied linguistics/SLA and in organizing and managing language curricula. As I have argued elsewhere (Levine, 2005), proposing a multilingual approach does not mean that we should throw the baby out with the bathwater, the baby being what we know about adult L2 acquisition and learning.

I close by returning to the Babel story invoked at the beginning of the chapter and asking, where do these social and sociocultural models of learning and acquisition get us in rethinking the Biblical tale? They give us the tools we need, not to resume construction of that fateful Tower nor to live in perpetual acceptance of God's curse as we dangle before language students the illusory promise of acquiring a brand new native speakership, rather to actually embrace the most precious aspect of the ostensible punishment, the ability by will and diligence to belong to one's own 'linguaculture(s)' (Crozet & Liddicoat, 1999) and simultaneously to pursue an intercultural third place, or any number of intercultural third places. If realized, this act has the potential to transform what was intended as a curse into something more akin to a gift, or to use Haugen's (1987) word, the blessing of multiple competencies, the ability to be not just a tourist in a 'foreign' culture, but to relish the role of sojourner in that culture (Byram, 1997).

Notes

1. At first glance, the ZPD appears to supplant Krashen's (1982) operationally difficult concept of $i+1$. However, there is no direct correspondence between the concepts. Dunn and Lantolf (1998) and Kinginger (2001) do a good job of analyzing the crucial ways in which they are fundamentally different. They are alike, in my view, only insofar as they offer a metaphor for understanding how development moves from one stage to the next.
2. Atkinson (2002) summarizes his understanding of connectionism as it relates to language acquisition as follows:

> Connectionism posits that meaning/knowledge exists largely in potential form in the human cognitive apparatus. That is, rather than having prebuilt cognitive structures, or schemas stored in the brain, all that exists is the potential for such structures to be formed basically online through the activation of various networks of neural associations. (Atkinson, 2002: 531)

3. According to Le Page and Tabouret-Keller (1985: 118), an 'act of identity' is defined as a projection 'onto others [of] images of the universe as they perceive it and of their own place and role in it in relation to others around them, by both what is said and the manner of saying it'. This notion of the role of perceptions enriches Gee's (1992) and Atkinson's (2002: 530) ideas about the relationship between the 'cognizing individual and the socially-constructed and mediated world'.
4. I only appeal to four of Tudor's seven guidelines, in part because three of them do not apply directly to conceptualizing a multilingual approach to classroom code choices.
5. Wenger (1998: 228) describes 'potential', 'active' and 'latent' communities of practice.

Chapter 3
What is a Code?
What is Code-Switching?

> "The Babel fish," said the Hitchhiker's Guide to the Galaxy quietly, "is small, yellow and leechlike, and probably the oddest thing in the Universe. ...It... excretes into the mind of its carrier a telepathic matrix formed by combining the conscious thought frequencies with nerve signals picked up from the speech centers of the brain which has supplied them. The practical upshot of all this is that if you stick a Babel fish in your ear you can instantly understand anything said to you in any form of language."
> "Meanwhile, the poor Babel fish, by effectively removing all barriers to communication between different races and cultures, has caused more and bloodier wars than anything else in the history of creation."
> (Adams, 1979: 59–61)

Language and Code

In Chapter 2, we moved toward a theoretical framework for rethinking code choice in the language classroom based on the tenets of sociocultural theory and an ecological perspective of language learning. The purpose of this chapter is to elucidate the issues of multiple codes and code-switching as a normal part of bilingual or multilingual communication. Along with the theoretical framework presented in Chapter 2, this discussion of code is essential to the curricular architecture presented in the coming chapters, because if we do not have a clear definition and understanding of what we mean by *code* and *code-switching* as L1 use in the L2 classroom, then we cannot easily design a curriculum or manage a classroom activity with a principled approach to code choice.

In the parody of the Babel story told in the epigraph above, Adams's *Hitchhiker's Guide* appears to convey that mutual *un*intelligibility is actually the blessing, while ubiquitous intelligibility is the curse, because if people can understand each other *too well*, then what ensues is not greater harmony and cooperation, but more opportunities for conflict and violence. Echoing Haugen (1987), in the last chapter I suggested that the world's multiplicity of codes should be regarded as a blessing rather than a curse, but Adams's Babel fish can serve as a healthy warning to us: in fostering a classroom environment in which all participants are given the means and power to communicate as they see fit, we should not also assume that this state of affairs will be harmonious or cooperative, or that it will happen in ways that lead to greater understanding, or even better language learning. Until a Babel fish is discovered here on earth, although the language classroom remains the front line in the struggle for mutual intelligibility and in developing an approach to multiple code use, the next step is (1) to define what we mean by *code* and (2) explore how we can best think about and analyze – with and for students – multiple code use, also known as code-switching.

What is a code, and how is the notion of code related to that of language? In my language courses over the years I have often cited Max Weinreich's (1945) maxim, 'a language is a dialect with an army and a navy', to help students think about language as the object of learning and see, in relative terms, relationships between the prescribed norms presented in the language textbooks and the vernacular forms they encounter everywhere but the textbooks.[1] For many years, I actually refrained from talking with language students about language in terms of *code* because I thought it would sound too technical or too 'linguisticky'. In recent years, however, I have come to view it as an indispensable part of language teaching to let learners in on some of what linguists and language teachers do, on the ways we think about teaching and learning and especially about the object of that learning. I have come to share with learners the secret that just as language and culture mutually constitute each other, so too are language and code interrelated in complex ways. The students hear from me: language is not a discrete entity at all, rather a mélange of multiple codes, just one among many possible semiotic systems. In a first-year German class, for example, there are German and English (in their academic, standardized versions), of course, but there is also non-standard usage of one or both of those languages, and there is gesture, body language, facial expression, graphic information such as pictures or charts, and not least, intentional silence (as a discourse tool); all of these modes, or modalities, are bona fide ways of making meaning, each with its own function and limitations (see van Lier's onion diagram in the previous chapter; also Blommaert, 2005). Of course, we could add more modalities, such as the ways that people present themselves physically, through dress or hairstyle and the like, as semiotic systems in their own right. This would all be part of what Atkinson (2002) described as the meaning with which social events are already saturated at the point someone opens her/his mouth to speak. As language professionals, it is imperative for us to take into consideration this wide range of codes in a pedagogically principled way, or else be fated to squeeze the square peg of a monolithic view of language into the round hole of the multiplicity of semiotic systems. And at the very least, limiting the pedagogical scope to just the L2, or even just the L2 and the L1, robs students of the chance to explore some of the ways in which the people in the target language/culture engage in meaning making in these non-linguistic modes in comparison with the ways that people in the students' own cultures do so.

Despite this complex understanding of code, we nonetheless refer most frequently to *linguistic* codes, such as Hebrew, English, German, Mandarin, L1, L2 and so forth. At all times, however, implicit in this conventionalized terminology should be the acknowledgment of many other sorts of codes, of the 'multi' in the multilingual classroom. In our discussion, however, I will limit myself to the linguistic codes, L1 and L2. Thus far, I have presented many theoretically motivated reasons why both codes should have a place in the language classroom. We now turn to detailing some ways of understanding the code choices that are made during classroom communication.

Code-Switching

What is code-switching? Since the phenomenon was first investigated systematically in the 1960s and 1970s, there have been numerous definitions ranging in specificity, and several theoretical models aimed at describing and explaining its many features and manifestations. Like any area of scholarly inquiry, the definitions vary depending on the purpose of the research. Some researchers have attempted to identify and model the formal linguistic constraints of code-switches (e.g. Myers-Scotton, 1997; Poplack, 1980; Sankoff & Poplack, 1979 to 1981). Others have investigated code-switching in social terms, seeking to explain the sorts of choices that people make as they use two languages (Gumperz, 1982; Myers-Scotton, 1993). Linguists working in the framework of conversation analysis (CA) have sought to explain the phenomenon in terms of the micro-interactional characteristics of turns in conversation (Auer, 1984; Li Wei, 1998, 2000). Though different in their orientation and purpose, two definitions would probably find agreement among the greatest number of scholars:

> Code-switching is the systematic, alternating use of two or more languages in a single utterance or conversational exchange.
> Code-switching is the systematic use of linguistic material from two or more languages in the same sentence or conversation.

Though both share that code-switching is systematic, there is a subtle difference between the two definitions. The first focuses on the directionality of the switch, on the act of switching; a speaker moves from one code into another. We can imagine the speaker's speech as a train riding one track, which we could call the 'L1 track', and then switching tracks within or between utterances to another track, the 'L2 track'. The second definition makes reference to the use of two or more languages, but whether the speaker moves, cognitively or verbally, from one language into another, remains either unexpressed or irrelevant. It's about the linguistic system making use of material from two or more languages; the empirical question is often whether it is comprised of two distinct systems, or whether the mixed variety represents a different sort of system of its own. In any case, in the second definition, we can imagine the two (or more) codes at the speaker's disposal like platters at a buffet. The speaker selects from different options in different ways at different times.

With either definition, one of the jobs of the analyst is to discover factors that influence or relate to the choices made in an utterance or conversation. These can be guided by (1) phonological, grammatical or lexical features of the speaker's languages; (2) discursive or conversational strategic considerations in the moment of interaction; (3) community or group social or historical norms (discourses) for code choice, or a combination of any of these. In this chapter and in Chapter 5, I will proceed with the assumption that choices in the first two categories themselves can be subsumed under the third: all code choices are part of discursive practices of bilingual or multilingual speakers, and our goal for the language classroom should be to move learners toward the discursive practices of the L2 culture. For the purposes of our discussion in this chapter and in the subsequent treatments in the remainder of this book, we will proceed with both definitions in mind; at times it will be appropriate to focus on the directionality of a switch, and at times merely on the fact that two codes are in play in a given utterance or conversation.

As mentioned in the introduction, it is not my aim to develop a new approach to code-switching overall, rather to hone a theoretical approach to code-switching that would be most useful for thinking about the role of code choice in the language classroom, to describe ways of influencing how talk could be managed by all class members and offer a pedagogical means to critically reflect on who speaks what to whom and in what contexts as an integral part of what goes on in the classroom. For any model of code-switching in the linguistics literature does not ultimately share our goal of seeking to *affect* speaker (learner) verbal behavior, rather to account for language use as it occurs among people. To this end, let us briefly examine three models of code-switching that seek to account for code-switching as social action and consider how each could be useful for pedagogical application. Though the third model is really an extension of the first, to make the competing claims of the models clear, I trace them in chronological order, beginning with the Myers-Scotton's Markedness Model (1993). The Markedness Model, derived from the work of Hymes (1972) and others, has been widely applied in studies of code-switching, but has also been the object of much criticism (e.g. Auer, 1998, 2004; Li Wei, 1998, 2005; Meeuwis & Blommaert, 1994). The second model is the interactional approach of Auer (1998), Li Wei (1998, 2005) and colleagues, which is based for the most part on the tenets of CA. In recent years, Myers-Scotton has addressed this criticism and revised the model in the form of the Rational Choice Model (Myers-Scotton, 2002), which is the third model we will examine.

Following a discussion of these three approaches to code-switching, I will consider the ways that any of the approaches presented help us to develop the tools we need for a multilingual approach to curriculum design and teaching from an ecological perspective. I will take up the question of whether a discourse-analytical approach might not get us what we need in order to *teach* code-switching and affect learners' code choices in order to, in essence, privilege the L2 over the L1 in the learning environment of the classroom. I will show that it is about the discourses that students as nascent L2 users and developing bilinguals take part in, or do not take part in, by which code-switching and code choice can be useful.

Markedness model

Myers-Scotton's Markedness Model offers a social account of code-switching as one aspect of multilingual speech that is determined or influenced by multiple levels of social context, such as the nature of the language contact situation (e.g. speech island, immigrant situation, two or more indigenous language groups competing for social dominance), the relationship of the speakers (e.g. peer communication, intergenerational communication) and so forth. The core premise is that any use of two or more codes in a conversation indexes what Myers-Scotton calls 'rights and obligations' (RO) sets. An RO set 'is an abstract concept, derived from situational factors, standing for the attitudes and expectations of participants toward one another' (Myers-Scotton, 1993: 85). The *unmarked* RO set, according to Myers-Scotton (1993: 84), 'is derived from whatever situational features are salient for the community for that interactional type'. When speakers in interaction make particular code choices, they choose either the marked or the unmarked code, based on the particular RO set of that exchange, and in doing so, 'index' that choice accordingly, that is, they position themselves socially and interactionally relative to their interlocutors. The unmarked choice is the one that accords most closely with the status quo of the community or group in question, the one that would, in any given context, arouse the least attention. The marked choice, by contrast, is used to assert, define or construct one's own position relative to the interlocutors. Consider the following exchange, recorded by Zentella (1997), the content of which may seem familiar to anyone who spends time around children.

Example 3.1[2]

[Context: Lolita (eight years old) pushes Timmy (five years old) off her bike, and Timmy tells the adults nearby.]

L to T:	Get off, Timmy, get off.
T to adults:	*Ella me dió!* ("She hit me.")
L to T:	*¡Porque TU me diste!* ("Because YOU hit me!")
T to L:	Liar!
Adult to L:	*¿Por qué* – [interrupted by L] ("Why?")
L to adult:	*Porque él me dió, pore so.* ("Because he hit me, that's why.")
	El siempre me está dando cuando me ve. ("He's always hitting me whenever he sees me")

(Zentella, 1997: 84)

In the Spanish-English bilingual situations described by Zentella in her detailed ethnographic study of a Spanish-speaking neighborhood in New York, children typically addressed elders in Spanish and siblings in English. Zentella noted that Lolita and Timmy always adhered to this particular norm, speaking in English to each other. In this exchange, Timmy used the unmarked code by addressing the adults in Spanish. Lolita, by contrast, addressed Timmy in the code that would have been marked if the two were alone – her use of Spanish suggests that the choice of code was intended to secure the adults' attention. Lolita violated the unmarked norms of the speech community – in this case the code choice norms of this family – in order to deflect the blame for having pushed her brother.

An interactional approach to code choice

The question arises of whether conversation-external social roles are being determined or perpetuated in the verbal behavior of these children, that is, whether we can conclude that this exchange merely *reflects* the social norms of this speech community, or whether the norms are in fact being negotiated and created in the situated context of this exchange. In this distinction lies the most central criticism of Myers-Scotton's model offered by Auer (1998), Li Wei (1998) and others, along with the central premise of the interactional approach. In proposing an analytical approach to code-switching based not on consideration of conversation-external, macro-social factors, rather solely on conversation-internal features, Li Wei (1998: 169) contends that understanding code-switching is not about understanding 'what bilingual conversationalists may do, or what they usually do, or even about what they see as the appropriate thing to do. Rather, it is about *how* the meaning of code-switching is constructed in interaction'. Li Wei (1998: 161) also asserts that '[b]ilingual speakers change from one language to another in conversation *not because of some external value attached to those particular languages* [my emphasis], but because the alternation itself signals to their co-participants how they wish their utterances to be interpreted on that particular occasion'. An example of this is offered in the following exchange, recorded by Li Wei of a Cantonese-English-speaking family. The conversation is between A, an eight-year-old girl, B, A's 40-year-old mother, and C, A's 15-year-old brother.

Example 3.2

    A   Cut it out for me (.) please.
    B   (2.5)
    A   Cut it out for me (.) mum.
    C   [Give us a look.

B   [Mut-ye?
    ('WHAT?')
A   Cut this out.
B   Mut-ye?
    ('WHAT?')
C   Give us a look.
    (2.0)
B   Nay m ying wa lei?
    ('YOU DON'T ANSWER ME?')
A   (To C) Get me a pen.
(Li Wei, 1998: 171–172)

To highlight what is going on here, in the community in which this family lives, the same pattern of code choice obtains as for Zentella's Spanish-English community: the adults prefer to interact in Cantonese while the children prefer English (Li Wei, 1998: 172). In addition, 'the authority structure of the family in the Chinese culture expects children to comply with their parents' (Li Wei, 1998: 172). Li Wei (1998: 172–173) suggests that while the mother was asserting her authority by her choice to remain in Cantonese, her daughter insisted on a divergent language choice by remaining in English. Within Myers-Scotton's Markedness Model, what is not clear is whether it was simply the unmarked pattern for each person to remain in her respective code of choice, but the subsequent communication breakdown does appear to indicate, at least on the daughter's part, an open flouting of the expected code choice, of the unmarked code. Crucially, this exchange is used by Li Wei to suggest that social context is not 'brought along' (Li Wei's term) or indexed in this exchange, as the Markedness Model would assert, rather that social context is, in fact, 'brought about' by it. Put another way, Li Wei claims that the exchange does not *reflect* conversation-external social or cultural conditions, rather it reflects, for the speakers in interaction, only the *momentary needs and goals* of each person. The social and cultural contexts are thus *created by* the interaction, not the other way around.

Rational choice model

In part in response to the criticisms, such as Li Wei's, of the Markedness Model, that identification of RO sets and markedness patterns relies too heavily on the analyst's judgment of speaker intentions, community norms and the like (Auer, 1998; Cashman, 2001; Li Wei, 1998, 2005; Meeuwis & Blommaert, 1994), Myers-Scotton developed a revision, or rather expansion, of the Markedness Model. The new model, called the Rational Choice Model (Myers-Scotton, 2002; Myers-Scotton & Bolonyai, 2001), asserts that marked choices are 'inherently potential sources of costs (in comparison with unmarked choices that largely validate the status quo)', but they are also a means of embracing new sets of values and negotiating new identities or multiplying existing ones (Myers-Scotton, 2002: 205–206). In my reading of the model, the notion of rational choice suggests a two-way relationship between situated conversational vicissitudes and what Myers-Scotton calls 'conversation-external', that is, social factors. In essence, Myers-Scotton attempts to build the interactional approach into her own model, but remains constant in her assertion that socially determined unmarked/marked patterns of code-switching exist in any given bilingual exchange, and that speakers follow or flout the unmarked pattern depending on how they wish to position themselves. Presumably, then, the analyst can identify these patterns by observing multiple code use in interaction and understanding the social norms and typical patterns of the speech community. In this point, we find a connection to Atkinson's (2002) assertion, discussed in the last chapter, that interactions come already infused with social meaning that language users must cope with, and with Gee's (2005) discourse-analytical approach to communication, which views the identities that people 'enact' through communication with others in terms of participating in societally normed discourses, which Gee labels 'big-D Discourses'. These are defined as those that 'existed before we came on the scene and... will exist long after we have left the scene' (Gee, 2005: 27). I will explain and consider further aspects of Gee's approach to discourse later in this chapter, and in Chapter 5, I will use this framework to analyze several classroom conversations.

Now, Myers-Scotton (2002: 206) admits that 'previous treatments under the Markedness Model have only picked out marked choices based on qualitative criteria that depend on analyses of the dynamics of an ongoing conversation and in reference to the expected language for the conversation, given community norms for similar conversations', that is, on the analyst's subjective assessment of context. But in this study, Myers-Scotton also offers quantitative data, intended to triangulate with and support the qualitative data; her results show markedness based on frequency of code-switches by different interlocutors.

The fundamental premise of the interactional approach (Auer, 1998; Li Wei, 1998, 2005) is that speakers create and negotiate conversations *only* in situated contexts, i.e. dictated and driven by the needs and desires of speakers in the here-and-now, by their respective motivations, desires and interests. In other words, as Li Wei (2005) argues, the interactional approach picks up with explaining code-switching where the Rational Choice Model leaves off. Even if motivations, desires and interests are influenced by what we acknowledge as external factors, such as language prestige, an interactional approach posits that in situated interaction speakers do not consciously reflect on 'external' issues such as prestige. Speakers make conversational choices, such as holding, yielding or taking the floor, and they affect conversational repairs, such as overcoming breakdowns in communication (or not), in order to shape, maintain and change social context, not to reflect it (Li Wei, 1998: 163), not because they are concerned with larger social issues, but because they wish to maintain (or cease) a conversation, foster relationships, change the footing of the exchange (Goffman, 1981) and so forth. The issue for the interactional approach is to account for *how* speakers engage in code-switching; Auer, Li Wei and colleagues suggest that the Markedness Model is inappropriately concerned with *why* speakers code-switch. By contrast, a core tenet of the Markedness and Rational Choice Models is that in any given exchange, speakers are aware of the unmarked choice and choose to either follow or flout that norm. Further, the model considers it appropriate to look for 'messages of intentionality (implicatures) in the choices speakers make' (Myers-Scotton, 2002: 206), that speakers 'almost always have multiple identities' (i.e. a sort of repertoire of linguistic identities), that a code choice reflects the presentation or negotiation of one identity rather than another, and that speakers are 'rational actors' in that they are 'goal-directed' and seek to 'optimize their rewards' in conversational or identity terms. The process by which speakers make code choices can be explained in terms of rational choices (Myers-Scotton, 2002; Myers-Scotton & Bolonyai, 2001). In attempting to counter the critique of interactional approach proponents, Myers-Scotton (2002: 207) stresses that under this model, 'selection of choices is located with the individual, not outside forces', based on the idea that choices will always be rational: 'When faced with several courses of action, people usually do what they believe is likely to have the best overall outcome' (Elster, 1979: 22, cited in Myers-Scotton, 2002: 206–207). Myers-Scotton describes three 'filters' through which speakers make rational choices. The first is 'external constraints'. These include a broad range of sociological, sociolinguistic and pragmatic/conversation-related factors, such as socioeconomic status, gender, age and ethnicity. Following Elster (1979), external constraints translate into 'an opportunity set', the speaker's linguistic repertoire or 'arsenal of choices' (Myers-Scotton, 2002: 207), such as speech styles, dialects, languages, discourse strategies and culture-specific views about the appropriate use of any of these in interaction. These factors determine 'what individual speakers have at their disposal, but they do not directly determine the choices those speakers make' (Myers-Scotton, 2002: 207). With regard to Examples 3.1 and 3.2, external constraints consisted of what each person present 'knew' (though presumably not consciously or explicitly in that moment) about possible code choices. In terms of a multilingual approach to classroom code choice and this issue of conscious or unconscious attention to code choice practices, our goal is to raise learners' awareness of *opportunity sets* and help them critically reflect on ways they can or do manipulate or expand those opportunity sets in the classroom context.

The second filter, which Myers-Scotton (2002: 207) calls 'internal constraints', includes 'organizational aspects of the ongoing conversation in question', which are 'those micro-aspects of conversation that conversation analysts argue are critical to understanding any conversation'. Myers-Scotton lists this second constraint under two categories. Following Domasio (1996), the first category is labeled *somatic markers*, or 'features present in all organisms that help limit the "space" necessary for decision making and... call up experience and make decisions quickly. They are survival mechanisms... connected with human responses to social situations' (Myers-Scotton, 2002: 207). The second category is the *markedness evaluator*, a mechanism by which speakers 'take in information about how speakers/listeners behave and are perceived in specific interaction types' and 'abstract a reading of relative markedness of various linguistic choices' (Myers-Scotton, 2002: 207–208). Regarding the question of what speakers in interaction 'read', a parallel to Gee's (2005) discourse-analytical perspective can be noted:

> Thinking and using language is an *active* matter of *assembling* the situated meanings that you need for action in the world. The assembly is always relative to your socioculturally defined experiences in the world and, *more or less*, routinized ("normed") through Discourse models and various social practices of the Discourses to which you belong. (Gee, 2005: 67)

Importantly, somatic markers indicate the course of action for the best outcome, while markedness evaluations only compare outcomes of possible courses of action (Myers-Scotton, 2002: 208). In Examples 3.1

and 3.2, this involved assessing what personal outcomes might ensue from the marked and unmarked choices. With regard to code choice in the language classroom, this filter could be made salient to learners through strategies instruction, that is, through the identification and assessment of common markedness patterns or the normed discourses in which learners and teachers take part (see Chamot, 1994, 2001; Cohen, 1998).

The third filter Myers-Scotton calls 'rationality at work'. It is here that speakers make their code choices. Speakers consider their own and others' desires, values and beliefs, check these elements for internal consistency, and consider likely outcomes of choices. In short, speakers make a 'cost-benefit analysis' (Myers-Scotton, 2002: 208) each time they engage in multiple code use. Hence, the actual outcome of each exchange in Examples 3.1 and 3.2 was based on the rational choices of the interlocutors toward the greatest perceived benefit of and for each person. In the language classroom, learners could engage in overt analyses of this sort, based for instance on transcribed examples of their own or another class's conversations (such as those presented in Chapter 5), in order to identify, or at least raise awareness of, the 'costs and benefits' – in terms of language use and successful L2 acquisition – of their own code choices.

Let us briefly examine a further example of code-switching in order to try out the tenets of the Rational Choice Model. Example 3.3 (Block 2002), is a reported speech event that took place in Spain (this example will also be used in one of the curricular examples in chapter 6). David is a language professor living in Spain who speaks Spanish as well as Catalan, with Catalan being the L1 of most of the students at this language school. Jordi is an applicant to the school. In this exchange, David and Jordi meet for the first time in a placement interview for the language school. David wrote the following about the encounter:

> Part of my job at a large language school was to carry out placement interviews with prospective students. I normally began such interviews by speaking in Catalan as I wished to establish rapport and engage the prospective student in an informal conversation about his/her background before I proceeded to test his/her English. Beginning in Catalan instead of Spanish was not only a way of communicating to my interlocutor how I wished to position myself in the exchange, but also was an implicit recognition that most of our prospective students were Catalan dominant bilingual speakers. (Block, 2002: 129)

Example 3.3

David Bon dia, sóc David.
(speaking in Catalan) *Good morning, I'm David.*
Jordi Hola, soy Jordi, uh, Jorge.
Hello, I'm Jordi, uh, Jorge (speaking in Spanish, changing Catalan "Jordi," Catalan for George, to 'Jorge,' Spanish for George)
David Hola, Jordi. Molt de gust.
(still speaking in Catalan) *Hello, Jordi, Pleased to meet you.*
Jordi Ah, hablas Catalán. Muy bien. Estupendo. ¿Y cómo es eso?
(still speaking in Spanish) *Ah, you speak Catalan. Very good. Great! And how is that?*
David És que fa molt temps que visc aquí.
(still speaking in Catalan) *I've been living here for a long time.*
Jordi Sí, pero hay mucha gente que después de muchos anos aquí, no saben ni el castellano. Mira... por ejemplo, los extranjeros del Barça.
(still speaking in Spanish) *Yes, but there are a lot of people who after many years here, don't even know Spanish. Look at the foreigners [who play with] Barça (Barcelona Football Club).*
David Sí, supongo que sí. Bueno,...
(switching to Spanish) *Yes, I suppose so. Well,...*
(Block, 2002: 129)

This exchange is an example of dual code use motivated by the social conventions of the culture and society in which David and Jordi live and, considered in terms of the Rational Choice Model, was driven by the rational choices made by both speakers as they negotiated the local meaning of the exchange. The model would assert that accounting for the choices each speaker makes is possible only if we consider both 'external constraints' and 'internal constraints', which then led to each person's rational choices based on awareness (though perhaps not explicit awareness) of those factors. David's stated goal was to accommodate and acknowledge the status of Catalan in his encounter with the prospective student. Yet Jordi, while perhaps impressed with the professor's knowledge of his language or culture, was unwilling to acquiesce to David's desire to engage in conversation in Catalan. Appealing to social markedness principles, Jordi appeared unwilling to violate linguistic norms that apparently proscribe Catalan use with outgroup speakers; Spanish is the socially unmarked code and it was David's apparent desire to flout that norm for the sake of fostering intersubjectivity (according to David's own remarks about his intentions). The unmarked routine in a situation such as this would be to use Spanish; in overtly deciding to use Catalan, David reveals his awareness of this norm. While we cannot speculate on Jordi's intentions, we might, from the data alone, surmise a cost-benefit judgment by Jordi based on his desire to adhere to the unmarked norm, to retain his footing in the conversation or even to gain a sort of symbolic power relative to David (Bourdieu, 1991), who is both a professor and an interviewer. David's ultimate capitulation – as he switches to Spanish – lends support to the hypothesis that Jordi has assessed the situation in the moment, made what Myers-Scotton calls a 'cost-benefit' analysis and acted on it. If we accept the tenets of Myers-Scotton's Rational Choice Model, then we can and should consider as salient *both* the macro-social and the micro-interactional features of this exchange. Li Wei and Auer would probably object to this approach, noting that much of what we 'conclude' or at least hypothesize is based on speculation about markedness and even the nature of the cost-benefit analysis that Jordi or David might have carried out. They might counter that while one could analyze the exchange in terms of establishing or shifting footing or dominance, to bring in sociopolitical considerations based on tensions between Catalan and Spanish speakers is both unnecessary and of questionable validity. Admittedly, we could raise concerns regarding analytical validity, and in the case of David and Jordi, more data would be needed to establish such validity of our hypotheses about the *why* of this dual code exchange.

Yet, for the purposes of developing a multilingual approach to classroom code choice for curriculum design and teaching, two points should be made, and here is where empirical analysis of code-switching by researchers and pedagogical application of scholarship part ways to some extent. First, with regard to this one short encounter, this limited 'piece of language', to use Gee's (2005) way of describing verbal or textual interactions, in pedagogical contexts it would be unfortunate if we did *not* consider the socially and politically charged nature of the relationship between Spanish and Catalan in Barcelona as both an external constraint (as defining or delimiting the opportunity set of choices available to both speakers) and an internal constraint (the ways that speakers 'read' the relative markedness of various linguistic choices, or participate in discourses already infused with meaning prior to the exchange). After making a 'cost-benefit' analysis, it appears that Jordi and Davis make rational choices based on their perception of the social/cultural discourses of Catalan and Spanish, as well as that of a teacher and student. To accentuate the social/discursive dimension of this encounter, the reader would only need to consider how the conversation might have gone had the speakers made *different* choices, i.e. if Jordi had picked up on David's use of Catalan and continued in that language, or if David had acquiesced immediately to Jordi's choice of Spanish. In either case, the speakers could be said to make different cost-benefit analyses of the situation at the moment, though presumably against the same backdrop of social and cultural markedness information.

An ecological, pedagogical perspective of language use together with language learning allows us to engage Myers-Scotton's Rational Choice Model in designing a curriculum and analyzing with learners examples of learner code-switching, for it is indeed not just the *how* but also the *why* questions of code choices with which language class members can and should be concerned, even if these ultimately rest on subjective judgments. Pondering the *why* of code choice practices can lead to fruitful connections for language learning as part of humanistic inquiry, as a vehicle for critical thinking and as a component of the pursuit of intercultural communicative competence and translingual/transcultural competence. The interactional approach, though ostensibly unconcerned with the *why* questions in favor of the *how*, shows us that we probably *cannot* affect the details of code choices in situated interaction; these will always be driven by the local needs of each exchange (or perhaps by conscious awareness of social conventions or classroom power dynamics?); Lave and Wenger's social theory of learning and the notion of communities of practice resonates with this observation (that teachers can create conditions for learning, but not learning itself). The implication of the interactional approach for language pedagogy suggests that we should not attempt to control particular code choices through 'language-police'-like tactics. We should, however, consider what teachers and students *can* do, which is explore the *why* of code choice (along with some aspects of the *how*, of course) as a means of facilitating critical reflection about the nature and impact of their own (and others') code choices as part of L2 learning, of keeping in students' minds the complex nature of the many 'layers' of context at work in any social action. This now brings us to the pedagogical question: so how do we do this with students?

A discourse-analysis approach to code choice

In this section, I present an additional perspective of code choice in context through the tenets and methods of discourse analysis. Several scholars have regarded dual or multiple code use as discourse or in discourse-analytical terms (Heller, 1995; Rampton, 1995), though to date no one has performed a discourse analysis of code-switching in the instructed L2 context. Considering code-switching in discourse-analytical terms, Heller (1995: 159–160) regards code-switching as a 'means of drawing on symbolic resources and deploying them in order to gain or deny access to other resources, symbolic or material'. Following Bourdieu's (1977, 1991) concepts of symbolic capital and Gumperz's (1982) concept of speech economies and verbal repertoires, Heller (1995: 161) views code-switching as a tool to manage and control the linguistic 'marketplace' in which speakers draw on all their linguistic resources to accomplish conversational purposes. This approach grants context more than a place as an 'external' constraint or factor, it grants it an integral and concrete role in any human interaction, whether it involves one code, two or many.

In the many scholarly fields concerned in some way with discourse, there are numerous approaches to the analysis of discourse. In the broadest terms, discourse analysis is concerned with analyzing language beyond the level of the sentence. The discourse analyst studies the structures that organize authentic language in use, the ways political and social power obtain through discursive practices. Some scholars also move beyond the level of language itself to encompass all sorts of meaning making in discursive terms (Blommaert, 2005; Scollon & Scollon, 2003, 2004). For the purpose of defining and framing code-switching in the classroom context, we consider here meaning making only in its linguistic manifestation.

The tenets and techniques of discourse analysis are particularly well-suited to thinking about classroom code choice, for like Myers-Scotton's model, it takes into consideration the micro-interactional turns-at-talk as well as the macro-social, historical arc in which code choices happen. Scollon (2001) presents three principles for understanding what discourse is and how we can approach it theoretically. These principles do a good job of bringing several strands of discourse analysis and critical discourse analysis into harmony with one another, and they accord well with our pursuit of a set of principles for understanding classroom code choice:

> Principle one: The principle of social action: Discourse is best conceived as a matter of social actions, not systems of representation or thought or values.
> Principle two. The principles of communication: The meaning of the term "social" in the phrase "social action" implies a common or shared

system of meaning. To be social an action must be communicated. Principle three. The principle of history: Social means "historical" in the sense that shared meaning derives from common history or common past. (Scollon, 2001: 6–8)³

For the discourse analyst, discourse as meaning making is social action, which includes language. In line with sociocultural theory, language in this conception is not an abstract entity, independent of its use by and among people. Principle two means that people communicate because they have a shared system of meaning; Scollon, as well as Blommaert (2005), would contend that there are many systems of meaning beyond language, but language is a key shared system of meaning. This also compels us to regard language use as inextricable from the social action in which it occurs. The third principle, which derives in part from Bourdieu's (1991) concept of the habitus, helps us regard shared systems of meaning as part of historical patterns and trajectories. Blommaert (2005: 18) describes this aspect of discourse as 'historicity and process', whereby the 'historical conditions under which particular forms of communication become meaningful' (see also Atkinson, 2002). The key idea here is that 'every utterance displays a wide variety of meaningful features which, each in isolation, are pretty meaningless but become meaningful through their simultaneous occurrence in the utterance' (Blommaert, 2005: 126).

With its roots in Bakhtin's (1986) theory of speech genres, Gee's (2005: 7) approach or 'method' for discourse analysis lines up well with Scollon's principles. For Gee, users of language enact particular identities through language-in-use, called 'discourse with a "little d"'. Gee calls all aspects of context in which language-in-use occurs, '"big D" Discourse', which nicely reflects the consensus among several strands of discourse analysis:

> We are all members of many... different Discourses, Discourses which often influence each other in positive and negative ways... When you "pull off" being a culturally specific sort of "everyday" person, a "regular' at a local bar, a certain type of African-American or Greek-Australian, a certain type of cutting-edge particle physicist or teenage heavy-metal enthusiast, a teacher or a student of a certain sort, or any of a great many other 'ways of being in the world," you use language and "other stuff" – ways of acting, interacting, feeling, believing, valuing, and using various sorts of objects, symbols, tools, and technologies – to recognize yourself and others as meaning and

meaningful in certain ways. In turn, you produce, reproduce, sustain, and transform a given "form of life" or Discourse. (Gee, 2005: 7)

Young (2009: 53) succinctly summarizes Gee's notion of big-D Discourses as 'ensembles of semiotic systems that must be considered not only to have a history but whose history is part of the way in which participants construct meaning'. To analyze discourses in these terms, Gee offers seven 'building tasks'. Whenever we speak or write, asserts Gee (2005: 11), 'we always and simultaneously construct or build seven things or seven areas of "reality"'. These are significance, activities, identities, relationships, politics (the distribution of social goods), connections and sign systems and knowledge. For each building task, Gee poses a discourse-analytical question related to what the language user enacts or what 'piece of language' is made significant within that task.

If we use this approach as a lens to focus on code-switching in general or dual code use in the language classroom in particular, then we are challenged to consider *any* use of the L1 as possible enactment of Gee's building tasks, of social action as meaning making, and certainly as a discursive tool based on a common history and common past of classroom code-switching. Any instance of L1 use in this framework can be analyzed through aspects of language-in-use, such as the conversational functions of code-switching and turn-taking (and here an interactionist approach helps us to understand the ways that speakers position themselves through code choices) as well as through the multiple Discourses in which the switch takes place, where L1 use plays a part in enacting identities and recognizing one's self as 'meaning and meaningful' in certain ways. The sociolinguistic concept of markedness and rational choice for code-switching thus helps us to define what aspects of context we are to look for, while Gee's method provides us with the analytical tools for understanding the ways that the L1 is used in the discourse community of the language classroom (Olshtain & Celce-Murcia, 2003). The key point is that L2 classroom code-switching as social action, as communication and as historicity is arguably a Discourse in its own right, in which students and teachers make use of the L1 and the L2 to enact identities and index a range of other Discourses. In Chapter 5, I analyze code choice in two classroom conversations using Gee's building tasks.

Summary and Conclusion

I began this chapter by clarifying what I mean by *code*, pointing out that codes as semiotic systems (ways of making meaning) can be both linguistic and non-linguistic in nature. I offered two definitions of code-switching, and thereafter described three scholarly approaches to code-switching. While the interactional approach to the analysis of code-switching places the researcher's emphasis on the observable course of code choices in turns-at-talk, the pedagogical emphasis on the language learner and teacher need not be constrained to the explanation of the *how*; students and teachers have the luxury, in the safety of the language classroom, to engage in reflection and (subjective) analysis of both the *how* and the *why* of code choices. For this reason, the tenets and tools (in terms of social markedness and rational choice filters) of Myers-Scotton's Rational Choice Model are useful, not only for rethinking the ways that language classroom code choices are made, but also – and perhaps most importantly – for allowing for the possibility to overtly influence learners' and teachers' approach to 'managing' code choices. For this purpose, a concept of markedness is not only necessary, it is the vehicle by which we can make engagement with the very issue of code choice possible for all class members. Viewing code choices in terms of rational choices made against the backdrop of the 'filters' of 'external' and 'internal' constraints allows us to analyze classroom code-switching through the *how* of turns-at-talk as well as the *why* relationships between those turns-at-talk and the many 'layers' of context at work in any interaction (van Lier, 2004). At the same time, while the Rational Choice Model is helpful in making the concept of markedness operational for approaching classroom code choice, I further suggested that the tenets of discourse analysis could be helpful for understanding what L2 learners do with multiple codes. As observed in Chapter 1 about the 'myths' that underpin approaches to language teaching and code choice in the classroom, learners and teachers, of course, manage turns-at-talk in situated interaction, but in using the L2 and L1 in particular ways, they also participate in, perpetuate and modify multiple Discourses with a big-D; bringing aspects of those code choice discourses to our conscious attention for consideration and reflection is crucial for curriculum designers as well as teachers and students in classroom interaction. This will be the instrumental purpose of Part 3 of this book, but first, in Part 2, we must sketch out the status quo of classroom code choice. For if we don't have a good sense of what classroom participants do with code choices, we cannot establish a viable curricular architecture for a multilingual classroom community of practice.

Notes

1. In the original Yiddish, Weinreich (1945: 13) wrote, '*A shprakh iz a dyalekt mit an armey un a flot*'.
2. Conversation data reproduced from other sources follow the transcription conventions of the original.
3. Each of Scollon's (2001) principles includes several corollaries, but for the purpose of outlining a discourse-analytical approach to code-switching, a summative look at these principles is sufficient.

Part 2
Empirical Support

Chapter 4
The Code Choice Status Quo of the Language Classroom

> The teacher emphasised an environment of "No Chinese!". Because Mandarin Chinese is our mother tongue, when we found we didn't know how to say something in English, we would speak Chinese. But the teacher told us not to speak Chinese in class. Over a period of time, this became a class rule. When you spoke Chinese, all the other classmates would say, "No Chinese!". Of course, there were some naughty children. They disobeyed the rule and kept speaking Chinese in class. Everyone could feel that they were bad; we would put a negative value on them and think they were children who disobeyed the rule. We felt in our hearts that their behaviour was not allowed and bad and wrong. We would still talk to them, but not very often indeed.
> (Dörnyei & Murphey, 2003: 40)

> I don't like the fact that [the university] is forcing me to take a language when I could be learning something I like or will use. So, I refuse to speak it to my peers unless explicitly told to do so, and since the teacher answers in English if I ask in English, I stuck to what I know and like better.
> (First-year university Spanish student)

The First Language Elephant in the Room

Why is it that the two statements made by these students will probably both ring true and not sit right with many language teachers? In the first quote, the students have certainly bought into the monolingual/immersion principle laid down by the teacher, stigmatizing along with the teacher any use of the L1. In the second quote, which was written on an end-of-course survey, the student clearly links his dissatisfaction with having to study a language at all with the flouting of the expectation to speak the L2 'unless explicitly told to do so', pointing a finger at the teacher as equally guilty of violating the presumed convention. I headed up this chapter with these two comments on code use conventions to foreground the very complexity of the issue, for ultimately in this chapter I will distill and simplify numerous complex issues for the purpose of establishing what I call the code choice default condition or the code choice status quo for the language classroom.

Let's cut to the chase: in any language class, even the English class referred to by the Chinese student, in which L1 use was expressly forbidden, students' L1 will be used. It will be used at the very least for small talk among learners, or when pairs or groups of students negotiate for meaning in a language task, between the instructor and students at the beginning and end of class, and if used in none of these contexts, then we cannot deny that learners' private speech (Vygotsky, 1978) will often be in the learners' L1. In addition to these contexts, the L1 will probably be used to present or discuss L2 grammar and usage rules, course policies and the like. These assertions or assumptions about some common roles for the L1 probably won't strike the reader as especially controversial; they likely coincide with many people's intuitive understanding of what happens in language classes. For supporters of certain versions of CLT, these contexts for L1 use represent a sore point, an undesirable set of contexts for L1 use. And on the face of it, I would concur. When the L1 is used in these sorts of contexts, the tenet of maximal or optimal L2 use may be undermined. But my objection, as a classroom teacher, to students using the L1 for unscripted, off-record talk (small talk), or for the negotiation of tasks during pair or group work, is based more on the notion that class members engage in this sort of L1 communication *without awareness and critical reflection* about why or how they are doing so. But this is putting the cart before the horse: before we can address problems of the code choice status quo, it is necessary to demonstrate some evidence of it beyond the intuitive, anecdotal awareness of language teachers. If this reality is borne out by empirical support, then what are the implications for a multilingual approach to classroom code choice? In the introduction and Chapter 1, I argued on a conceptual and theoretical basis that a monolingual approach to code choice is undesirable, unrealistic and untenable. In this chapter, empirical evidence in support of that position is presented. It will be shown that in typical US university-level language classes, the unmarked code is often English in several crucial communicative contexts and the marked code is the L2. It will also be shown that in the absence of critical reflection about code choice issues, learner and instructor code choices generally do not contribute to the creation of conditions for the L2 as the unmarked code. I call this state of affairs, the 'code choice default condition' or 'code choice status quo' of the language classroom, which will be taken up in pedagogical terms in Chapters 6 and 7. The evidence is drawn from several sources. First, I review some of the literature on classroom code choice, including the results of a questionnaire study on L2 and L1 use, first published in Levine (2003). Thereafter, I report on a case study of two university-level language classes, in which amounts and instructional contexts of code use were recorded using an observational chart system.

Empirical Research on Classroom Code Choice

Interest in the topic of code choice in the classroom garnered scholarly attention from time to time prior to the current generation. A century ago, Büttner (1910: 2) railed against the dogma of the direct method (Krause, 1916) with its banishment of all translation and use of the L1 in language learning, believing that forbidding learners to use their L1 and the act of translation would make language learning 'futile and aimless, because it is based on false premises'.[1] Unfortunately, his ideas did not get much traction, then or in the ensuing generations as the audiolingual method and its variants based on behaviorist principles were developed (e.g. Bloomfield, 1942), which also saw the L1 as interfering rather than helping with language learning. It is, in any case, interesting that what most approaches since earlier grammar-translation methods have in common is the view of the L1 as an interference or a hindrance in L2 learning. This idea carried over to our time, despite the paradigm shift underlying the development of CLT (Hymes, 1972; Krashen & Terrell, 1983/2000) with its rejection of pedagogical principles based on behaviorism. At this juncture, if we value and wish to enrich the gains of CLT as an overall approach, it is crucial to have a picture of what really happens in classrooms, as diverse and variable as these events are in the particulars; we can indeed get a generalized sense of how the L1 and L2 are used.

Therefore, the purpose of this relatively brief literature review is to get at this question of just how much the L2 and the L1 are used in L2 classrooms, and how it is used: who speaks what, to whom and in what contexts. This discussion is limited to empirical studies, though there are many useful theoretical and pedagogical treatments of the issue (e.g. Blyth, 1995; Butzkamm, 2003; Butzkamm & Caldwell, 2009; V.J. Cook, 1999; Turnbull & Arnett, 2002). I will highlight studies whose aim was to either quantify the amount and type of L1 used by teachers and/or students, or describe or explain the ways the L2 and the L1 are used in the language classroom. Because of the flurry of relatively recent scholarly interest in this issue (e.g. Butzkamm, 2003; Butzkamm & Caldwell, 2009; de la Campa & Nassaji, 2009; Dailey-O'Cain & Liebscher, 2009; Edstrom, 2006; Ford, 2009; Kim & Petraki, 2009; Kraemer, 2006; Liebscher & Dailey-O'Cain, 2004; Littlewood & Yu, 2009; Thompson, 2006), and because many of the studies appear to repeat or confirm similar findings, I will focus only on studies that help us develop a picture of a code choice status quo in US language classrooms that also differ somewhat from each other. First, we will consider studies that measured the amount of L1 use among both teachers and students and categorized the functions of L1 use. Thereafter, I will focus on studies that delved into the intersubjective or sociocultural dimensions of L1 use specifically among learners. This will be followed by a description of an exploratory study I conducted of an introductory Spanish class and an intermediate-level French class.

Quantifying and categorizing classroom first language use

One of the earliest studies explicitly about classroom code choice, itself building on several studies from the 1950s through the 1970s, was reported by Wing (1980) in her doctoral dissertation. This study of teacher code choice in 15 Spanish high school classrooms addressed the interrelationships between two dimensions of teacher 'classroom verbal behavior', native versus target language and linguistic versus communicative functions. Linguistic functions were defined as the 'use of language in which the primary intent is to demonstrate, elicit practice of, and reinforce responses in the phonological, morphological, structural, and lexical systems of the language' (Wing, 1980: 14). Communicative functions were defined as the 'use of language in which the primary intent is to transmit and receive messages that express ideas, information, opinions, desires, commands, and feelings' (Wing, 1980: 14). Recordings of classroom communication were transcribed and analyzed according to these variables and numerous sub-variables. Not surprisingly, the descriptive picture arrived at demonstrates the full range of ratios of L2 to L1 use, with the L2 being used from 7.1 to 91.3% of the time! However, on average, Wing (1980: 191) found that the 'foreign language teacher uses the target language slightly more than half of the time while speaking in the classroom and slightly less than half of the time while speaking in the Communicative Function'. Also interesting was the finding that teachers with low overall L2 use spent a greater percentage of the time talking *about* language (the linguistic function) overall, and they were also more likely to use the L1 in the so-called communicative function. Conversely, those teachers who tended to use the L2 more, also tended to devote more time to communicative over linguistic functions overall, and to use the L2 for linguistic functions.

Another early study of classroom code choice was conducted by Guthrie (1984), which also focused primarily on the verbal behavior of the instructors. Exploring the question of optimal classroom conditions for L2 acquisition, Guthrie investigated the code choice practices of 6 university French instructors during 10 recorded hours of instruction. Like Wing (1980), Guthrie found that even in a multisection course at a single institution, there was a great degree of variability in the amounts and purposes of L2 and L1 use. Yet, overall, Guthrie concluded that most instructors used the L2 a great deal of the time. Of the six subjects, five apparently used the L2 83–98% of the time. Guthrie also measured the amount of L2 versus L1 used by the students, finding greater variability in a range from 68 to 93%. However, the study did not apparently focus heavily on the students' use of language because, importantly, in the classes recorded, students did not actually talk very much overall (in either language); they spoke from 9 to 24% of the time.

Also considering the amount of L1 to L2 use, Duff and Polio (1990) carried out a qualitative study of instructors' code choices in 13 university-level language classes. Like its predecessors, this study also yielded a very broad range in the ratio of L2 to L1 use, from 10 to 100%. In their discussion of the results, the researchers speculated on several factors that may have affected the amount of instructor L2 use, namely, language type, departmental policy on target language use, lesson content and objectives, pedagogical materials and formal training. They noted that the instructors opted to use the L1 in many administrative or other situations in which the L2 could have been used. In their opinion, using the L1 in these contexts deprived students of many good opportunities to hear and process the L2 for a range of communicative functions. The reader thus notes that despite observing the many functions of the L1 in the classroom, in line with long-standing beliefs about the pedagogical value of the L1, the authors also seem to see the L1 as interfering with L2 learning or use. And this despite the authors' finding that students in their study claimed to be satisfied with the status quo of their particular class, regardless of the recorded amount of instructor L2 use.

Four years later, Polio and Duff (1994) revisited their data and considered the question, when do teachers tend to use English, rather than the L2, and for what functions? In this paper, they focused on what they saw as one of the reasons for the students' general lack of success in the L2 acquisition endeavor: 'Students are simply not engaged in meaningful interaction in the foreign language during class time' (Polio & Duff, 1994: 313). Through a discourse analysis of judgment samples of the data, they considered the type of L2 available to students vis-à-vis 'the contexts in which English is used in lessons instead of the target language' (Polio & Duff, 1994: 313–314). They demonstrated how some of the instructors in the study appeared to engage in frequent intrasentential code-switching and often dealt with communication breakdowns by switching to English rather than negotiating in the L2. Last, the authors echoed Wing's finding that many instructors appeared reluctant to teach grammar ('linguistic function') or engage in classroom management in the L2. According to Polio and Duff (1994: 320), some instructors appeared unaware of 'how, when, and the extent to which they actually use English', apparently believing that they used the L2 exclusively and 'urged the students to use it too, but would not necessarily do so themselves'.

Departing somewhat from these earlier studies, in that it focused on the language use of both teacher and students, but still focusing on quantifying L1 and L2 use and categorizing its functions, Nzwanga (2000: 73) found that while the L1 as part of code-switched utterances did have a place in the language classroom, in the 14 hours of recorded university-level French classroom conversation, instances of L1 use by the instructor and students were relatively scarce. Indeed, the instructors in this study explicitly forbade the use of the L1 and avoided its use. Importantly, however, Nzwanga concluded that whereas communicative approaches to instructed L2 acquisition may have dictated maximal or exclusive L2 use, the L1 did and should have a role to play. He found that code-switches were most likely to occur during pair or group work (presumably among the students), before a quiz or during the presentation stage (presumably by the instructor), but that these appeared to be an important and integral part of what happens with language in the classroom (Nzwanga, 2000: 104).

Macaro (2001) was interested in how much instructors use the L1, why they claim to use it and what factors appear to influence their decision to use it. Similar to Duff and Polio (1990), he investigated how the decision to use L1 was influenced by beliefs about L2 and L1 use, pedagogical training, or governmental or institutional policy. Like Nzwanga, however, Macaro discovered that overall, in the classes recorded, very little L1 was used by either the instructor or the students. When instructors initiated a switch to the L1, it appeared that they did so for the sake of efficiency and expediency, or to impose discipline or keep control of the group (students were 11- to 14-year-olds). Considering the low proportion of L1 use overall, Macaro concluded that there is little reason to advocate for the exclusion of the L1 from the classroom. This assertion in *The Modern Language Journal*, along with similar assertions made by V.J. Cook in *TESOL Quarterly* (1999), begged the question of whether the prevailing taboo against the L1 might not stifle reflective practice among instructors (Macaro, 2001: 545), that is, that the dogma of exclusive L2 use might not limit what we could accomplish in the classroom. Still, in line with Polio and Duff, Macaro suggested that rather than going the path of least resistance by switching to L1, certain contexts present themselves as opportunities to expand students' vocabulary and hence the range of functions of the L2, and argued that that we need 'a framework that identifies when reference to the L1 can be a valuable tool and when it is simply used as an easy option' (Macaro, 2001: 545).

In Levine (2003), I was also interested in the amount of L1/L2 and contexts of use for both students and teachers, based on self-assessments. At the very least, it was interesting to compare self-reports of estimates of code use, and attitudes toward and beliefs about it, with the 'reality' of the classroom to uncover the extent to which we can count on those reports as reflecting what goes on. In the 2003 article, I focused primarily on the relationships between reported L2 use and anxiety. In the present discussion, I focus mainly on L2 and L1 use overall, and on some interesting differences and similarities between the student and instructor data. In order to complete the picture, I will tie in this questionnaire study with the next section of this chapter, in which I report the results of a classroom observational study of L2 and L1 use.

Shifting the focus from the instructor alone, as with many previous studies, to both instructor and students, I carried out a questionnaire study to measure learner and instructor beliefs about and attitudes toward L2 and L1 use (Levine, 2003). The questionnaire, administered anonymously over the Internet, probed the interrelationships between estimations of L2 and L1 use in that academic term, and it sought to obtain information about learner anxieties about L2 use. In the case of instructors, the survey gauged their assessment of their students' use of L1 and L2, and the students' anxieties about L2 use (indirect but nonetheless instructive). The main goal of the project was to begin to develop a descriptive model of code choice, necessitating a focus on both learners and instructors, and not only on absolute amounts of L2 and L1 use but, like Wing (1980), on functions of use, and further, on constellations of interlocutors, that is, who speaks what language and to whom.

In contrast to the typical small-scale observation-based study, for this investigation I chose to sample the largest possible segment of the population of university-level L2 learners and teachers. This is also part of the reason that the study dealt with people's *estimations* of L2 and L1 use rather than with actual measurements of the same. The study was guided by the following research questions (Levine, 2003: 347):

(1) What do students and instructors believe goes on in the language classroom with the L2 and L1? Specifically,
   (a) How does reported L2 use differ for different interlocutors?
   (b) How does reported L2 use differ in different communicative contexts?
   (c) How do instructors and students perceive L2-use anxiety, particularly in different communicative contexts?
(2) How do reported amounts of L2 use and L2-use anxiety relate to each other and to personal or classroom variables?

In order to address these questions, a questionnaire was devised that would measure first- and second-year language students' and instructors' (a) estimations of the quantity of L2 use in different contexts in university-level classes; (b) beliefs about the importance of L2 use; and (c) beliefs about student anxiety experienced through L2 use, also with regard to specific classroom contexts. Two versions of the questionnaire were created, a student version and an instructor version. Both were posted on the internet, and email appeals were sent out for participants at about midterm in the fall semester of 2000. Six hundred language students and 163 instructors responded to the study, representing primarily the most commonly taught languages in the USA (French, German and Spanish; this despite concerted efforts to engage the participation of language classes in the so-called less-commonly taught languages). Obviously, the self-selected nature of the sample meant assuming a certain skewing of the results from the outset, for it excluded large numbers of language students and instructors who either did not make regular use of the internet or who simply did not wish to participate in the study. The student sample was also made up of more highly motivated, higher performing students than a random sample would have involved. Still, the statistically significant relationship found between expected grade, motivation and L2 use (see Levine, 2003) suggests that similar relationships would have been obtained if the sample had been more representative.[2]

The Code Choice Status Quo of the Language Classroom

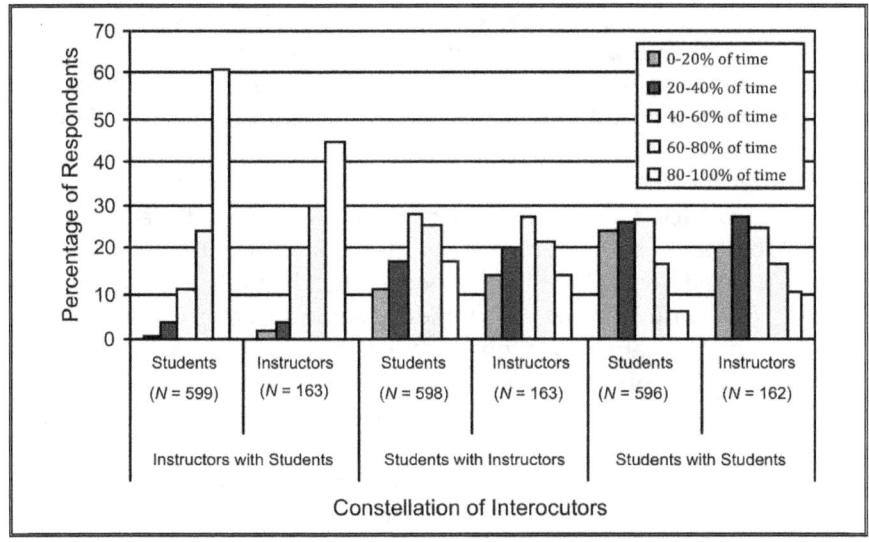

Figure 4.1 Comparison of student and instructor estimates of target language use among different interlocutors (Levine, 2003: 349)

Here, I reproduce the main findings with regard to ratios of L2 and L1 use. Figure 4.1, which represents student and instructor estimates of the amount of L2 use by different sets of interlocutors, reveals several important patterns of interest. First, about 60% of students reported that their instructors used the L2 80–100% of the time when speaking to them (the students). Second, students acknowledged that their instructor used the L2 much more frequently than they did, though they reported using it more when speaking to their instructors than to each other. Third, in comparing the student and instructor responses, it is interesting that learners generally reported greater L2 use than the instructors. Fourth, while the frequencies of responses may be different between students and instructors, the patterns of responses coincide remarkably.

Comparing this study with the earlier studies of amounts of L2 and L1 use, because these results indicate that in 40–60% of the language classes the instructor used the L2 80–100% of the time, the L2-to-L1 ratio appears to be as variable as was reported by Duff and Polio, Ellwood, Guthrie, Macaro, Nzwanga and Wing. Yet, while there is great variability within each interlocutor rubric, it is most important to note that the L2 was used most by instructors when speaking to students, less by students when speaking with their instructors and still less overall when students spoke with other students. In seeking to determine what the code choice status quo of typical classes is, this finding supports the imperative to have students talk more, and to find the means for them to use more of the L2 when doing so.

Considering the next rubric, communicative context of use, in Figure 4.2 we see a wide range of responses among both learners and instructors. Here, the student and instructor patterns largely coincide in the first context, 'topic/theme' (i.e. which was defined as those contexts dealing with cultural content or topics of some sort and corresponds to Wing's 'communicative function'), though the overlap is not as clean as with constellation of interlocutors. And here the context in which inverse responses appear should be noted: with the contexts 'grammar' and 'tests', learners report less L2 use, instructors report more L2 use. By and large, this chart shows us that the most L2 is used for so-called 'topic/ theme-based' communication, less for communication about L2 grammar and still less for communication about administrative aspects of the class (e.g. discussing tests). While not surprising, these data contribute to the picture of the code choice status quo I am attempting to sketch by suggesting that in contexts often deemed most important to students,

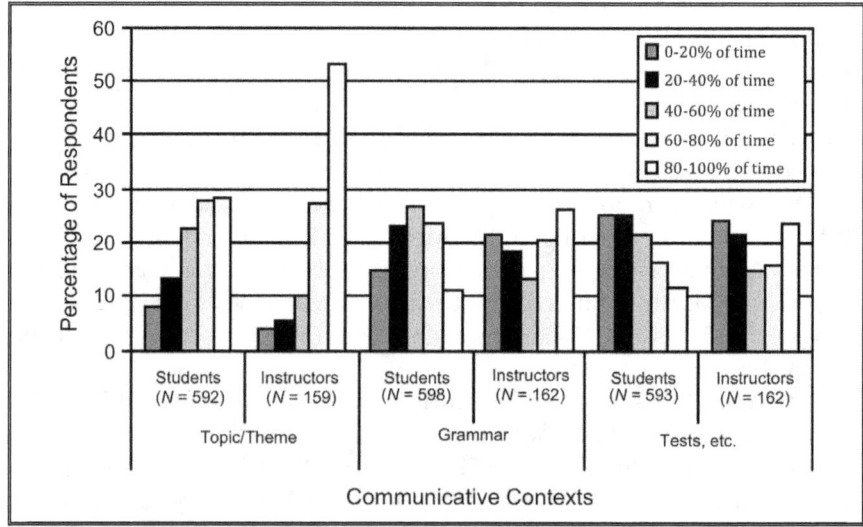

Figure 4.2 Student and instructor estimations of target language use in different contexts

such as gaining information about tests and course policies, or learning overtly about L2 features and structures (grammar), the L1 appears to be the default choice a good deal of the time.

Although my main focus is on the overall picture of code choice, a brief report of the study's results with regard to anxiety must be included here, because they help us both identify the code choice status quo and provide support for seeking to address problematic aspects of it. After establishing that none of the nominal variables in the questionnaire (year of instruction, expected grade, bilingual background, etc.) predicted reported amounts of L2 use as well as reported anxiety about L2 use, a least-squares regression analysis of questionnaire responses comparing estimated amounts of L2 use (found to be a factor through factor analyses of all responses) and reported levels of anxiety about L2 use (also identified as a factor) revealed a highly significant inverse relationship between the two factors. This means that learners who reported that they use the L2 more frequently themselves, also reported feeling less anxious about L2 use. The instructor responses followed the same pattern and yielded a similar, inverse relationship (−0.308). Admittedly, this simple but significant set of results indeed underscores the importance of maximal L2 use, but it also raises the question of the optimal conditions for it. The results suggest that for classes in which more L2 use and low anxiety about it was reported, the L2 was functioning more as an *unmarked language* (than in classes with low L2 use). Although the parameters of her analysis were different, Wing's study also seems to echo this conclusion.

What do these questionnaire results tell us about what is 'typical' for language classes, at least at the university level in the USA? What do they tell us about the relationship between more or less L2 use and markedness? There are three observations to be made. First, the responses indicate that the L2 is the most frequently used code by instructors, in accord with the results of earlier studies. Second, that learners use the L2 less frequently than their instructors is also supported by this study and the other studies described. Third, it appears that the L1 is the preferred code for communication about course policies, tests, assignments and L2 grammar. Whether the L2 is the unmarked code for communication about other things, such as interpersonal language functions typically included in mainstream CLT textbooks, cannot be answered from the questionnaire results or other research to date. At the same time, studies such as Antón and DiCamilla (1999) or Swain and Lapkin (2000), which I will describe in the next section, suggest that the

L1 may be the unmarked code for so-called meta-communication, language used by learners to negotiate and carry out an L2 task.

Intersubjective and sociocultural dimensions of classroom first language use

Moving in the direction of Vygotskyan sociocultural research and a shift in emphasis from language *acquisition* to language *use* as the object of study, and from the teacher to the students, rather than quantifying ratios of L2 to L1 use, Antón and DiCamilla (1999) moved the investigation of L1 use toward the discourse functions of L1 during L2 classroom interaction, studying the verbal interaction of five pairs of adult learners of Spanish as they worked collaboratively on three Spanish writing tasks. Departing radically from the base assumption that L1 use is something to be avoided, Antón and DiCamilla (237) concluded that, 'L1 use provides, through collaborative dialogue, an opportunity for L2 acquisition to take place'. L1 served not just as the code that learners resorted to when language ability proved inadequate, rather it served three main functions: 'construction of scaffolded help, establishment of intersubjectivity, and use of private speech' (245). L1 is not simply a metalinguistic tool, but rather a 'means to create a social and cognitive space in which learners are able to provide each other and themselves with help throughout the task' (245). The authors argued that the relationship between L1 and L2 in the classroom cannot be viewed in simple terms of how much L2 versus how much L1 is used. Underscoring the inextricable nature of language and thought, and rejecting the notion of a simple prohibition of L1, the authors appear to concur with Macaro (2001) that a principled framework is needed in which L1 serves as one of many communicative or semiotic tools. However, it must be noted that the linguistic gains demonstrated in this study are primarily in lexical acquisition, rather than grammatical or intercultural gains.

Similar to Antón and DiCamilla, Swain and Lapkin (2000) investigated the ways learners make use of the L1 to complete L2 tasks. In their study of 22 pairs of adolescent French immersion students, the authors described the ways in which the learners made use of the L1 in two different types of story-writing tasks. Swain and Lapkin concluded that learners make important, creative use of their L1 in order to complete L2 tasks. Here, too, is an overt rejection of the exclusion of L1 from the language classroom. And here, too, most of the language gains demonstrated are in the lexicon.

Focusing on the ways that L2 learner identities are performed and negotiated through code-switching and cultural 'crossing' (Rampton, 1995), Ellwood (2008) analyzed several classroom interactions in which adult English as a second language (ESL) students with different L1s aligned themselves to the role of 'student' or resisted some aspects of it. 'Acts of alignment' are those 'in which the student attempts to align both with the task and the role of good student in order to avoid any loss of face' (Ellwood, 2008: 544). They are 'proactive attempts to get "on board"' with a given classroom task (553) in which the student desists in 'presenting identities that are not institutionally desired' (Canagarajah, 2004: 120, cited in Ellwood, 2008: 544). Students performing acts of alignment through switching to their L1 in off-record interaction do not wish to be seen as not understanding the task or the language of the teacher and use their L1 to clarify and understand the task or the teacher.

In contrast to code-switching for the purpose of alignment, Ellwood also explores examples of 'classroom resistance', which are defined as the 'active resistance to or rejection of student roles' and constitute 'criticisms of some aspect of the classroom activity' (545). Acts of classroom resistance manifest through a 'flaunting of the conventions of "good student" physical behavior' (545).[3] Although Ellwood offers us this interesting dichotomous mode of analyzing the social or identity-related functions of classroom code-switching, she also warns against 'essentialist typologies' alone, asserting that 'given the fluid complex of identity formation, drawing upon pregiven categories is likely to fail' (547). Many other factors influence code choices in situated interaction; in the case of Ellwood's study participants, these include potential reading difficulties or proficiency issues.

In relating students' off-record use of L1 to pedagogical concerns, Ellwood's data 'demonstrate the fluidity and idiosyncrasy of identity and highlight the importance of recognising that students' classroom identities necessarily consist of more than the normative role of student' and that 'attempts to categorise students or to ignore the heterogeneity of individuals in classrooms is bound to go awry' (554). Also, beyond manifesting or indexing learner identities, code-switching as an act of resistance may 'index a critical response and, as such, provide a form of feedback on a variety of difficulties with or resistance to the task' at hand in the classroom (554). In other words, when learners flout L2-use norms by using their L1 in the classroom, the teacher should consider whether the code-switching also marks a critique of the teaching, the task, or the materials.

The final study to be considered delves not just into the question of whether and to what extent the L1 is used in the classroom, but on the question of *who* is using the L1, and why. Dailey-O'Cain and Liebscher (2009) use a conversation-analytic approach (based on Auer, 1998) to compare code-switching by students and teachers with code-switching in societal bilingual situations. From this conversation-analytic approach and sociocultural perspective, the authors stress that 'conversational moves in the first language can have different functions – or have different meanings – depending on whether the person using them is a student or a teacher' (Dailey-O'Cain & Liebscher, 2009: 133). Their data are from two classrooms at a Canadian university, a conventional second-year German language course, and a third-year applied-linguistics course taught in German. Focusing in this paper on what Auer (1998) called 'discourse-related' switches, or switches that 'serve to structure and organize conversation by flagging particular conversational items as functionally different from the parts of the conversation that preceded them' (Auer, 1998: 135), the authors' analysis shows how the same sort of code-switching appears to have different functions or carry different sorts of meaning when used by the teacher or the students. Crucially, their study provides evidence from naturally occurring – i.e. not elicited – classroom communication that both teachers and students use code-switching to structure and organize interactions using the L1, but that students' use of the L1 and code-switching is not modeled on that of the teacher. Dailey-O'Cain and Liebscher (2009) conclude that,

> envisioning the foreign language classroom as a bilingual community does not entail saddling the instructor with the task of formally training learners to behave as bilinguals, or even modeling the conventional codeswitching norms found in non-classroom bilingual communities. In fact, burdening the teacher with the task of explicitly teaching codeswitching has limitations, since some of the codes-witches take on different meanings depending on whether the students or the teacher perform them. (Dailey-O'Cain & Liebscher, 2009: 143)

In Chapters 6 and 7, in which I offer a framework for integrating multiple code use into the curriculum and classroom practice, I will address Dailey-O'Cain and Liebscher's admonition against 'burdening the teacher with the task of explicitly teaching codeswitching', differentiating 'teaching codeswitching' from systematically raising teacher and learner awareness of code choices in conversation, both in and outside the classroom, and of using this awareness to foster a multilingual classroom community of practice that also promotes avid L2 use, and hopefully L2 acquisition.

Several of the studies described here have the common aim of providing a straightforward description of what goes on in language classes with code-switching and code choice practices, and within the parameters of each investigation, they largely succeed. The overall picture that comes into focus is that, in terms of the overall *amount* of L2 used, the ratio of L2 to L1 use is highly variable (from practically no L2 use to nearly 'exclusive' L2 use) and is affected by a wide range of factors, such as the pedagogical approach, instructional content, teacher training, official policy, personal beliefs about L2 use, dynamic, fluid learner identities and so forth. For the classes studied in which little or no L1 use was observed, the interesting question is instructor control of classroom communication. For instance, in a class hour in which the instructor did most or all of the talking, and did this in the L2, it would follow that the subsequent report would reflect high L2 use. The question remains open as to whether in such classes the *learners* also used mostly or only the L2 (or whether they got to speak at all).

In the SCT-based studies of L1 use for completion of L2 tasks (Antón & DiCamilla, 1999; Dailey-O'Cain & Liebscher, 2009; Ellwood, 2008; Swain & Lapkin, 2000), the focus was not centrally on the amount of L1 to L2 use, rather on the discursive and conversational functions of code choices; the goal was to uncover the creative, interpersonal ways that teachers and learners make use of their full linguistic repertoire in order to carry out classroom tasks and communicate in the classroom context. Learners made use of the L1 for 'scaffolded assistance' and for structuring and organizing interactions and learning. Interestingly, with the exception of the students in one of the classes studied by Dailey-O'Cain and Liebscher, the uses of the L1 in all these studies occurred in ways that were neither principled nor in some way subject to conscious reflection by learners. Put another way, the status quo of most of the L2 instructional contexts studied is that the L1 appears to remain an *un*marked code, that is, the most natural choice in a range of situations. Even in Antón and DiCamilla's and Swain and Lapkin's studies, the L1 was certainly useful in a metalinguistic sense (to clarify or learn L2 word meanings), but it did remain the unmarked code and L2 the marked code of the interactions used in the analysis. Ellwood's (2008) study, too, showed that the L1 remains unmarked for learners. In looking at off-record learner code-switching to uncover some of the complexities of the ways that L2 learners enact dynamic and fluid identities in the classroom, the author demonstrated that learners engaged in varied and creative use of their L1s, but there was no principled awareness of the ways that L1 use related to classroom communication or learning.

Before proceeding to a description of my own exploratory study, let us summarize what these studies collectively appear to be telling us about classroom L1 and L2 use in typical language classrooms. First, whether instructors and learners use mostly or only L2 is highly variable, influenced by a wide range of factors. However, many scholars have found, in measuring actual L2 versus L1 use, that teachers in language classes are pretty good at using mostly the L2 most of the time. That said, the L1 appears to be prevalent in particular contexts or functions, i.e. for communication about any sort of administrative aspects of the course, discussion of tests, classroom procedures and certainly for off-record communication. This begs the important question of whether, in typical language classes, the L1 is being reserved for the contexts and functions that students and the teacher regard as most important. The questionnaire study described earlier gives a strong indication that this problematic condition may represent the reality. Third, it appears that in classes in which the L2 was shown to be used most or all of the time, we must be cautious in drawing conclusions, because the indication is that in such classes, instructors do most of the talking. Relatedly, in classes in which learners are allowed or encouraged to use the L1 to complete tasks, we must also consider whether the ways that the L1 is used in fact contribute to the perpetuation of the L1 as an unmarked code and the L2 as a marked code. In addition, the question of the differential significance of L1 use in classroom interactions should be considered. The collective findings of these studies point toward a generalized default condition, whereby the L1 remains the unmarked code for several key contexts of use.

A Case Study of Two Language Classes

In order to connect the estimations and beliefs expressed by learners in the questionnaire study with classroom observation and determine the contexts in which the L1 or the L2 are typically the unmarked code in the classroom, let us look at two language classes: a first-year Spanish class and a second-year French class. Both took place in the 2002 summer session, at my home university. The goal of the study was largely descriptive: from classroom observations and recordings, I sought to derive a picture of the ways that the L2 and the L1 were used. Specifically, my aim was to identify, if possible, the socially marked code throughout each class hour, and determine whether any markedness patterns could be identified across the six observed hours of each class, or between the two classes. The research questions guiding the study were as follows, built in part on the classic sociolinguistics question: who speaks what, to whom, and in what contexts?

(1) *What codes* are used in each class, and across all sessions recorded?
(2) *Who* is speaking to whom, and *what code* do they choose? Or *Who* controls the classroom discourse?
(3) *What contexts* are observable, and *what code* do speakers choose for them?

The instruments

Because I was interested in patterns of communication among all class members, I encountered several methodological problems in the design of the instrument. Following many of the tenets of ethnographic methodology (see Saville-Troike, 2003), and owing to concerns for the observer's paradox, my role as researcher and university professor (and, sadly an *older person* in a room full of people in their late teens and early twenties), I needed a means of observing and recording how code choices were made by and among all class members (not just by the instructor) in ways that were the least intrusive and conspicuous. Therefore, videotaping was not considered, and audiotaping as the primary means of recording classroom communication (for transcription of all classroom communication) was also not a viable solution, because during group or pair work an untranscribable din results. Hence, what was needed was an observational chart that would provide a detailed record of who was speaking what language and to whom at a given moment in time in a holistic manner. After considering both Wing's (1980) interesting coding chart and Spada and Fröhlich's (1995) COLT observational chart systems, I generated an observational chart that would help me record what was going on in the classroom with the following variables:

- Constellation of interlocutors, including speaker and addressee(s).
- Function or context of communication, particularly in terms of instructor versus learner control of the discourse.
- Code choice, i.e. L1, L2 or a clear instance of dual code use.

Finding grid-based observational chart formats personally too cumbersome, I opted to employ the conventions of syntactic tree diagrams, remaining (mostly) loyal to the restriction of binary nodes. The chart is

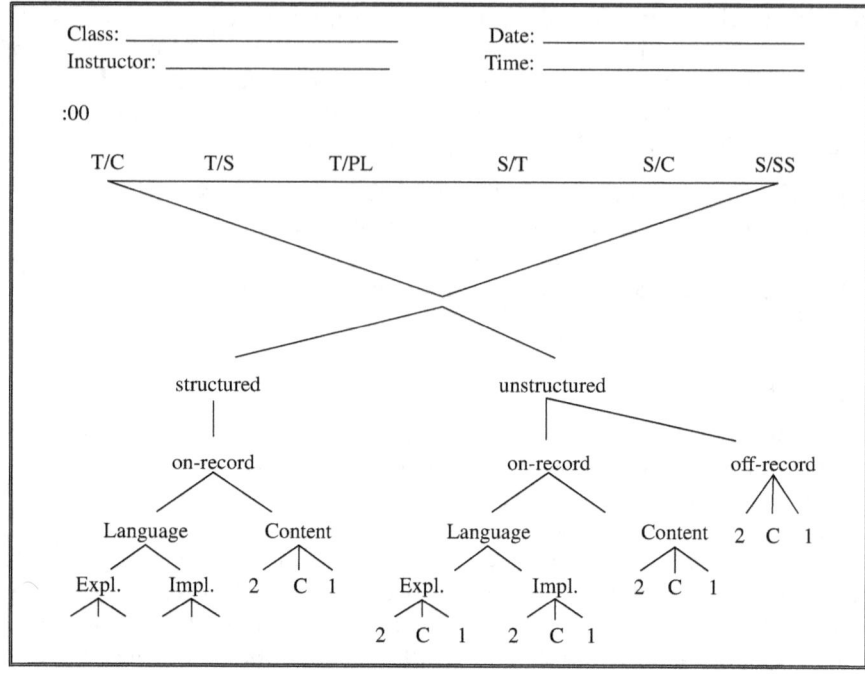

Figure 4.3 Observational chart

reproduced in Figure 4.3. This graphic layout was selected in part to force the observer to make on-the-spot either-or choices, even though this necessarily meant settling on levels of abstraction that might endanger representing the 'reality' of what was going on in the classroom. Ultimately, this chart represents making the best of a difficult situation: recording what a few dozen people are doing with language simultaneously in a room with fairly poor acoustics.

After several, more and less complex versions of the chart were created and discussed with friends and colleagues, this chart was piloted in four different German classes in my own department. Using a digital stopwatch, a research assistant and I took readings every 30 seconds, meaning two charts per minute. In all four classes, there was a nearly 80% correspondence between the assistant's record and mine, which was deemed an acceptable level of inter-rater reliability. Also, most of the mismatch between my observations and the assistant's occurred in one area of the chart, the variables under 'communicative context', that is, when judgments were called for whether the language being used at that moment was structured or unstructured (vis-à-vis scripted or unscripted), on or off-record or whether it dealt with language or content, and was explicit or implicit in its orientation.

The chart divides the three variables (interlocutor, context/function and code choice) across the three levels. The variables were converted into three sets of questions that the observer must answer at 30-second intervals. The top line addresses the question, who is speaking, and to whom? and is referred to here as 'constellation of interlocutors'. The second level, including the next four nodes, encompasses the questions, what function is language serving at this moment, that is, what is the context of communication? This rubric was the most difficult to arrive at, because of the problematic nature of concluding that an exchange is structured or unstructured, that it is mostly about language or content (something other than linguistic forms or usage), and when it is about language, whether it is dealing with it explicitly or implicitly. The issue of on-record versus off-record communication (see Hancock, 1997) was somewhat less problematic. The third question was also more straightforward, namely, what code/codes is/are being used at this moment in time, L1, L2 or dual code? Dual code use at each interval meant either (1) an individual speaker was using two or more languages in an utterance or exchange or (2) both languages were being used by multiple individuals at that moment. In the latter instance, this often meant that during pair or group work, some learners were using the L2, some the L1 and some were switching back and forth. It is important to note that in this sort of measurement, the concern was not with the exact function or nature of the code-switch, rather simply whether the L1 or the L2 was being used.

Data collection

I arranged to visit the two classes on six different days. These classes took place five days per week from 9:00 am until just before noon. My visits took place either at the beginning of the day or after one of the several breaks in the long sessions. I usually recorded for an hour, but in several instances the time span was dictated by the class's break schedule (the Spanish class took more frequent breaks than the French class).

Results

In the following, I address each of the research questions in turn, employing frequencies and their corresponding percentages to make comparisons between these two classes, to establish areas of difference and similarity.

What codes are used in each class, and across all six sessions recorded?

The observations of code choice allow this study to be compared with earlier studies in which the ratios of L1 to L2 use was reported, except that here I add the rubric 'dual code use' as a variable between the L1 and the L2. As mentioned, 'dual code' was recorded either when one speaker was using more than one language in an utterance, or when multiple speakers were heard using English and the L2.

Table 4.1 presents the aggregated frequencies for code choice in all six sessions of each class. I deal with each class separately in order to compare them and because aggregating the results from all 12 sessions would mean assuming general heterogeneity across languages, between two different teachers, two separate classroom communities of practice, etc.

In the second-year French class, the L2 was used 67.6% of the time in the six recorded sessions. Both French and English were heard 14.1% of the time, and class members used English 18.3% of the time. In the first-year Spanish class, somewhat more English was used (33% of the time), but about the same percentage of observations were made when both Spanish and English were used (14.1%). The reader should keep in mind that these results are based on looking at all six hours together (424 and 701 observations, respectively), which at least allows us to conclude that in both classes *English plays an undeniable role in classroom communication*

Table 4.1 Code choice frequencies for each class (six sessions each)

Language class	Code choice			Total
	L1	Dual code	L2	
Spanish				
Frequency	140	65	219	424
%	33.0	15.3	51.7	100
French				
Frequency	128	99	474	701
%	18.3	14.1	67.6	100

over time but that *the L2 is used a majority of the time*. Beyond this, though, based solely on these numbers, the two classes do not appear to be that different. Before we jump to the conclusion that we have already arrived at some sort of 'typical' pattern, however, we should look at code choice frequencies for each hour individually. Figures 4.4 and 4.5 present these data in graphic form.

When looked at across the observed sessions, the apparent similarity between the two classes dissolves. In line with numerous earlier studies, what becomes clear here is that there is always variability from one session to the next with regard to how much of each language is heard and used. In the Spanish class, L2 use ranges from 21 to 89.5%. In the French class, L2 use ranges from 35.6 to 90.5%. The bar charts reveal that over all sessions, more L2 was used in the French class overall than in the Spanish class. While the reasons why this may be the case relate to a large range of personal or curricular variables, we are compelled to examine the classes more closely in terms of the other two rubrics under investigation, constellation of interlocutors and communicative context.

Who is speaking to whom, and what code do they choose?

At 30-second intervals, the observational chart recorded who was speaking and to whom they were speaking. Figure 4.6 presents the frequencies in percentages of constellation of interlocutors for each class

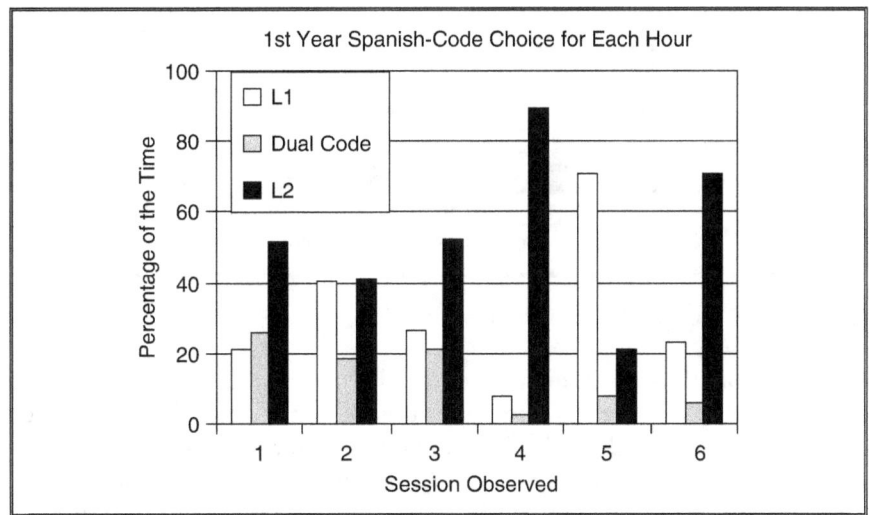

Figure 4.4 First-year Spanish – code choice for each hour

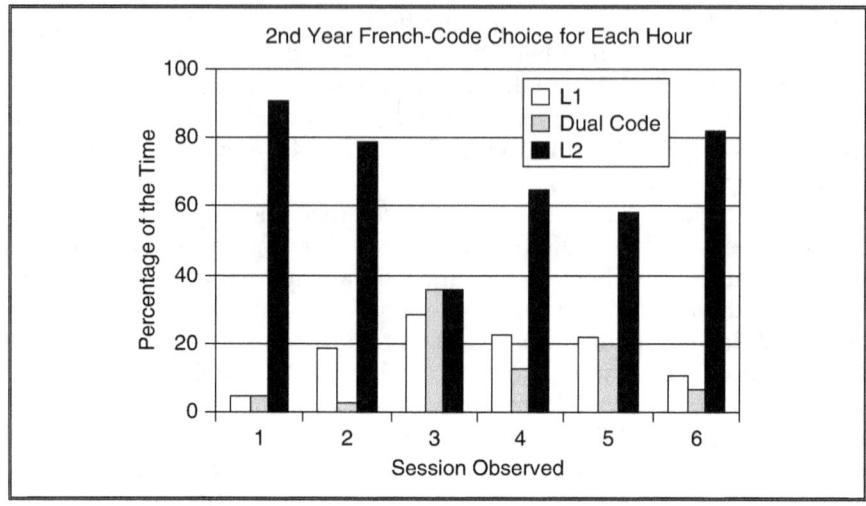

Figure 4.5 Second-year French – code choice for each hour

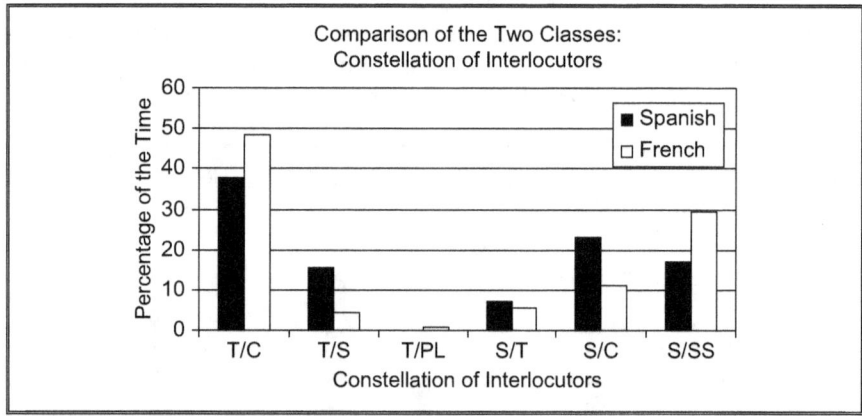

Figure 4.6 Constellation of interlocutors

(the sum of all six sessions of each). In contrast to the code choice patterns, what is most striking about this comparison of the two classes over the six hours is their similarity. The instructor spends a good deal of the time (37.7 and 48.4%, respectively) talking to the whole class. If we divide the categories into teacher talking and students talking, then another interesting similarity between the classes appears. In the Spanish

The Code Choice Status Quo of the Language Classroom

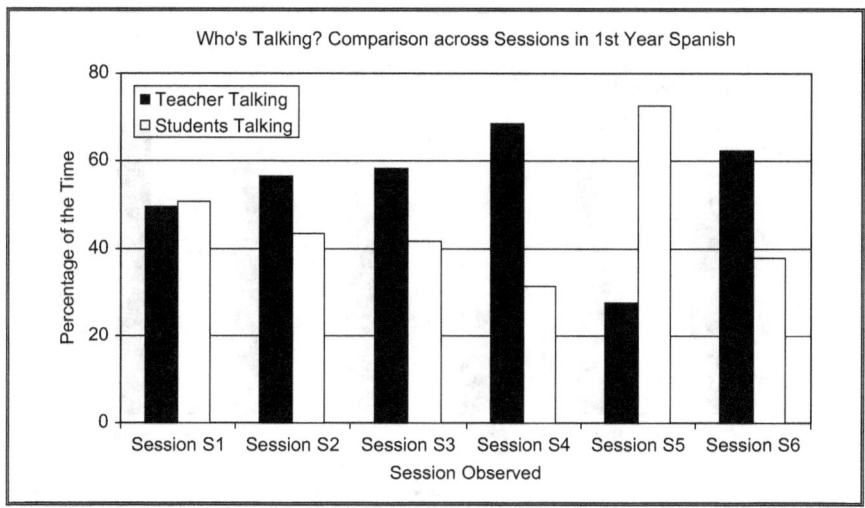

Figure 4.7 Who's talking? Comparison across sessions in first-year Spanish

class, the teacher was recorded talking 53% of the time and the students talked 47% of the time. In the French class, the teacher talked 53.7% of the time and the students talked the remaining 46.3% of the time. What this means is that over the six sessions of both classes, the teacher did the talking over half of the time.

As with aggregating code choice over all six sessions, here too it would be helpful to determine whether and how interlocutor constellation varied from session to session. Figures 4.7 and 4.8 divide the six interlocutor constellations between teacher and students to answer the simple question: who's talking? As with code choice, there is also a great degree of variability, and the two classes appear very different from each other. These data show that sometimes the teacher dominates classroom talk time, as in sessions S4, S6, F2 and F6, and sometimes – less often in the 12 sessions observed – the students do most of the talking in a given session, as in sessions S5 and F3. In F3, this was because students prepared skits that they were to present later on. In both classes, however, the students appeared to talk routinely for 40% of the time or less. In a typical 50-minute class, this would mean that students routinely talk for about 20 minutes.

The next important question related to constellation of interlocutors is, what code do people use when they're talking? Figures 4.9 and 4.10 present the frequencies of code choice according to interlocutor

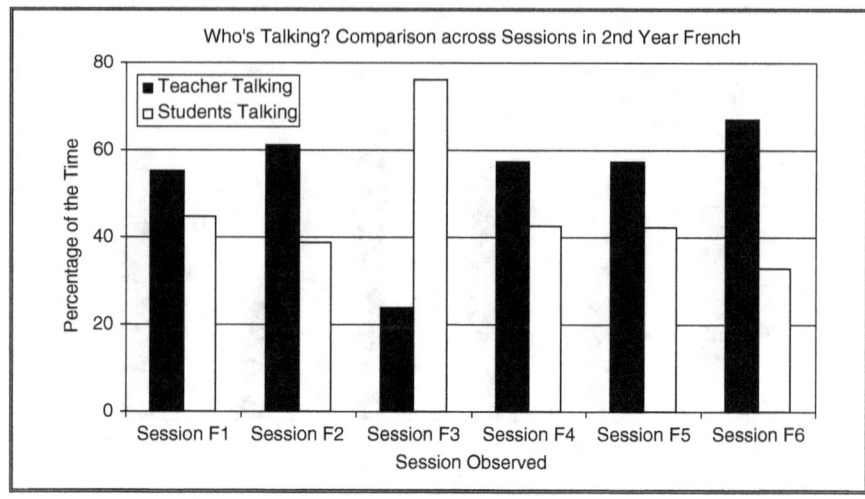

Figure 4.8 Who's talking? Comparison across sessions in second-year French

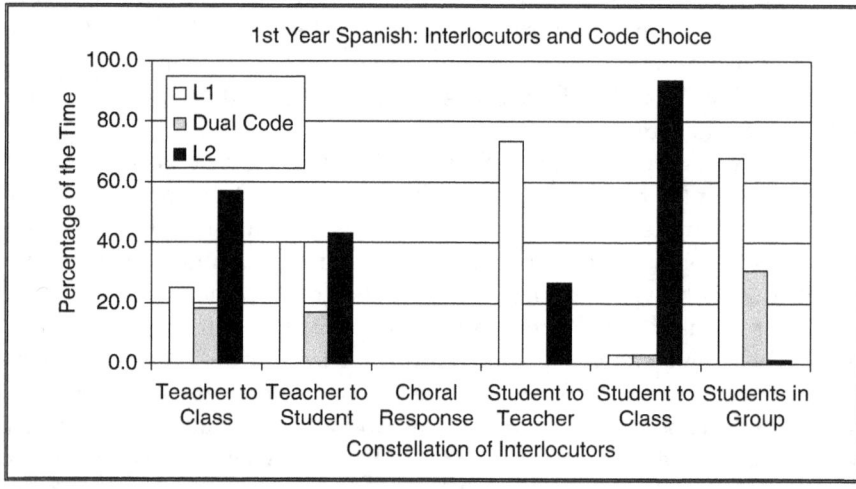

Figure 4.9 First-year Spanish: Interlocutors and code choice

constellation. Looking first at the Spanish class, the data show that the instructor, while using the L2 a majority of the time (56.9%), opted to use English 25% of the time when speaking to the whole class. When talking to individual students, he was even more inclined to employ English.

The Code Choice Status Quo of the Language Classroom 93

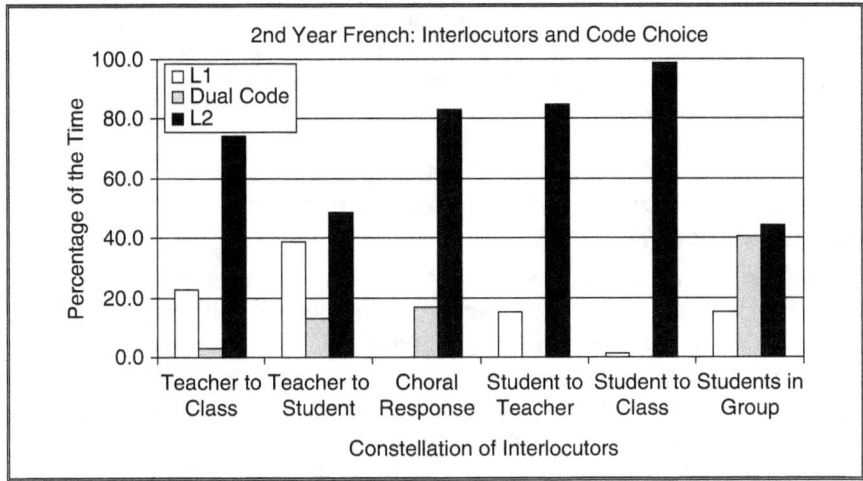

Figure 4.10 Second-year French: Interlocutors and code choice

The students' use of English and Spanish is also very interesting. Not surprisingly, when speaking to the whole class, usually in the context of an elicited response to a textbook activity, students most often stayed in Spanish. When speaking to the instructor or to fellow students, however, they were strongly inclined to switch to English.

The code choices made in different constellations of interlocutors manifested differently in the French class. Here we see a great deal more use of French overall by both the instructor and students. When speaking to the class, the instructor chose French 74.3% of the time. In the few instances of initiating choral responses from students, the instructor also used French most of the time. When speaking to an individual student, however, he chose French about half the time (48.4%), similar to the Spanish teacher.

In this French class, the students were much more inclined to use the L2 than the students in the Spanish class. While they were equally inclined to use the L2 when speaking to the whole class, when speaking to the teacher, they tended to choose the L2 much more than the Spanish students did. However, in pair or group work, students in both classes appear to opt for the L1 a great deal more of the time (than when speaking before the whole class or in other contexts).

With regard to observations of dual code use in both classes, more instances of dual code use were observed in the Spanish class than the French class, but by and large, it was surprising how little overt code-switching went on. Most of the instances of dual code use by students occurred when both the L1 and the L2 were being used in the room at that moment, i.e. during group work some learners used the L1 only and some used the L2 only.

What contexts are observable, and what code do they choose?

The next issue to be considered is communicative context, namely, what functions or contexts of language were observed in the 12 sessions, and what code was used for them? Figure 4.11 is a bar chart displaying the frequencies of the communicative contexts observed. As mentioned earlier, this was the most difficult variable of the class to judge and record, because of the problematic nature of calling a particular exchange structured or unstructured, i.e. scripted or unscripted, dealing solely or mostly with language or with cultural context (a literary text, a movie, an aspect of the L2 daily life, etc.), and if it had to do with language, did the communication deal explicitly or implicitly with it? For example, if the instructor was reading a text to students about a famous painter and the text contained recurring instances of a particular grammatical feature also under study in that part of the course, and if the instructor was making this in some way salient as the text was read, without explicitly 'teaching' this grammar feature, then this was labeled implicit,

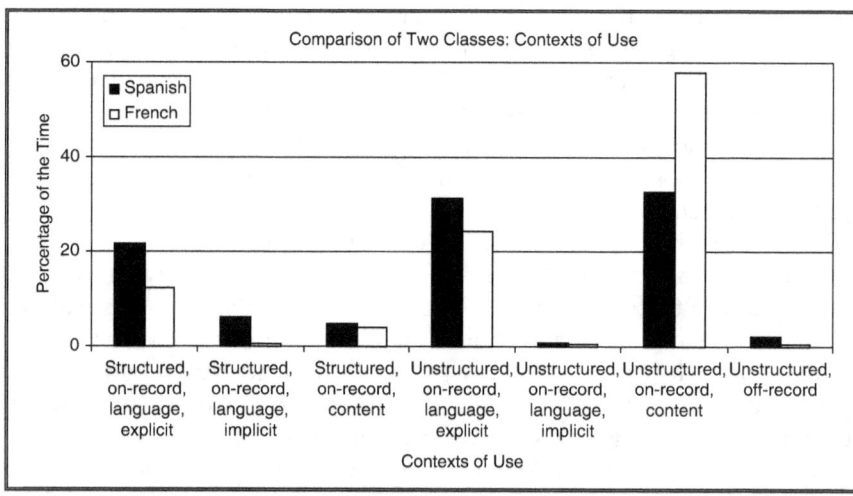

Figure 4.11 Comparison of two classes: Contexts of use

unstructured communication about language (the fifth of the seven columns in Figure 4.11). The issue of whether a particular instance of talk was on- or off-record was usually not a problem.

The data in Figure 4.11 show us two interesting things. First, in both language classes the context was about language as the topic of communication, i.e. vocabulary, linguistic structures or rules, 60.1 and 37.7% of the time, respectively. Second, of the on-record communication (almost all observed communication ended up being on-record), it was unstructured or unscripted 65.1 and 82.6% of the time, respectively. These findings indicate that a significant amount of communication in the language class may be about language as the topic of communication, but that, quite often, it is not scripted or elicited by curricular materials. These numbers in any case point to one unsurprising area of difference between the first- and second-year classes, that 'content' is dealt with more frequently overall in the second year than the first.

With this variable, communicative context, it is not necessary to examine variation from session to session, as it is assumed that in any language class, communicative context can and should vary greatly not only from session to session, but from moment to moment; it would, in fact, be remarkable to not find great variation from class hour to class hour. Let us move straight away, then, to a cross-tabulation of communicative context and code choice, presented in Figures 4.12 and 4.13.

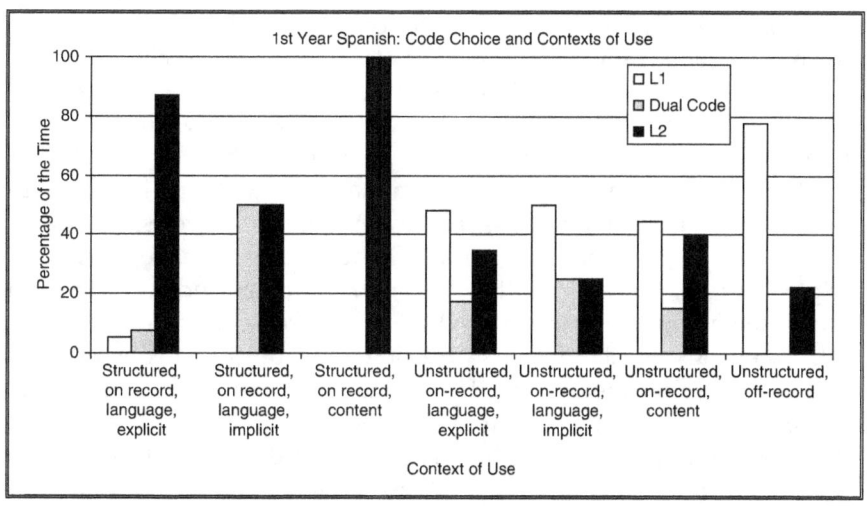

Figure 4.12 First-year Spanish: Code choice and contexts of use

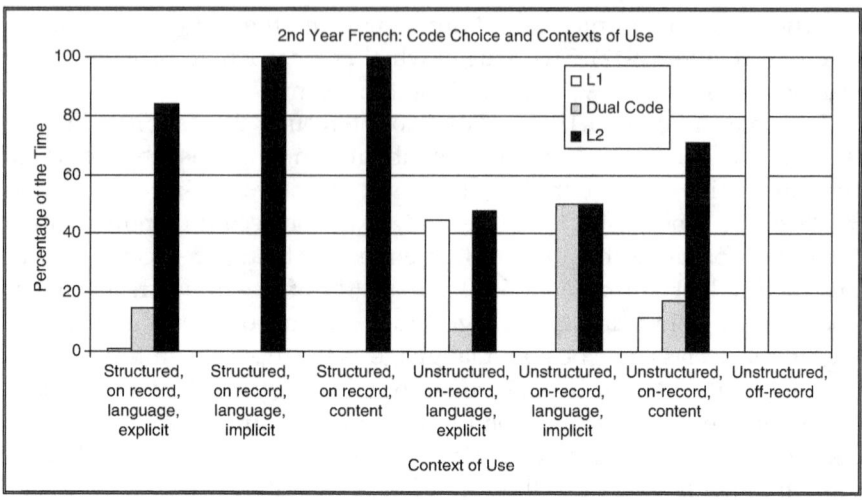

Figure 4.13 Second-year French: Code choice and contexts of use

In the first-year Spanish class, the L2 was used predominantly in structured or scripted activities, activities largely determined or guided by the textbook or worksheets. For unstructured or unscripted communication, class members clearly used more English than Spanish. For the mere nine instances of off-record communication observed, seven were in English.[4] And as with constellation of interlocutors, the contexts in which dual code use was recorded was less frequent overall.

As with constellation of interlocutors, communicative context and code choice also manifested quite differently in the introductory Spanish class and the intermediate French class. First, for scripted or structured contexts, whether about language or 'content' (in this class this meant talking about class readings), the French class members almost always remained in the L2. When communication was not scripted per se, but still dealt with language, then students appeared equally likely to use French or English, or a mixed-code format of some sort. When talking about course readings and the like ('content'), the class was more inclined to use the L2 than the Spanish class; this is, of course, not a surprising difference between a first-year and a second-year class. Finally, as with the Spanish class, for the few instances when off-record communication was observed (only 4 of 701 observations), English was the language chosen.

Discussion

Each of the three research questions has been addressed by the descriptive data obtained through classroom observations of these two classes. It was found that the amount of L2 varied greatly from hour to hour, but that, overall, the L1 was generally used in both classes from one third to nearly half the time, enough of the time for us to conclude that regardless of communicative-approach methodology, the L1 served numerous functions.

For the question of who speaks to whom, it was found that the instructor in both classes generally talked for about half of most observed sessions. Whether this is a 'typical' pattern for language classes must, of course, remain an open question because of the small sample size, but I suggest that this finding would surprise few language teachers. It was found that the instructor used the L2 more than the students overall, in accord with the findings of my earlier questionnaire study (Levine, 2003) and the findings of earlier studies (e.g. Guthrie, 1984).

In looking at the code choices made by different constellations of interlocutors, clear differences between the two classes were apparent, and one crucial similarity. In the Spanish class, learners were very likely to use the L1, unless they were addressing the entire class; in the French class, in many instances the students appeared to use the L2 more readily than the instructor, except when they were talking in groups. In this case, the Spanish and French students appeared to use the L1 as often as the L2. This finding alone points toward what I see as a serious problem in typical language class communication, namely that the common use of pair and group work in CLT classrooms may involve the most use of the L1 to complete tasks. The issue is not whether this use of English supports L2 learning and task completion, for surely it does in many cases, as Swain and Lapkin (2000) found; it's about whether the teacher and students have reflected upon its uses in this or other contexts and make principled use of L1. This will serve as the cornerstone of the curricular proposals made in Chapters 6 and 7.

With regard to contexts of use, the classes observed accord with communicative patterns discussed by van Lier (1996) and others: a frequent, central topic of conversation in the language class is the L2 itself, though in the second-year course, class members communicated about 'content' more of the time than did the people in the first-year class. The code chosen for different contexts likewise revealed differences between the two classes, though we cannot say if this is a function of language level or some other factor. In the Spanish class, the L2 was used predominantly for structured or scripted contexts and the L1 in unstructured/unscripted contexts, in the French class people were more likely to use the L2 in unstructured contexts, or rather, they were generally equally likely to use the L1 or the L2.

How do these observations help us in determining a norm or baseline set of assumptions about code choice on which to build a curricular architecture? The similarities between the two language classes serve to indicate potential directions, points of overlap that allow us to suggest commonalities among language classes in general, but what of the differences, which are clearly more numerous than the similarities? Admittedly, some of the differences may be a function of language level, but one can't say for sure. In my own observations of numerous language teachers' German classes, I can assert that in many first-year classes the L2 is used even more of the time than we saw in this second-year French class, and correspondingly, in many second-year classes the L1 is used more than in this French class. This anecdotal assertion alone makes establishing a default condition problematic, no matter how you turn it, yet it is important to make the attempt.

To move in this direction, in the following I would like to pull together the findings from research presented earlier in this chapter and from this study, in order to argue that the default condition in typical language classes is indeed *marked L2 and unmarked L1* in particular key contexts. Further, the heterogeneity within and across language classes, while perhaps an impediment to successfully modeling the process of L2 acquisition, can be viewed as an advantage in our goal of developing a multilingual approach to code choice in the language classroom, of transferring autonomy and power over classroom communication to learners. For in acknowledging the inherent complexity and heterogeneity of the classroom, our job becomes assigning workable principles to manage it, not to 'control' it per se (heterogeneity is by definition impervious to overt control).

Teasing out a Default Condition

Based on the review of the empirical literature and the descriptive study of an introductory Spanish and an intermediate French class, I believe that we have come to the point of being able to identify a default condition of classroom code choice on which to build our curricular architecture (Chapter 6) and articulate it horizontally and vertically in multi-section language programs (Chapter 7). Although a great many aspects of code choice vary from person to person, from class to class and from hour to hour within a given class, there are many points in common among the several sources of information about code choice considered in this chapter, factors that appear to apply across the board in introductory and intermediate university-level language classes regardless of language level, the language being taught[5] or other factors. From these common features or factors, we can synthesize a code choice default condition:

- *L1 serves important functions.* All the studies described in this chapter, including my own questionnaire and case studies, indicate that the L1 clearly serves important communicative (discourse), cognitive and social functions in the classroom, and in L2 learning in general. As such, its use must be considered as given in the language classroom, a position supported by the arguments and empirical evidence brought by numerous scholars.[6]
- *The instructor uses the L2 more frequently than the student.* The two studies described in this chapter show that compared to the students, the instructor uses the L2 far more frequently in many situations.
- *The instructor does a disproportionate amount of the talking.* The questionnaire and classroom case studies demonstrated that the instructor appears to do a great deal of the talking in any given hour; she/he appears to hold the floor for around half of the time on average. This means that consideration of how much time is spent using the L2 in any given hour must be weighed against the fact that the default condition indicates that the instructor talks a good deal of the time.
- *The L2 is unmarked in many scripted contexts; the L1 is unmarked in many unscripted contexts.* It was also shown that we can't simply consider code choice at the broadest level, in terms of simple ratios of L2 to L1 (though this is an important first step): we must also consider communicative context. Here, the most important generalization about a code choice default condition can be made: it appears that when class members communicate in structured or scripted ways, that is, through textbook activities, they are more likely to use the L2 more than the L1, in keeping with expected practices in CLT activities and tasks. Yet, when talking in unscripted ways, whether about language as a topic of conversation or about 'content', class members tend toward selecting the L1. Further, when the topic of conversation is language itself, both the instructor and students often favor using the L1, even at the intermediate level

when learners presumably could deal with this sort of context in the L2. This is supported by the questionnaire study, which suggested that for communication about grammar and course policies, tests and the like, the L1 is often the preferred code, and by the observation study, where it was also shown that learners favor the L1 to discuss linguistic structures and rules (see Figure 4.11).
- *Learners prefer the L1 when talking among themselves.* Also related to the contexts-of-use issue, when learners meet in groups, they lean very heavily toward using the L1. This is supported by my own studies, as well as by the evidence offered by Antón and DiCamilla (1999), Ellwood (2008) and Swain and Lapkin (2000), who showed how learners use the L1 in diverse and creative ways and contexts.

Given that we probably cannot influence the fact that instructors dominate the floor in language classes about half the time on average (that would be the topic of another book; see van Lier, 1996, Chapters 8 and 9), we have to consider what aspects of this default condition we could affect toward the goal of providing greater affordances for L2 and L1 use that supports L2 use. While the L2 is clearly an unmarked code in numerous contexts in many language classes, such as during structured or scripted activities, enough of the typical communicative contexts in the classroom proceed in an unmarked way in the L1 to accentuate the imperative to help teachers and learners to critically reflect on code choices and code use, to socially and 'artificially' mark the L1 in those contexts and work toward unmarking the L2. Through this process it is hoped that the domains and contexts in which the L2 becomes unmarked will increase, thereby optimizing L2 use overall. Of course, if in the process we can find ways to get the teacher to talk for less of the time overall, too, then so much the better.

Summary and Conclusion

In this chapter, a survey of previous research as well as my own case study of two language classes helped to establish what I call the code choice default condition or the code choice status quo of typical CLT classes in US universities. I also suggested that it is not sufficient to simply 'allow' the L1 a role in the classroom in the absence of critical reflection about it, for unchecked it will be used most frequently in communicative contexts that might undermine rather than support maximal L2 use. In closing, and to return to the two student statements in the epigraph of this chapter, the proposed curricular architecture should facilitate the means of marking L1 in certain contexts without stigmatizing it, as the L1 clearly was marked in the first student's situation. Additionally, it should avoid forcing on students a particular viewpoint or top-down set of rules to be defied or undermined, as was the case for the second student. In short, we must offer a means for students to be the masters of their own classroom discourses, with code choice as one of the most salient and flexible features of those discourses.

Notes

1. My translation of Büttner.
2. In the 2003 paper, the L2 is referred to as the target language (TL).
3. Ellwood (2008: 548) analyzes a third category in her study, which she calls 'acts of global identity', in which the study participants, who hailed from multiple language backgrounds, engaged in crossing behavior (the use of other students' L1s) in order to 'present themselves as having a "global" or "cosmopolitan" identity'. This part of Ellwood's study in not included here because our focus in this book is the university foreign-language classroom in which students share the same L1; while crossing and acts of global identity surely obtain in some situations, this sort of code choice behavior lies outside the scope of this book.
4. So few instances of off-record communication were recorded, not because class members did not engage in this sort of communication, rather because it was usually whispered or spoken very softly between interlocutors, therefore what was being talked about or what code was being used could not be determined (see Hancock, 1997).
5. Admittedly, the extant literature on code choice, including my own questionnaire study and the study reported in this chapter on the Spanish and French classes, deals almost exclusively with European languages, primarily English, French, Spanish and German. Duff and Polio (1990) study classes in which languages other than these are taught, but by and large, this represents a large gap in the scholarly investigation of code choice. Therefore, generalizations made should be considered to apply to the genetically related languages most commonly taught in US university courses.
6. For example, Antón and DiCamilla (1999), Belz (2002, 2003), Blyth (1995), V.J. Cook (1999, 2001), Crozet and Liddicoat (1999), Duff and Polio (1990), Ellwood (2008), Guthrie (1984), Kramsch (1993, 1998 and elsewhere), Levine (2005), Liebscher and Dailey-O'Cain (2004), Littlewood and Yu (2009), Macaro (2001), Nzwanga (2000), Polio and Duff (1994), Swain and Lapkin (2000), Turnbull and Arnett (2002) and Wing (1980).

Chapter 5
Classroom Code Choice: Toward Becoming Bilingual

> *If I have no idea who you are and what you are doing, then I cannot make sense of what you have said, written, or done.*
> (Gee, 2005: 22)

Discourse Analysis as a Tool for Understanding Classroom Code Choice

Using language, or 'languaging', is one of the most powerful things human beings do (Larsen-Freeman, 2003; Phipps & Gonzalez, 2005). And, of course, everyone has an opinion about language, particularly about foreign languages and bilingualism. Yet, it is ironic that the individual acts involved in communicating as we go through our days often remain opaque to most speakers; we do not consciously consider the ways we slip in and out of different communication patterns, or discourse routines. While individual utterances certainly vary, allowing us to create infinite novel utterances – an observation that drove Noam Chomsky's original thinking about the problem of language acquisition (Chomsky, 1965, 1988) – the very meaning of the language–culture link means that any use of language is never just that, a use of language, rather it is a piece of the unceasing, massively collaborative enactment, recreation, modification and nuanced manipulation of our cultural and social realities (Bourdieu, 1990). In the classroom context, the range of these social-cultural frames are less opaque, perhaps, than in the so-called 'real world' outside the classroom; this sets up limitations, of course, but also affordances for curriculum designers and teachers for efficiencies of communication, and of learning. With regard to code choice, in the educational setting, the choices we make to use the L1 or the L2 interact with and influence how communication takes place, and how learning might happen. Yet, here again the irony is that most participants in classroom interactions – teachers and students alike – are not usually overtly aware of how and when they make code choices

(Dailey-O'Cain & Liebscher, 2009; Polio & Duff, 1994). This does not mean that they do not flout the conventions established by the pedagogical context, of course, but even here, learners and teachers in interaction may not be aware of it when they do so.

The goal of this chapter is thus to bring some aspects of code choices in classroom interaction to our conscious attention, and to analyze some of the discourse patterns of L1 and L2 use, in order to provide a further layer to the case for a principled approach to classroom code choice. The analysis aims to show that any code choice made by students or teachers is embedded within multiple contexts; awareness and consideration of these contexts must also be part of any curricular architecture. In Chapter 3, models were presented whose goal was to account for code-switching as social action. I argued that an interactional approach is useful for understanding some of the ways that speakers code-switch in order to orient and position themselves in interaction, basically to 'get things done' by using the L1 in L2 interaction, but I raised the question whether disregarding other spheres of context, factors that are often thought of as 'conversation external', is appropriate in considering L2 learner code-switching. I suggested that looking at all aspects of context might be the way to gain a fuller understanding of code choice in the language classroom, as well as provide a means for integrating learning of and about code choice into the language curriculum.

I then examined Myers-Scotton's Markedness Model and its more recent revision, the Rational Choice Model, to determine whether it serves us better in analyzing the code choices made by learners toward the goal of establishing principles for classroom code choice. The idea of markedness, I argued, is indeed a useful construct for classroom discussion of code-switching with students, because it opens a space for contextual, social and cultural factors to influence code choices; in Chapters 6 and 7, I will integrate this concept into a set of curricular proposals. Although Myers-Scotton's Rational Choice Model allows us to consider issues of context that include and then go beyond talk-in-interaction, the model does so in a way that remains problematic, for two reasons. On the one hand, the dichotomy external-internal appears based on the assumption that anything can be 'external' to a particular social act, such as a conversation. This is, of course, a key objection of the interactional approach to the very idea of markedness, namely, the appeal to 'conversation-external' factors to analyze talk-in-interaction (Auer, 1998). Second, viewing the act of code-switching as a rational choice that has passed through the three filters is a compelling metaphor, but it sets up the moment of code choice as the culmination of a linear sequence of events, even if the speakers are not overtly aware of the affect of those filters. Yet, considering all the aspects of context, the RC Model itself mandates that the influence of contextual factors on code choices is multifaceted, dynamic and variable according to the situation, and hence non-linear. A solution, I suggested, lies in reframing this notion of filters from a discourse-analytical perspective, which accords well with the sociocultural and ecological frameworks presented in Chapter 2 (see also Levine, 2009). Gee's (2005) discourse-analytical 'method' (of talk-in-interaction) is a synthesis of several strands of discourse analysis and conversation analysis, and it allows us to consider all aspects of what is usually understood as context in discursive terms, to regard the moment of code choice as the enactment (not simply the reflection or indexing) of a range of little-d discourses ('doing things with words') and big-D Discourses, which obviates the need to dichotomize conversation-internal and -external factors, and it moves beyond the choice to use the L1 or the L2 as a linear process, as the Rational Choice model requires. Viewing the individual act of code-switching in this way brings all these 'levels' or 'layers' of meaning making into consideration as interacting in complex and not necessarily linear or hierarchical ways. It also removes the imperative to deduce or interpret in some final and potentially inaccurate way the intentions or thoughts of speakers in interaction (Li Wei, 1998; Walsh, 2006). Instead, it allows us to view them as actors within multiple discourses, and we can then consider the ways that code choice contributes (or not) to the enactment of those discourses. For, ultimately, we are interested in locating students in this analysis as nascent or developing bilinguals, which to my mind must also take account of the social, cultural and institutional aspects of context. Or rather, it should consider how individual instances of code choice in interaction relate not only to the situated vicissitudes of conversation, but how learners in interaction embody, or respond to, discourses already infused with meaning by social and cultural norms (Atkinson, 2002; Bourdieu, 1990; Levine, 2009; Young, 2009). Whether or not the students and teachers in interaction are consciously aware of it, while engaged in pedagogically oriented communication in the classroom environment, all participants enact discourses for learning and communication with at least the ostensible goal of learners becoming 'proficient' in the L2, of bringing some aspects of a new language and culture inside themselves, regardless of the long-term outcome of that process. In addition, all communication in the classroom takes place in an institutionalized, educational setting, irrespective of the pedagogical approach of a particular curriculum; this also establishes for us aspects of context that are of use for analyzing what is going on in individual 'pieces of language' (Gee, 2005; see also Drew & Heritage, 1992; Walsh, 2006).

To illustrate this combined emic/etic approach to classroom code choice for pedagogical purposes, in the following we will closely examine two classroom interactions. In the first excerpt we will see that the default condition for classroom code choice attested in the last chapter obtains, and that this default condition represents the enactment of several learner-specific discourses, of Gee's 'building tasks'. These tasks are things that are usually considered conversation-external (by analysts such as Myers-Scotton), but which are elements of the very context being enacted in the moment. Gee uses these building tasks as a frame for asking questions about what speakers do with language in interaction, about the things they 'enact' or build as they perform social acts, which includes using language. 'Big D' Discourses are semiotic systems that have a history, but whose history is also part of the way in which interlocutors construct meaning (Gee, 2005; Young, 2009: 53). The seven building tasks are as follows, with the questions the analyst can pose in analyzing a 'piece of language':

(1) Significance. How is this piece of language being used to make certain things significant or not and in what ways?
(2) Activities. What activity or activities is this piece of language being used to enact (i.e. get others to recognize as going on)?
(3) Identities. What identity or identities is this piece of language being used to enact (i.e. get others to recognize as operative)?
(4) Relationships. What sort of relationship or relationships is this piece of language seeking to enact with others (present or not)?
(5) Politics (the distribution of social goods). What perspective on social goods is this piece of language communicating (what is being communicated as to what is taken to be 'normal', 'right', 'good', 'correct', 'proper', 'appropriate', 'valuable', 'the way things are', 'the way things ought to be', 'high status or low status', 'like me or not like me' and so forth)?
(6) Connections. How does this piece of language connect or disconnect things; how does it make one thing relevant or irrelevant to another?
(7) Sign systems and knowledge. How does this piece of language privilege or disprivilege specific sign systems (Spanish versus English, technical language versus everyday language, words versus images) or different ways of knowing and believing or claims or knowledge and belief? (Gee, 2005: 11–13)

In the following, I analyze two longer 'pieces of language' and consider, in turn, five of these seven questions with regard to the ways code choices appear to assign significance, enact activities, identities and relationships, and privilege specific sign systems. In the present analysis, I omit politics and connections because of the content of these two examples; as Gee points out, we cannot always easily analyze every piece of language according to these seven building tasks; the more data we can gather, the more we can address all these tasks. Hence, based only on excerpts of two interactions, we cannot accomplish everything we would wish to with the analysis.

Let us further clarify the twofold purpose of this analysis. First, it is intended to show that *any* use of language in the classroom, whether a single exchange between two people or an entire conversational event, represents the enactment of numerous discourses; there is no such thing as 'just talk' in any setting, including the language classroom. Every time someone opens her/his mouth to speak to another person, whether this language is his/her own or whether he/she is delivering the script of someone else's words (such as is common in many language classroom activities), that speaker is enacting discourses bound to, constrained by and simultaneously manifesting context in a particular time and place (Scollon, 2001). Every such exchange of words between people is about making meaning, about being a particular person making meaning and about relating to others as they make meaning. The particular focus of our analysis is on the ways this meaning making and identity enactment takes place through code choices.

The second goal follows from the first: I wish to contrast the two examples in this chapter to demonstrate how discourses enacted through code choice differ depending on the different roles and discursive goals of the speakers in interaction. It is also intended to support the imperative for a principled approach to code choice, and for considering L2 learners in the language classroom as emerging bilinguals.

The transcript excerpts presented here were recorded in two classes, one first-year and one second-year German course. The courses were taught by graduate student instructors. Recordings were obtained using a small hand-held digital voice recorder. Students were asked to pass the recorder around during classroom activities or place it on the teacher's desk when he and the class were interacting. Therefore, the recordings generally captured just a few interactions in the classroom in any given class hour.[1] Six class sessions were recorded in the second half of a first-year course, and six sessions were recorded in the middle of the second-year course (fifth of six quarters).[2] The first hour's recording of each class was discarded, leaving a total of ten 50-minute class periods. These were transcribed, with English use marked in boldface. The present analysis is based, as mentioned, on two classroom interactions. Each is rather long, yet as will become clear this is necessary to address questions about five of Gee's building tasks.

Example 5.1: An Activity in an Introductory German Class

In the class in which this exchange was recorded, the curriculum and teaching approach of which is based on the tenets of CLT, no mention was made of code-switching or the sanctioned use of English as part of the German class, and no effort was made to influence students' code choice practices. This exchange is between two students as they worked on an activity in their first-year German textbook. The activity has one student ask the other questions, and the other answer the questions.

Example 5.1[3]

S1 = male student   S2 = female student

1 S1 (reading) mit wem sprechen sie wenn sie probleme mit einem kurs haben?
       with whom do you speak when you have problems with a course?

2 S2 eh, mit freunden
       eh, with friends

3 S1 ich auch
       me too

4 S2 **excuse me?**

5 S1 ich auch
       me too

6 S2 **oh, ok** um (reading) besuchen sie pro- professor professorin in die sprechstunde?
       oh ok um do you visit the professor professor + fem. suffix in the office hours?

7 S1 um (..)

8 S2 **yeah**

9 S1 sprechstunde sprechstunde
       office hour office hour

10 S2 **speaking hour office hours?**

11 S1 **oh yeah yeah yeah** (..) **uh** (.) ja
       oh yeah yeah yeah uh yes

12	S2	warum?
		why?
13	S1	um (.) weil (.) sie helfen haben (.) mm (.) idees for (.) besser arbeit machen
		um because they help to have mm ideas for doing better work
14	S2	besser arbeit machen?
		doing better work?
15	S1	**uh huh**
16	S2	**how to do work better?** ja (reading) wie oft haben ihren professoren (.) oder
		how to do work better? yes how often do your professors or
17		professorin
		professors (female)
18	S1	eh
19	S2	eh (reading) sprechstunden
		eh office hours
20	S1	ich wisse nicht (.) oh ich wisse nicht
		I don't know oh I don't know
21	S2	ich weiss nicht?
		I don't know?
22	S1	ich weiss nicht (.) aber ich denke (.) um drei stunde im woche (..)
		I don't know but I think about three hours in the week
23	S2	sehr gut (laugh) und ich eh ich besuche um (.) mein professor oder professorin
		Very good and I eh I visit um my professor or professor+ fem. suffix
24		in der sprechstude (.) wenn ich (..) fragen haben? ich fragen abe (.) ja (..)
		in the office hours when I have questions? I have questions yes
25		(reading) haben sie schon mal ein gruppenproject gemacht?
		have you already done a group project?
26	S1	um (.) ja (.)
		um yes
27	S2	**ja?** (laughs) **simple answer!**
28	S1	**ok let's see** (..)
29	S2	**I hope this is picking up** (.) **we'll check afterwards** (.) (reading) was ist
30		passiert?
		what happened?
31	S1	um (.) **howdya say remember?**
32	S2	**uh** (.) **like to be reminded of**
33	S1	(flipping through book – long pause) um (.) ich erin (.) erinner e mich?
		um I remem- remember?

34	S2	**it is reflexive so you're gonna have a** mich [**in there**
35	S1	[ich mich *I +accusative refl. pron.*
36	S2	**or a** [mir *or a me* (dative reflexive pronoun)
37	S1	[erinnieren *remember*
38	S2	**might be [dative (..) probably should turn the page** (..)
39	S1	[**um xxx um**
40	S2	**ok** (reading) was war gut was war schlecht? *ok what was good what was bad?*
41	S1	ich habe Gruppenprojekt nicht gern (..) *I don't like group project*
42	S2	nicht [gern? *not like?*
43	S1	[und du? (reading) haben sie schon mal ein gruppenproject gemacht? *and you? have you done a group project before?*
44	S2	ja (.) **I've done one** [aber *yes I've done one but*
45	S1	[was ist [passiert? *what happened?*
46	S2	[passiert? passiert auf english? ich weiss nicht *happened happened in English? I don't know*
47		ich (.) **I forgot** was passiert ist auf English *I forgot what passiert is in English*
48	S1	**oh, what hap like how** [**was it?**
49	S2	[ah! eh
50	S1	**or what happened?**
51	S2	(laughter) (..) eh (.) er I war gut (..) **nothing important er boring old project** *eh er I was good nothing important er boring old project*
52		(clears throat) wir haben viele xxx in der gruppe gemacht or gehabt (.) ja *we did or had a lot xxx in the group yes*
53	S1	[**ok ok that's** gut *ok ok that's good*
54	S2	[**yeah** (.) **are we done?**

As an example of introductory language class interaction, there are of course many 'typical' things going on here, such as error-correction or repair (Kasper, 1985; van Lier, 1988), elicitation techniques (Seedhouse, 2004; Walsh, 2006) and scaffolded learning through interaction (Swain & Lapkin, 1998). Additionally, of course, there is a good amount of code-switching and multiple uses of the L1 and the L2 in alternation by both speakers. Before we conclude simply that English is the unmarked and German the marked language in this interaction (which might be as far as we would go if reading this transcript with language class students as part of an awareness-raising activity), let us formulate a few hypotheses. Let us pose the hypothesis that S2's private speech (Vygotsky, 1978) remains primarily or exclusively in English in this meeting; for her, German appears to remain simply a bunch of words to use to get through the interaction, and perhaps, in the first half of the conversation anyway, to drive her enactment of certain discourse routines, which we'll examine shortly. By contrast, let us hypothesize that S1 remains in some way consciously aware that the point of the course is to become good at using German, and that this very interaction functions as practice toward that end. Put this way, we can ask ourselves whether S1 is attempting to 'mark' English in some way, or whether S2's utterances serve to keep English unmarked.

Second, in terms of the epigraph at the head of this chapter, let us hypothesize that these learners are enacting through language – and through choice of English and German at different points – specific sorts of activities, identities and relationships. Lastly, we can hypothesize that some of the ways English and German are used reveal a privileging of English in this interaction.

Assigning significance

Gee (2005: 110) sets up the task for assigning significance in part with the question, what are the situated meanings of some of the words and phrases that seem important to the situation? By 'situated' we mean that particular words or phrases carry significance bound to this specific context of the interaction. He illustrates with the example of a square room: 'There is no clear "front" or "back" to the room. But I speak and act in a certain way... and, low and behold [sic], where I sit becomes the "front" of the room' (Gee, 2005: 11). In our discussion, we are interested in the ways that these sorts of situated meanings are part of or relate to code choices. This begins at the start of the excerpt. In line 2, S2 responds to the textbook question that S1 read. In line 3, S2 replies *'ich auch'* (me too), which S2 either did not hear or did not understand. In any case, in line 4, she chooses to speak English when she says 'excuse me?' Apart from the situated meaning of 'excuse me?' here – it is meant as a request for S1 to repeat himself – we can ask whether her choice to use English for the question might not also have been an implicit prompt for S1 to repeat himself in English. Next, jumping ahead to line 25, S2 reads the question from the book, to which S1 responds simply *'ja'* (yes). In line 27, S2 switches to English with 'simple answer!' Apart from the mere fact that S2 judges S1's response to be too short, her use of English appears to add extra emphasis to her view that one-word answers are not acceptable here. One need only imagine a question such as the one S1 read in line 25 being asked in a conventional, that is, non-pedagogical, social encounter outside the classroom. An answer such as S1's in line 26 would likely go uncommented. At the very least, the questioner would ask a follow-up question, such as 'Really, what sort of project was it?' In this exchange, then, the switch to English makes significant that one-word answers do not accord with the pedagogical purpose of the activity. S2's utterances, 'excuse me?' and 'simple answer!' appear to foreground, or assign significance to, the very pedagogical aspect of the activity and the interaction. This is one of several examples in which one speaker positions herself/himself as a sort of surrogate teacher. Another example of this, as scaffolded assistance, is in line 34, when S2 offers a clarification of a grammar point, in English: 'it is reflexive so you're gonna have a *mich* in there'. A further example of this, though code-switching is not involved, can be seen in line 21, in which S2 recasts a grammatical error made by S1, which S1 then restates correctly in line 22.

Enacting activities

The idea of enacting activities is also context bound and context determining. It relates to the fact that we talk and act differently in different situations. Gee (2005: 11) asks, 'What activity or activities is this piece of language being used to enact' or 'get others to recognize as going on?' Put another way, I use different words and speak in different ways when I am giving an academic lecture from when I am in a café talking with friends. This can relate to register (formal to informal), speech variety and, of course, among bilingual speakers, code choices. The very choice of words or code is a marker of the activity itself; it both reflects it and helps to create that activity. In this exchange there are three instances in which S2 asks S1 to give or confirm the meaning of a word or phrase by using English: in line 10 with 'speaking hour office hours?'; in line 16 with 'how to do work better?'; and in line 47 with *'ich* I forgot *was also passiert ist auf englisch'* (I forgot what *passiert* is in English). In line 31, S1 asks in English 'howdya say remember?' In each instance, the speaker indicates a gap in her or his lexical knowledge and uses English to do it. Apart from the fact that requesting such information tends to occur only in this sort of classroom situation, and much less so in spontaneous social interactions, we can ask whether the activity being enacted, what each speaker was getting the other to recognize, would have been the same if entirely in German. By asking for this information in English, the speaker appears to get the other to recognize, at yet another level, that the activity of the moment is word and grammar learning, not actually communicating about professor's office hours and group projects. This alternation, back and forth, between the German needed for the activity and the English meta-communication about words and word meanings, is the enactment of discourse routine both participants are aware of, though perhaps not consciously, and feel comfortable with.

Enacting identities

It is difficult to make strong claims about identities enacted from such a short interaction, and especially one based on contrived communication such as this one. Yet, it is important to do so because language teachers do not often reflect on questions of who their students are when they perform language tasks in the classroom (Kramsch, 2009). Returning to Liddicoat's (2003) well-put questions, the language learner should ask herself/himself: who am I when I speak this language? and how am I me when I speak this language?; the language teacher can consider how learners need both to explore who they are or could be through the L2 and how they can retain their sense of self within the discourses of the L2. In this interaction, we see some evidence of what we might call the imposition of the L1 self at the very outset. The interaction begins with S1 reading the prompt from the language textbook (line 1) and S2 answering the question (line 2). S1 follows up S2's response with a statement giving his own response to the textbook's question, which S2 does not understand. She expresses this with 'excuse me?' in English. S1 then repeats himself, S2 acknowledges his answer and they continue with the activity. Because S2 does know the German for the phrase (*wie, bitte?*), we could hypothesize that S2 chooses English here in part in order to assert or retain her identity as an English speaker. This is supported by the fact that in the 22 clear instances of L1 use in this exchange, 14 are uttered by S2.

By contrast, there is evidence in this exchange that S1 is attempting to remain in the L2, and we can hypothesize that he seeks to identify himself – as much as is possible in this sort of limited classroom activity in an introductory German class – with or through the L2. In addition to S1's overall stronger attempt to complete the task in the L2, the first specific indication appears in line 9, when he seeks explanation or clarification of the word *Sprechstunde* (office hour) by repeating the L2 word. Next, in line 21, when S2 offers S1 corrective feedback in the L2, S1 stays in German, correcting the verb form and continuing with his response. Lastly, at the end of the exchange (line 53), S1 begins to switch to English but then moves back into German with 'ok ok that's *gut*'. This suggests at the very least the effort to make German the language of conversation. These examples suggest that in typical classroom activities, learners constantly either assert, or in some ways forfeit, aspects of their identity as speakers of their L1, and that this can be noted by their code choices.

Enacting relationships

Related to the issue of enacting identities is that of marking or reinforcing relationships. In some classroom interactions, scaffolding behavior often occurs in an asymmetrical way, with one learner positioning herself/himself as a sort of surrogate teacher, as we have seen in this example. This is especially true when one participant in an exchange possesses superior abilities in the L2 (Swain & Lapkin, 1998). In this exchange, however, despite S2's more frequent use of the L1, we see two learners providing each other with a good deal of assistance in order to complete the task. In particular, each participant provides the other with word meanings at different points using the L1, as in lines 10 ('speaking hours office hours?'), line 16 ('how to do work better?'), line 32 ('like to be reminded of') and lines 48/50 ('what hap like how was it... or what happened?'). In addition, from line 34 to line 38, the students use the L1 to briefly clarify a grammar point for the usage of the reflexive verb *sich erinnern* (to remember). In three of the four instances of glossing, the L1 translation of the target word was offered with clearly rising intonation. This suggests that the person offering the information perhaps was not sure of the translation, but it may also be intended to mark the speaker's equal status in this exchange, to avoid appearing overbearing with the information. Throughout the excerpt, we see both students attempting to respect and yield to the knowledge of the other, and the L1 appears to be one tool used to mark this relationship.

Privileging sign systems and knowledge

Based on the topic of this book, I might have given prominence to this particular building task, for in nearly any exchange between L2 learners and others this question relates well to the issue of markedness: what sign systems and knowledge are privileged in this exchange? What language is made relevant or irrelevant? Although we can say that S2 appears to privilege English more than German, a close look at the code choice patterns reveals that the relevance of English or German shifts for both speakers.

S1 begins by asking the first question in the activity (line 1), which S2 answers (line 2) with *'mit freunden'* (with friends). S2 responds with *'ich auch'* (me too), which S2 either does not hear or does not understand, for she says 'excuse me?' By the end of introductory German, all students in the class have learned several ways to express non-comprehension in German. Yet, S2 chooses to do so in English. At this point, let us hypothesize that she is stressing the significance of English here, that she is, to use Gee's term, *privileging* English as a sign system. In line 5, S1 repeats his *'ich auch'* and the interaction proceeds. In accord with the instructions for the activity, S2 asks the next question. After brief difficulty with the word *'sprechstunde'* (office hour), in which S2 confirms the meaning with a translation (line 10), S1 answers the question in German with a simple *'ja'* (yes). S2 asks the follow-up question *'warum'* (why) (line 12) to which S2 again responds in German, albeit with difficulty, in line 13: *um weil sie helfen haben idees* for *besser arbeit machen* (because they help have ideas for doing work better). S2 parrots this response and then immediately translates it for herself into English (line 15). This already provides support for our hypothesis that in this conversation, S2 assigns greater significance to English over German.

We then see S2 take over asking the remaining questions of S1, who works to answer each question in German. In lines 23 and 24, S2 answers a question herself in German, with no appeal to English at this point, then moves straightaway to the next question in the activity (line 25). S1 answers the question with a simple *'ja'* (yes), to which S2 exclaims (line 28): 'simple answer!' Again, for S2, English appears to hold both a significant and a privileged position.

Ultimately, it appears that code choice itself, rather than some thematic aspect of the activity, holds some significance for the students. It also appears that each participant privileges a different language: S1 German and S2 English. Whether this represents successful communication or an affordance for learning cannot be determined from this conversational excerpt alone, but we could surmise that the students, at the very least, left the exchange having added to their lexical knowledge of German, specifically with the words *Sprechstunde* (office hours) and *sich erinnern* (to remember). With regard to whether L1 use here is 'good' or 'bad' in pedagogical terms, we should ask whether this conversation would have even been possible entirely in German, and if so, if the same sorts of mutual, scaffolded assistance would have taken place.

To summarize, even in this relatively short excerpt from a conventional introductory German class, both participants use English and German in creative and interesting ways. German clearly remains the object of study as the activity dictates, rather than as a means for 'real' conversation. This is admittedly the discursive and pedagogical norm in introductory language classes, evidenced by the fact that neither student appears inherently interested in the issue of professors' office hours.

Example 5.2: A Discussion in an Intermediate German Class

In the second-year German class in which Example 5.2 took place, the students were asked to conceptualize and create a 'Museum of German Culture' (see Levine *et al.*, 2004). The discussion here is about the groups that will work on the various exhibits in the museum, and one student, S1 (a different student from S1 in the other two excerpts), raises concerns about working with the same group over many weeks and about the composition and tasks of a few of those groups.

Example 5.2

S1 = female student   SX = unidentified student   CL = class
S2 = male student   TR = teacher

1   TR ok so wir haben jetzt im prinzip um sieben ausstellungen eins zwei drei vier fünf
        ok so we have now in principle about seven exhibits one two three four five

2   sechs sieben (.) das ist auch ok =
        six seven that is good too ok =

3   S1 = yeah (.) wir haben nur ein eine gemacht weil sie so (.) **comprehensive** (.)
        yeah we only did one one because it so comprehensive

1   TR sie können auch xxx leute haben so das wäre auch ok yeah die meisten die in die
        you can also have xxx people so that would be ok too yeah most of those in the

2   gruppen wir müssen jetzt gruppen bilden haben sie eine frage?
        groups we now have to form groups do you have a question?

3	SX	nein
		no
4	TR	oh ok (.) **and uh** die gruppen sollen drei personen haben mit drei personen um pro
		oh ok and uh the groups should have three people with three people um per
5		thema um das mit dieser kulturkarte sie können vier haben das wäre cool xxx was
		topic um that with this culture map you can have four that would be cool xxx which is
6		ein grosses thema ist und um dann reicht es eigentlich wenn wir sieben haben (.) um
		a big topic and um then it's enough actually if we have seven um
7		tja ich weiss nicht wie wir das am besten machen (.) um ich könnte einfach jetzt die
		well I don't know how we can best do this um I could simply now say the
8		ausstellungen (.) sagen und wenn sie sich dafür interessieren heben sie die hand (.)
		exhibits and if you are interested raise your hand
9		**we'll see how we can try to** =
10	S1	= ich habe eine frage
		I have a question
11	TR	**yeah** bitte
		yeah please
12	S1	auf englisch? bitte
		in english? Please
13	TR	**yeah**
14	S1	**are we going to decide among those which ones we want to work with?**
15	TR	[xxx
16	S1	[**ok so the groups we're making now are not like the permanent groups**
17		**for the** (.)
18	TR	um das [sind
		um those are
19	S1	[für die [ausstellungen
		For the exihibits
20	TR	[die gruppen für die nächsten um ja eigentlich für die nächsten vier
		the groups for the next um yes actually for the next four
21		fünf wochen
		five weeks
22	S1	**ew ok**
23	TR	(responding to a raised hand)(NAME: S2)?

24	S2	also wir werden diese ausstellungen haben unseren gruppen
so we will our groups will have these exhibits
25	TR	uh huh
26	S2	ok (.) die [werden
ok they will
27	S1	[**because** (.)
28	S2	also jede gruppe hat zwei forscher xxx
so each group hat two researchers xxx
29	TR	mehr oder weniger **yeah**
more or less yeah
30	S2	jede gruppe hat nur drei oder vier (.) wir lassen es geteilt einfach so?
each group hat only three or four we leave it divided up that way?
31	TR	naja wir müssen jetzt um es könnte sein dass jemand eine a- an einer anderen
well we have to now um it could be that someone wants to work on another
32		Ausstellung arbeiten möchte und nicht unbedingt wo sie waren (.) deswegen will
exhibit and not necessarily where they were therefore I want
33		ich vielleicht die chance geben zu wechseln
to perhaps give the chance to switch
34	S1	**yeah but what I think is that like for instance the beer and** essen (.)
35	TR	mm hm
36	S1	**would be included in the** kulturkarte **if we decide to do the** kulturkarte (.)
37	TR	[xxx
38	S1	[**so there is no point to have three separate** ausstellungen **when two of them are**
39		**inside** (.) **you know what I mean?**
40	CL	xxx xxx (multiple students commenting simultaneously; laughing all around)
41	S1	**a lot of that's why we thought of putting it in the** kulturkarte
42	TR	**y'know** orga organisatorisch müssen wir später xxx
y'know orga organizationally we have to later xxx
43	S1	[ok
44	TR	[aber um ich überleg wie sie gesagt ich hab das auch gesagt bier ist ein grosses thema
but um I'll consider as you said I said that too beer is a big topic
45	S1	grosses ja
yes big
46	TR	dieses mit der kulturkarte kann auch als übergreifendes xxx gesehen werden werden
this with the culture map can also be be seen as a comprehensive xxx

Before we examine the use of English in this exchange between the teacher and S1 from several perspectives, it is important to note that most of the exchange, and indeed most of the communication in this class overall, was in German. A second key piece of contextual information is that S1 was, in fact, one of the top-performing students in the class. She was highly motivated and participated fully, and almost always in German, in the course projects and activities. One of the things that makes this exchange noteworthy, then, is her request in line 15 to ask a question in English. From our knowledge of her performance in the class overall, it would have been possible for her to ask her question in German. This is, in any case, an example of formally sanctioning L1 use through an explicit request to use English; this class discussed and agreed on the convention at the start of the term. In the following, let us examine the exchange in terms of several of Gee's building tasks.

Assigning significance

Just as with Gee's front-versus-back-of-the-room example, in line 15 we see S1 marking the coming exchange as significant by virtue of her request to use English. She appears to feel strongly about her concerns regarding the activity, and the switch to L1 itself serves to make those concerns significant for the teacher and the other students present. This significance-marking through code choice is then repeated later on, after the teacher attempted to clarify his position in lines 34–36; in lines 37–43, S1 comes back in with English in order to expand on and explain her opinion about the composition of the working groups. Thus, her use of English appears to focus more attention on her objections and concerns than, presumably, use of German only might have done.

Enacting activities

The activity being performed by the teacher and his students is, of course, the clarification of roles and tasks for planned class work. All those present are familiar with the 'rules' of this sort of situation; there are certain things that happen. The teacher makes some sort of explanatory statements. Some – but usually not all – of the students ask questions or seek clarification of details. The teacher may write things on the board or project instructions on a screen (this did not happen here) and some or all the students may write notes on what is said. The activity usually ends with the teacher sending the students off to perform the planned tasks, either in the same session or outside class time. Of concern for us is how code choice relates to the enactment of this activity. When S1 indicated in line 13 that she has a question, she enacted the activity within expected parameters. Her request to use English in line 15 also accords with this class's framework because rules for English switching had been agreed on. Her statements from line 17 to 20 and the teacher's response in lines 21–23 also match with expectations. Further, S2's participation in German (lines 27–33) also conforms with the expected scope of this sort of activity; it's still about the students asking for clarification and the teacher providing answers. Thus, we cannot say that the use of English itself by S1 either supports or undermines the enactment of this activity or discursive genre. All we can say is that both German and English are in play here; both have an overlapping function in terms of enacting activity.

Enacting identities

In any language classroom there is a power differential; no matter how equitably a teacher deals with students, ultimately all are aware, even if not consciously or continuously, that the teacher retains the final say over what happens in the classroom (Gebhard, 2002/2004). This is exemplified in this exchange by the teacher's implicit refusal to accommodate or yield to S1's concerns; both are aware that it is his right to call the shots. So S1's switch to English, and her remaining in English for the most part, along with the teacher's choice to remain in German, appears to serve two purposes. First, at some level it reinforces each person's identity in context: teacher and student. Hence, we can hypothesize the perceived need to switch to English in order to move beyond or above those limitations; had S1 chosen to carry on the discussion in German, her more limited ability to express herself (relative to the teacher's) might have served a simple identity-reinforcing function, as appears to be the case with S2 remaining in German, reinforcing her position as student/learner. In an apparent effort to position herself on a more equal footing with the instructor, however, S1 opts for English.

Enacting relationships

This is an exchange in which the relationships enacted overlap with the identities being enacted, though as mentioned we might conclude that S1's code choices signal a challenge to the unmarked teacher–student relationship here. In addition, S2's use of German to move the discussion along might signal a solidarity relationship to the teacher and a distancing from S1.

Privileging sign systems and knowledge

Although S1's German is strong enough to allow her to carry on this exchange with the teacher in that language, she appears to make use of the L1 as a tool to privilege English. The message: In order to assert my position and ensure that I am heard, I use English. In some ways, this appears to offset the teacher–student power differential; he sanctioned the use of L1, and S1 uses it to express her concerns and objections.

By contrast, where the exchange becomes interesting in terms of code choice begins in line 27, when S2 enters the exchange. He obviously does not switch to English, but remains in German throughout (lines 27–33). It is unclear whether he shares S1's objections to the plan, but in his choice to engage in this activity in German, he appears to privilege German use. We can imagine how the conversation might have gone had S2 and/or other students chosen to switch to English to enact this conversation. The fact that only S1 chose this code choice path thus appears significant in itself.

The Code Choice Status Quo

The exchange in Example 5.2 between the teacher and two students is arguably fairly typical of many intermediate-level language classes, at least those that are task or project based. Details of the project must be worked out, and the choice to use the L2 or the L1 is involved in the discursive building tasks to accomplish this. In this example, looking only at the turns-at-talk does not give us all we need; from a discourse-analytical perspective, considering contextual factors such as the institutional or power relations among the speakers as they interact gives us useful guidance in understanding, or at least hypothesizing in helpful ways, the code choices the participants make. It helps us to surmise that while German is here surely more *un*marked in this exchange, English still performs significant interactional and social functions. Hence, it also matches with the code choice status quo detailed in Chapter 4.

Example 5.1 also appears to be fairly typical of many introductory language classes. The uses of German and English accord with the findings of many descriptive studies of classroom code-switching, as well as with my own observational study presented in Chapter 4. The students' purpose for using German, as dictated by the textbook activity and the norms of the CLT classroom, is almost entirely, if not entirely, pedagogical in nature; English remains the unmarked code for both, though S1 demonstrates a willingness to use German in the framework of the activity. Even in their use of L1 to scaffold the activity, provide each other with assistance and assert their identity as English-dominant speakers, the students, in essence, enact and respond to routines they know, that have been part of their educational socialization and are part of the norms of the CLT classroom.

Summary and Conclusion

In this chapter, I presented a brief discourse analysis of excerpts from two university German language classes. The goal was to examine the functions and characteristics of code choices in the classroom context, using Gee's building tasks. I attempted to show how learners, and in Example 5.2, the teacher as well, chose to use the L1 or remain in the L2 to assign significance, enact identities, activities and relationships, and privilege sign systems and knowledge. There is resonance in Gee's approach with Barthes's (1972) observations about myths as ways of making meaning that have come to be or feel natural, as well as with Bourdieu's (1990) notion of habitus, or discourses as embodied practices; the situated meanings worked out in these two classroom exchanges should be considered against the backdrop of the historical, discursive arc, which allows for certain things to happen or to be said, and precludes other things. Thus, in my analysis, I sometimes framed what the conversational participants said in terms of what they *did not say*; the aim was to highlight the ways that the discourses are always constrained, as participants engage in what Gee calls building tasks; raising awareness of these constraints can help to bring into focus the historically and socially constructed nature of code choice practices, particularly those related to the ways that speakers position themselves *in situ* to engage in building tasks through code choices.

One goal of the analysis was thus to show that any 'piece of language' in the classroom, whether a single exchange between two people or an entire conversational event, is never 'just talk' and that code choice is a significant factor in the analysis. A second goal was to demonstrate how discourses enacted through code choice differ depending on the different roles and discursive goals of the speakers in interaction, their particular roles in the exchange vis-à-vis the positions they adopt in interaction. These analyses should add a further layer of evidence that a principled approach to code choice, one that takes no aspect of classroom communication for granted, including code choice, should be part of the language curriculum and integral to learners' and teachers' experience in the classroom.

Notes

1. There were several methodological reasons for this minimal approach to recording classroom proceedings. I would have preferred videotaping the class, but our classrooms are quite small and the acoustics are poor. Second, as both researcher *and* language program director (and as such, the instructors' immediate supervisor), I did not want to be present in the room while the recordings were made, in part to minimize any feelings of intimidation. Any instances in which I could not understand the context of an interaction (which were few), I was able to ask the instructor for details.
2. An additional detail about the second-year course in which the recordings were made should be noted. The course was a simulation-based course in which the learners were given a great deal of control over classroom events. In addition to formalizing code choice using some of the tenets of the multilingual approach, in this course the students were accustomed to critically engaging with many aspects of the curriculum, not just code choice. This is a crucial difference to our more conventional first-year course (for more about this course, see Levine *et al.*, 2004).
3. Transcription conventions used for original conversational data in this book:

italics	gloss in English
bold	code-switch
(..)	pause
:	lengthened or sustained vowel
?	noticeably rising intonation
=	end and beginning of two utterances are immediately adjacent
[	overlapping speech begins here
()	commentary on aspect of context or speech act
xxx	speech could not be transcribed

Note that in transcription of speech, orthographic conventions are not followed; this means, for instance that German nouns, proper nouns, the first word of a line, etc. are not capitalized. The exception is the English first-person pronoun 'I'.

Part 3
Curriculum

Chapter 6

An Architecture of Classroom Code Choice

> *Few encounters ever take place according to plan, but we do find the plans helpful nevertheless.*
> (van Lier, 1988: 215)
>
> *One can produce affordances for the negotiation of meaning, but not meaning itself.*
> (Wenger, 1998: 229)

Realizing the Multilingual Classroom Community of Practice

In this chapter, we will bring to bear the theories, concepts, arguments and empirical evidence of the preceding chapters, to build what I call a curricular architecture based on multiple code use in the language classroom. Working with a sociocultural and ecological perspective, each component will attempt to take as its starting point the complexity of any linguistic situation, the dynamic relationships at work between situated interaction and other levels of context. Most of the proposals in this and the next chapter are oriented toward raising learner awareness of code choice in a variety of ways, both in the classroom and in other settings. This raised awareness is intended as a vehicle for communication and interaction, of personal development for the learner, and in sociopolitical terms, of giving the learner an active role in her/his own learning. In terms of language classroom practice, a central goal of the proposed curricular architecture is to create affordances for optimal second language (L2) use, but not just any L2 use, rather L2 use informed by an understanding of multilingual norms in and outside the classroom.

I would like to begin with an anecdote to illustrate part of the goal of a multilingual approach to classroom code choice. In my town, there is a private elementary school that has operated successfully for several decades. Part of the school's approach and philosophy is to foster knowledge of and appreciation for languages. Each morning, the day begins with a half-hour 'language circle', in which the children learn and practice phrases and songs in a particular language. Each week, they hear and learn about a different language; in the course of the year, the children are exposed to a good deal of German, Spanish, French, Japanese and other languages. Around the school, labels and signs hang with the names of various objects and frequent classroom expressions in these languages. During the day, staff members address the younger children in these languages, which usually involves instructions and requests of various sorts. The older children take part in content instruction for part of each day in whatever language their teacher is most proficient. This is not immersion instruction in a fully articulated way, but the playful, dynamic, open-ended use of both English and different other languages.

While, unfortunately, I have not yet collected any linguistic data from this environment, I have observed several interesting things that are pertinent to this discussion of a multilingual approach to classroom code choice at the university level. First, while the children in the school do not become bilingual in all the languages to which they are exposed (though apparently some do achieve this with at least one of them), the noticeable cumulative effect among the students is related to language socialization. At the very least, the children appear to accept as a matter of course that the world speaks many languages, that people who know more than one language make regular use of the languages in their repertoires, and importantly, that this is a good thing. At best, this environment appears to provide affordances for the children to acquire the cognitive and social tools for engaging in meaningful cross-cultural communication, and hopefully, for approaching 'otherness' with tolerance and appreciation. Second, and perhaps most compelling in support of a multilingual approach, is the empowerment of the children at the linguistic level. It is fairly uncontroversial that children have greater skill in acquiring language to a 'native-like' level than adults (Birdsong, 1992, 1999; Coppieters, 1987); in this school situation, the curriculum appears to be structured around this belief and the children appear to be comfortable with it. To illustrate this point, one day I was present for the language circle, and the main activity that day was singing songs. The teacher leading the group allowed individual children to select some of the songs, and some she selected herself. At one point, she chose a Japanese song that she apparently did not know very well herself (she was not a speaker of Japanese). She asked the children to sing her the song so that she could learn it, and as they sang, she jotted down the lyrics. She then sang it back on her own, and in the process apparently mispronounced several words. The children were adept and apparently well practiced at correcting her errors and helping her get through the song. The teacher was open to correction and appreciative as she overtly deferred to the expertise of the children. All in all, it was a fine example of collaborative, (largely) learner-centered learning, and crucially, of learner empowerment. Here was a situation in which the learners, rather than the teacher, were the final authority or experts on a particular matter.

How does this situation relate to our goal of creating the best conditions for a multilingual language classroom? The answer lies in what this school accomplishes at an educational level: with a clearly articulated approach or set of principles and consistently applied pedagogical tools, the teachers appear to succeed in subverting the widespread monolingual bias typical in the US educational establishment (Horner & Trimbur, 2002; Reagan & Osborn, 2002) and facilitating a fair degree of learner autonomy and collaborative learning through language learning and language use. They also convey the message that learning other languages and about other people is not only important, but it is an inextricable part of all other sorts of learning. It is exactly these accomplishments that overlap with the goals of a multilingual approach to language classroom communication.

One of the central arguments of this book is that the language class is a ubiquitously multilingual place, and that any pedagogical approach that does not take this into account must be considered inadequate or incomplete. In Chapter 4, I supported this observation through a review of the literature on classroom code choice and a presentation of some of my own research. It was shown that while the classroom is indeed a multilingual environment, the default condition of 'typical' language classes might not be the most conducive to the principle of maximal or optimal L2 use. Evidence was offered that suggests that the L1 may remain the unmarked code for many class members in particular communicative contexts even in the second year, when learners' lexical and grammatical knowledge presumably supports greater unmarked L2 communication. In Chapter 5, through an examination of two conversational excerpts, I demonstrated how these conditions play out in classroom interaction. In this chapter, I explore some of the ways we might intentionally influence this default condition, or rather, create conditions that will allow learners and instructors to do so. The term I will use in this presentation of a curricular manifestation of a multilingual approach to classroom code choice is *principled heterogeneity*. I define this as the condition whereby class members co-construct norms based on their own motivations, perceived needs and interests. Any given class proceeds differently from all others, but they do so according to common principles. The ways these principles serve to unify and articulate curricula horizontally and vertically despite this intrinsic heterogeneity will be taken up in Chapter 7. The principles that underpin code choice practices have, of course, been explicated throughout this book; the problem addressed in this chapter is how to make them accessible and operational to learners and teachers in the classroom. The structure and content of this discussion is based on Tudor's (1995) treatment of the learner-centered language curriculum, on some of the tenets of Reagan and Osborn's (2002) interpretations of critical pedagogy and on Dörnyei and Murphey's (2003) discussion of group dynamics in the language classroom. I divide the treatment of a multilingual classroom community of practice into five component task types, presented graphically in Figure 6.1.

These rubrics derive from the leadership styles and roles described by Hersey and Blanchard (1982) with regard to organizational psychology and adapted to the language classroom situation by Dörnyei and Murphey (2003), as follows:

- *Telling* entails providing a task orientation with a clear explanation at the beginning of group life.
- *Selling* entails convincing students that the tasks are helpful for their learning. However, as the best salespeople know, convincing is a relationship and improving relationships among the class members is probably one of the best ways to increase the value of the activities in the classroom.
- *Participating* means allowing students to interact with the material and each other rather than merely listening to the teacher, giving them lots of time on task.
- *Delegating* entails letting students in on the process of choosing and directing activities. This is when teachers get to learn a lot from their students. (Dörnyei & Murphey, 2003: 98)

For the multilingual classroom, *telling* and *selling* can be manifested in what I call learner training, for the development of terminology, concepts and techniques needed to even think about code choice as a salient, important part of classroom language learning. Learners as a group must not only develop a sense of the importance of code choices in the language learning process, they must also feel comfortable with the idea that they can regulate code choice practices in the long term as an autonomous group, that is, in cooperation with the instructor, but largely

An Architecture of Classroom Code Choice   129

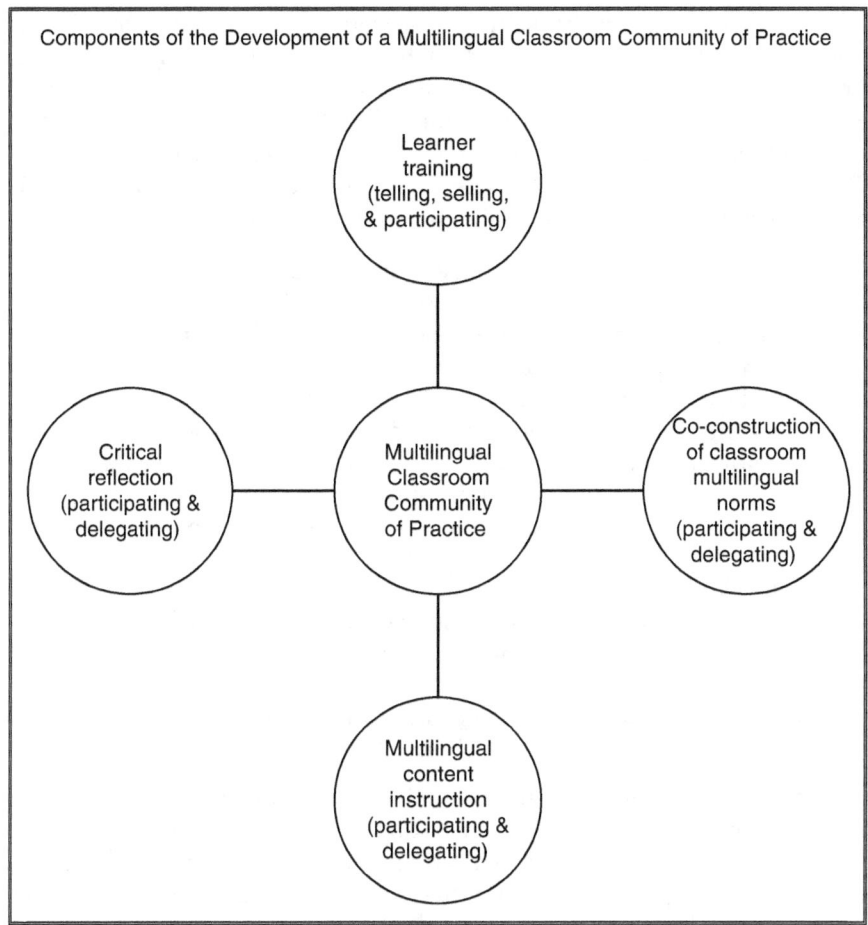

Figure 6.1 Components of the development of a multilingual classroom community of practice

independently of her or him. *Participating*, while also driven by the leadership of the teacher, is also part of learner training toward the goal of co-constructing workable code choice norms. Co-construction of norms, engagement with multilingual content or learning about multilingual speakers and communities, and critical reflection all involve *participating* and *delegating*. The instructor delegating these activities to the learners also has the function of contributing to the learners' ability to reflect critically on code choice practices.

In the following, I address, in turn, learner training, co-construction of norms, multilingual content instruction and critical reflection, and present examples of classroom tasks associated with each. The sample activities included here follow the guidelines for learner-centered teaching and learning outlined by Reagan and Osborn (2002; following Grennon Brooks & Brooks, 1993 and Kaufman & Grennon Brooks, 1996) as fundamental to what they call 'constructivist teaching':

(1) Use raw data and primary sources, along with manipulative, interactive, and physical materials.
(2) When framing tasks, use cognitive terminology, such as classify, analyze, predict, create, and so on.
(3) Allow student thinking to drive lessons. Shift instructional strategies or alter content based on student responses.
(4) Inquire about students' understandings of concepts before sharing your own understandings of those concepts.
(5) Ask open-ended questions of students and encourage students to ask questions of others.
(6) Seek elaboration of students' initial responses.
(7) Engage students in experiences that might engender contradictions to students' initial hypotheses and then encourage a discussion.
(8) Provide time for students to construct relationships and create metaphors. (Reagan & Osborn, 2002: 60–61)

Reagan and Osborn (2002: 61) call these characteristics 'structured introduction' or 'guided discovery'. They point out that these things are not necessarily part of just constructivist teaching, rather good teaching in general, and these provide a theoretical foundation to what good teachers have long done intuitively.

Learner Training

Learners, of course, come to any educational endeavor with a great deal of prior knowledge. One of the most challenging aspects of teaching is accommodating and adapting to the diversity of experience and knowledge that a given group of learners has in helping them to learn something new. At the same time, teachers know that in order to learn or do something truly new, learners need preparation and training, and most often this endeavor occurs prior to or separately from the learning itself. In Dörnyei and Murphey's (2003: 97) terms, this entails the assertive, structured leadership of the teacher, based on the provision of a 'clear and straightforward framework within which early development of cooperation and autonomy can safely occur' as well as on cooperative exchanges and autonomous practices on their own. In Vygotskyan terms, the learner training phase involves other-regulation toward the goal of self-regulation (Dörnyei & Murphey, 2003: 98).

In most language classes, just communicating in the L2, and perhaps language learning overall, represent a novel experience, and as a matter of course, effective teachers develop and teach techniques for helping learners to be successful language learners. With regard to managing code choice practices, there are two areas in which class members would presumably benefit from explicit training in order to succeed. One is based on minimal or no prior knowledge about effective ways to communicate in the L2 or through dual code use, and one is based on critically examining several popularly held conceptualizations of both language learning and code-switching.

Tudor (1995: 37) defines learner training as 'the process by which learners are helped to deepen their understanding of the nature of language learning, and to acquire the knowledge and skills they need in order to pursue their learning goals in an informed and self-directive manner'. Crucially, learner training is not simply about imparting information or techniques to learners (though it sometimes is about this), rather it is also about 'the creation of a forum within which teacher and learners exchange insights and perceptions of the learning process and thereby initiate the shared exploration of language learning which lies at the heart of a learner-centred approach' (Tudor, 1995: 37). Even here, it is important to note that learner training can and should have significance, politically and socially, that goes beyond the parameters of the task itself.

To a large extent, learner training involves strategies instruction. Strategies instruction, in its simplest conceptualization, entails identifying the characteristics and practices of successful learners and then 'teaching' these characteristics to learners so that they might benefit from them (Chamot, 2001). Tudor (2001: 39) observed that 'it would be misleading to assume that these strategies [of successful learners] can be neatly pedagogized and "taught" to learners in a straightforward manner' because what constitutes effective strategies varies by context and a range of factors, such as the nature of the task, the learning stage, the learner's age, individual learning styles or cultural differences. Strategies instruction should therefore not just be about teaching a particular set of techniques or skills, but more generally 'fostering learners' understanding of language, of language learning, and of their own subjective interaction with the processes of language use and learning' (Tudor, 2001: 40). Put another way, learner training to co-construct and manage code choice practices should provide learners with new information about the task, but it also must ask learners to engage critically with pertinent information and ideas. This critical approach at the front end should also bolster the critical work to be done at intervals throughout the establishment of a multilingual classroom, and later on in the critical reflection stage.

So, what sort of training would be needed in order to bring about a classroom community of practice that supports dynamic code choice practices and the optimal use of the L2? Three types of learner training are considered:

- Critical reflection about human communication in general and language use in particular.
- L2 discourse strategies instruction.
- Instruction in basic code-switching concepts.

'Multilingual content instruction', or learning about speakers and communities, could also contribute to learners' ability to make informed decisions about what is workable in the classroom, but I will discuss this later on in its own section. These three components of learner training need not be dealt with in this or any particular chronological order, rather in response to learners' collective prior knowledge and situated needs analyses. That said, I place them in the order that I would teach them in my own language class.

Critical reflection about human communication in general and classroom language use in particular

Before learners can be expected to engage in dual or multiple code use, it would be important for them to engage first with the entire notion of human communication in general and language use in particular. Most adult learners come to the university-level language class with some experience of classroom language learning, usually from high school, which means they have at least developed, whether consciously or unconsciously, certain strategies for approaching L2 learning and L2 communication, and perhaps certain assumptions about the value or usefulness of language learning. Yet, it would be reasonable to assume that most learners' prior L2 class experience has not asked them to think or talk about:

- How and why language is used, whether inside or outside the classroom.
- Differences between classroom communication and 'real world' communication.
- The relative status and prestige of the L1 and the L2.
- Curricular and institutional structures and how these relate to ways that all class members interact.

Hence, a first step is to ask learners to engage critically with some or all of these issues. Sample Activity 1 provides a framework for thinking about contexts of communication out in the 'real world' in relation to those of the L2 classroom.

Sample Activity 1

Comparing 'real-world' communication with language classroom communication

(A) Together with one or two classmates, please discuss the following questions. Take notes so that you can efficiently present the results of your discussion to the class.
- In what sorts of contexts, or for what functions, is language used *outside* the classroom? You may consider contexts and functions as related to:
  - places, such as the airport, the bank, the university, the coffee shop;
  - people we communicate with, such as parents, friends, employer, professor;
  - what people *do* with language, such as tell a story, get information, make an argument, make small talk.

  Write your collective conclusions in a list.
- Now consider the language classroom. In what sort of contexts, or for what functions, is language used *inside* the classroom? Write your conclusions in a second list.
- How do your two lists compare? Where do they overlap and where are they different?

(B) With the leadership of the instructor or another class member, please transfer the groups' collective responses to the board, overhead transparency or digital presentation. The class should then collaboratively address the following questions:
- What sort of communication takes place both inside and outside the classroom, that is, what are the areas of overlap?

- What sort of communication takes place that seems to be specific to the language class?
- Are there particular language choices (whether to speak English or the foreign language) associated with each of the functions unique to the language class? For instance, if someone said, 'communicative strategies instruction' (like this activity) as one context of classroom communication, what language would be most frequently used for this context, English or the foreign language? How does language level relate to this choice? Apart from simple lack of linguistic knowledge to engage in a certain type of communication in the foreign language, why would a student or a class choose one language over another in a given context? Think of an example or two to support your position.

(C) Meet with the same students from part (A) of this activity and discuss the question, 'What have we learned from this activity that could be converted into active classroom practice, into practices that could positively affect our classroom as a language learning environment?'

This or similar learner training activities, of course, raise the question of language choice for or within the activities themselves, so allow me to briefly to address this point. Obviously, at the introductory level, it would not be possible for learners to engage in this sort of discussion in the L2, and this fact might not sit well with some language teachers. Still, the sample activities presented in this book, with their common goal of raising learner awareness about language use and code choice, are intended to directly benefit learners' ability to use the L2 by creating a framework for critical awareness of language use, of moving the making of code choices from an unconscious to a conscious act. At the intermediate level, whether they could be carried out in the L2 will vary by the number of contact hours available, overall learner proficiency, specific instructional goals and numerous other factors. At the advanced level, it might be preferable to conduct the sessions in the L2, but even here the larger goal of facilitating learner insights into issues of communication and code choice should be considered to override the need to use the activities concurrently as a forum for language practice or development. For example, the main goal of Sample Activity 2 is to create a forum for reflection and analysis of classroom communication and code choice. When I have used this activity with my students, several have commented that it was the first time they ever considered questions of what constitutes 'important' communication, and what language might match with the most important forms of communication. So, ultimately, regardless of the language chosen for this activity, its content should contribute to learners' ability to optimize L2 use.

Sample Activity 2
What is 'important' classroom communication and which language should be used for each?

(A) For each of the following, please provide two pieces of information:
- Check off which language you believe is most appropriate for the situation.
- Express how personally important you find each situation for your German class. Mark each with a number according to the following 5-point scale:

1	2	3	4	5
totally unimportant	unimportant	a little important	important	extremely important

Situation	German or English?	Importance (1=least and 5=most)
Discussing your or others' family members (in a class activity)		
Asking the teacher to explain a grammar point you did not understand		
Receiving directions for a class activity		
Receiving directions for a section of a test		
Discussing people's professions (in a class activity)		
Asking a classmate to tell you what the teacher just said (you didn't hear it)		
Asking the teacher to repeat or explain what she/he just said (you didn't understand it)		
Discussing the content of the next test with your instructor		
Ordering food from a German menu (in a class activity)		
Shopping for presents for your family (in a class activity)		

Informing your teacher that you have to be absent tomorrow		
Discussing details of tomorrow's homework with your instructor		
Planning weekend activities with classmates (in a class activity)		
Planning weekend activities with classmates (for real)		
Chatting with a classmate about what she/he is doing after class		
Discussing what you like to do in your free time (in a class activity)		
Talking about the weather in Germany (in a class activity)		
Other		

Now extract all the items that received a 4 or 5 and list them here (abbreviations are ok!), placing them in the appropriate box:

German	English
_____	_____
_____	_____
_____	_____

(B) Together with one or two classmates, compare your responses and decide what is noteworthy or interesting about the information in your tables. Do your responses differ? Can the situations in either column be organized into categories? Be prepared to share the results of your discussion with the class.

Second language discourse strategies instruction

Toward the goal of facilitating the conceptual and linguistic scaffold for co-constructing code choice conventions, to mark the L1 and unmark the L2, learners should engage in activities that help them develop effective discourse strategies. Primarily, this means working on ways to take part in meaningful L2 communication despite their still limited lexical and grammatical knowledge. Considering the finding that learners often carry out much of their meta-communication (talk about language tasks or talk to negotiate completion of language tasks) in the L1 (Antón & DiCamilla, 1999; Swain & Lapkin, 2000; the classroom case study in Chapter 4), helping learners to engage in meta-communication in the L2 would be a useful step in facilitating optimal L2 use. To help them use the L2 in culturally appropriate ways, Crocker and Kramsch (1990) proposed the learning of 'gambits', unanalyzed speech 'chunks' (VanPatten, 1995) as a useful starting point. Sample Activity 3 is designed to accomplish this at the introductory level. The aim is for learners to essentially 'own' the authentic L2 phrases they use, even though they may not yet be able to produce such utterances spontaneously. In Kramsch's (1998: 23) terms, lack of access to such phrases impedes 'potentially bilingual outsiders from becoming integrated into a group'. In this regard, this sort of activity goes beyond the simple provision of 'useful classroom expressions', as is common in mainstream language textbooks. This format underscores the goal of learner autonomy and the long-term goal of facilitating more L2 use.

Sample Activity 3

*The Bilingual Club: Identifying and learning phrases
for communicating in the foreign language*

In working through the activities in your language textbook, you are learning ways of talking about the classroom environment, yourself and your interests, your habits and routines, to describe your classmates, aspects of this new culture, the weather, etc. Also important is the language you use to negotiate your way through class activities on these topics, and while your book contains some guidance here, there is much more to be learned. For example, do you know some ways to express that you did not understand something a discussion partner said, to express agreement, to offer an opinion? Usually, we let you wait until you are an intermediate or advanced language student before we let you in on these sophisticated ways of talking! This activity is designed to help you brainstorm, learn and record some of these ways of talking that we hope will enable you to communicate in the foreign language in culturally appropriate ways right from the beginning. Welcome to the Bilingual Club!

(A) Together with a classmate, write down one or two phrases that you might use in English to express the following:
  (a) Non-comprehension
  (b) Agreement
  (c) Acknowledgment (of someone's point, perhaps designed to keep the conversation going)
  (d) Disagreement

(e) Request for clarification
(f) Self-clarification
(g) Objection
(h) Acquiescence (to do something or agree to something)
(i) Incredulity (over something someone has said)
(j) Other

Write the results of your conversation on a piece of paper or overhead transparency and be prepared to share them with the class.

(B) A matter of 'register'. Register is a linguistic term that basically refers to the degree of politeness or formality you use when speaking with others. It's sort of the difference between saying 'How do you do?' and 'What's up, dude?' In the table, take two or three of your favorite phrases from (A) above and write them in the appropriate box. Then reformulate these phrases in the other box so that they are culturally appropriate for that register.

'Polite'/formal	'Colloquial' (or 'impolite')/informal

(C) Still working with the same classmate, and with your teacher's assistance if necessary, determine what the corresponding foreign language phrases would be for each phrase you have written in the boxes in (B). Be prepared to share these with the class.
(D) Writing the foreign-language phrases on a large sheet of paper (poster board or butcher paper), accompany each phrase with visual support or an English 'translation' of some sort, or both. Include in the presentation some indication of the register of each phrase.

Instruction in basic code-switching concepts

This sort of learner training may appear to students as the most 'foreign' of all forms of training. Firstly, many or most students will have never considered dual code use to be a viable mode of communication, either in or outside the class, even if they are themselves bilingual or multilingual. My experience as a language teacher has shown me that learners can be among the most fervent linguistic purists coming into the classroom, and a large part of the *sell* and *tell* modes of leadership entails convincing them of the usefulness and inherent value in dual or multiple code use. Or at least the normalcy of code-switching in societal bilingual situations. Of course, the case is bolstered by multilingual content instruction, which will be addressed later in this chapter.

The short version of this type of learner training is: help learners understand (1) what code-switching or dual code use is and (2) that it actually can be a useful means of keeping their communication in the L2. How can we best accomplish this? By first conveying some basic linguistic terminology, buzz words that learners can use in developing multilingual norms later on. Sample Activity 4 is preceded with a handout presenting these terms and introduced by a group discussion of what they might mean. The reader will note that this activity represents a classroom manifestation of several of the ideas and arguments presented and developed in Chapters 2 and 3. In addition to asking learners to think through Kramsch's (1993) and Crozet and Liddicoat's (1999) concept of an intercultural 'third place', some of the terminology of Myers-Scotton's Markedness Model is brought to bear. Note that learners are asked to make value judgments, to speculate as to the *why* of code-switching, something that is ultimately rejected by code-switching scholars, such as Auer, Li Wei and others. The point is that learners speculate on some of the reasons one would want to use more than one code in or outside the classroom, not to be or act like a linguist or other sort of social scientist.

Sample Activity 4

What is code-switching?

(A) Some important terms and concepts. Read the following about four terms that are important for understanding, talking about and using more than one language to greatest benefit in our language class.

Code-switching: The alternating use of two or more languages in a conversational exchange, either within a sentence or between sentences.

Here are a couple of examples, recorded in first-year German classes (exactly as the students produced them):
(1) "Ich denke, der Junge in dem Bild ist wirklich *crazy*. Denkst du das auch?"
(2) "Die Katze schlafen *in the corner.* Neben der kleine Tisch."
(3) "*I don't know, my father* kommt nächste Woche nach L.A."
(4) "Am Wochenende gehe ich zu meine Elterns Haus. *They live in San Diego and they'll only be in town for a day or two before they're off on their vacation.*"
(5) "*I was in the Louvre and I saw all those* Bilder, *the ones* wir sehen *in the books and stuff.*"

Socially 'marked' language or code: The 'marked' language is the one that in a particular conversational exchange would feel the most '*un*natural' to most or all speakers. For example, in an immigrant family household in which, say, Spanish is the dominant and most-often used language, younger family members' use of English may be 'marked' to elder generation speakers. Further, younger speakers may be aware of this fact and use English in part to intentionally 'flout' (resist) the markedness 'rules' of the household.

Socially 'unmarked' language or code: The 'unmarked' language is the one that in a particular conversational exchange would feel most 'natural' to most or all speakers. In our Spanish/English example, the unmarked code in many household contexts is probably Spanish, even for younger speakers. When these same speakers exit the house, however, English is probably the socially unmarked code.

Multilingual language classroom: A foreign language classroom that is 'multilingual' is one in which all the languages known by learners and the instructor come into play and are acknowledged as important and useful in different contexts. Obviously, all language use in the language class should have as its goal the maximization of opportunities to hear and use the foreign language. Yet often, and perhaps ironically, this may be accomplished by using English (or another language) in certain ways and at certain times. The class's job (teacher and students) is to determine together when and how those other languages (English, Spanish, Chinese) can or should be used.

The intercultural 'third place': Language classes usually make a dichotomous distinction between the 'native' language and the 'target' language and culture(s), with the presumed goal to help learners move from the former to the latter, to acquire 'native-like' competence in the foreign language. While this is a lofty goal, in the 'real world' it seldom actually happens. Hence, an alternative goal is for learners to strive for a 'third place', a cultural and linguistic competence that is no longer simply the learners' native language/culture, but also is not the native language/culture. In other words, learners strive to become what they can be: competent, intercultural *bilingual* speakers of English and German or Spanish or Chinese.

(B) Group activity 1. Together with one or two classmates, invent a short dialogue between two or more people. The dialogue can be about whatever you'd like (money? love? language learning? plans for the weekend?), but decide in advance what the unmarked code of the conversation will be. This will necessitate considering the reasons why one or the other code is unmarked (based on the context, the location, who is talking, etc.). At least one person in the dialogue should make some use of a language other than the unmarked code of the conversation. Be prepared to present or act out your dialogue to the class!

(C) Each pair or group should present its dialogue to the class. While your classmates present their dialogues, take notes on the following:
   (a) How do the speakers make code choices and *why* is a second (or third) language used in this conversation (other than that this activity required you to write it that way!). For example, do they use the other language because they are missing the words from their vocabulary, to draw attention to or emphasize a particular point, to gain control of the conversation, etc.? Rampant speculation is perfectly ok here!
   (b) Would this use of code-switching be applicable or imaginable in the language classroom? Why or why not?

In addition to thinking and talking about concepts and constructs, learners, even as non-linguists but just as human language users, are qualified to think and talk about examples of real-world dual code use, of analyzing data. Sample Activity 5, which we have used in our German program at UC Irvine in German, asks students to read transcripts of verbal exchanges involving dual code use and speculate about their purposes or functions. This activity can be coupled with multilingual content instruction, as the class learns about the speech communities in which the conversations took place.

Sample Activity 5

Why do these people use two codes?

In previous sessions, we have been thinking and talking a good deal about the ways and reasons people use language, in particular why people would use two languages in the same conversation. This activity asks you to take the discussion one step further, to analyze examples of actual conversations among bilingual people.

Functions and meanings of code-switching or not code-switching

(A) Whole-class discussion
(1) The following example (1) was recorded in a group of male youths in the Altona quarter of Hamburg. Most of the youths in the group are of Turkish descent. One of them, Fahmi, is of Iranian descent. He uses Turkish in his conversation with his friends.

Information you should have: among Turkish youths the word '*lan*' is often used as a *discourse marker*. It means approximately the same as 'man' or 'dude' in English (e.g. 'Hey, man').

(1)

Fahmi: Iran, 15, male
Musa: Turkish, 15, male
Mutan: Macedonian. (already knew Turkish in Macedonia), 15, male

Musa → Mutan	**sen daha bir sey anlatacaktin bana**	
	you wanted to tell us something	
Mutan	später	
	later	
?:	ne (.) pscht	
	what	
Fahmi	((laughs)) **haydi lan**	
	come on, dude	
?	halts maul	
	shut up	

Notes:
Turkish is printed in **boldface type**.
"?" means that the speaker was not able to be identified in the transcription process.

(from Dirim, 2005: 21)

Discussion questions: How are Turkish and German used in this exchange? What do you think of how these three people use the languages? Why does a non-Turkish young man use Turkish? What does he achieve (if anything) in this conversation by choosing Turkish? Have you ever been involved in a similar situation? With which languages? Feel free to comment on any of these questions in German or English (or both if you want!).

The following example (2) took place in Spain. David is a professor who lives in Spain and speaks Spanish and *Catalan* very well. Catalan is a regional language in southern Spain. Jordi would like to study at the language school in which David teaches. In this exchange, the two meet for the first time. It is a sort of entrance interview for the language school. David writes the following:

> Part of my job at a large language school was to carry out placement interviews with prospective students. I normally began such interviews by speaking in Catalan as I wished to establish rapport and engage the prospective student in an informal conversation about his/her background before I proceeded to test his/her English. Beginning in Catalan instead of Spanish was not only a way of communicating to my interlocutor how I wished to position myself in the exchange, but also was an implicit recognition that

most of our prospective students were Catalan dominant bilingual speakers. (Block, 2002: 129)

(2)

David	Bon dia, sóc David. (speaking in Catalan) *Good morning, I'm David.*
Jordi	Hola, soy Jordi, uh, Jorge. *Hello, I'm Jordi, uh, Jorge* (speaking in Spanish, changing Catalan "Jordi," Catalan for George, to 'Jorge,' Spanish for George)
David	Hola, Jordi. Molt de gust. (still speaking in Catalan) *Hello, Jordi, Pleased to meet you.*
Jordi	Ah, hablas Catalán. Muy bien. Estupendo. ¿Y cómo es eso? (still speaking in Spanish) *Ah, you speak Catalan. Very good. Great! And how is that?*
David	És que fa molt temps que visc aquí. (still speaking in Catalan) *I've been living here for a long time.*
Jordi	Sí, pero hay mucha gente que después de muchos anos aquí, no saben ni el castellano. Mira... por ejemplo, los extranjeros del Barça. (still speaking in Spanish) *Yes, but there are a lot of people who aafter many years here, don't even know Spanish. Look at the foreigners [who play with] Barça (Barcelona Football Club).*
David	Sí, supongo que sí. Bueno,... (switching to Spanish) *Yes, I suppose so. Well,...*

(from Block, 2002)

Discussion questions: What is going on in this conversation? Why do you think each person sticks with his own language? Why does Jordi speak no Catalan with David, even though David apparently speaks Catalan so well? Why did David need so long to switch to Spanish? Or do you think he should have stuck with Catalan? What is the function or reason for David's switch in the last line? Have you ever taken part in a similar exchange? With which languages? With whom? You can discuss these questions in German or English (or both!).

(3)

Situation: Maike is visiting Tanja's house. Aischa comes by very shortly after Tanja got off the phone with Aischa.

Maike: German, 19, female
Tanja: Libian/German, 17, female
Aischa: Afghan, 20, female

Maike	( ) Tür geklingelt Tanja
	( ) *someone's at the door Tanja*
Tanja	warte mal (2.0) das ist Aischa
	wait a second that's Aischa
Maike	ja (.) schon so früh? korrekt
	yes already [here] so early? cool
Tanja	ha Aischa (.) **meraba kızım**
	hi Aischa hello my girl
Aischa	**n aber kız**
	what's up girl

((The girls greet each other with kisses on the cheek))

Tanja	**iyi misin?**
	you doing well?
Aischa	**hı iyim**
	I'm doing well
Maike	(echt) ich war beim Zahnarzt
	really I was at the dentist

((The conversation continues in German about the dental visit))

(from Dirim, 2005: 31–32)

    Discussion questions: What is going on in this conversation? Why do Aischa and Tanja use Turkish with each other, even though they are both fluent or even native German speakers? Why do they then switch to German and remain in that language? Have you ever taken part in a similar exchange? With which languages? With whom? You can discuss these questions in German or English (or both!).

Co-Construction of Norms

    In the previous section, I detailed just a few manifestations of learner training toward the creation of a multilingual language classroom community of practice. In the process, much of what I propose comes across as fairly prescriptive, and to some extent this is unavoidable, for the proposal of a multilingual approach ultimately must offer some concrete suggestions for addressing a code choice status quo in which codeswitching proceeds without reflection, possibly maintaining the L1 as an unmarked code. The learner training detailed in the previous sections is this oriented toward the main topic of this section, the co-construction of classroom norms for multiple code use.

Scholars involved with the study and analysis of code-switching in societal bilingual situations might reject the proposal that we can overtly manipulate code choice norms. Admittedly, it is largely uncontroversial that code-switching norms in societal multilingual situations – e.g. whether and when it is acceptable to engage in intrasentential code-switching – develop more or less organically, and usually between and across generations and over decades or centuries. Further, such norms are, for the most part, unconscious, that is, speakers who engage in code-switching probably could not articulate the specific rules for doing so. Even if one accepts a weak interpretation of markedness, speakers in societal bilingual situations have a good sense of the sorts of contexts in which the community allows for code-switching and of the value attributed to code-switching in various contexts (i.e. whether it is accepted as a creative verbal behavior or stigmatized as 'corrupt' usage), but most bilingual speakers could not make explicit the code-switching ground 'rules' of their community (Hymes, 1972).

In the classroom situation, because many of the functions and parameters of code-switching behavior accord with those of societal bilingual situations (Liebscher & Dailey-O'Cain, 2004), there is the indication that it would be difficult to manipulate learners' or even teachers' code choices. Chavez (2003) asserts that classroom diglossia is a reality, and that we should accept it, but she questions whether it is possible, or advisable, to intentionally influence how it goes on. In their 2004 study, Liebscher and Dailey-O'Cain suggested that we need pedagogical principles for understanding classroom code-switching, but they question the feasibility of intentionally manipulating code choice practices. As quoted in the literature review in Chapter 4, the findings of Dailey-O'Cain and Liebscher's 2009 study suggest that

> envisioning the foreign language classroom as a bilingual community does not entail saddling the instructor with the task of formally training learners to behave as bilinguals, or even modeling the conventional codeswitching norms found in non-classroom bilingual communities. In fact, burdening the teacher with the task of explicitly teaching codeswitching has limitations, since some of the codes-witches take on different meanings depending on whether the students or the teacher perform them. (Dailey-O'Cain & Liebscher, 2009: 143)

While it is true that we would not want to 'saddle' the instructor with a task that, as the authors' findings suggest, might not succeed anyway, I suggest that the proposed curricular architecture goes well beyond simply explicitly teaching code-switching, which alone would indeed have limitations. It's about awareness raising at the most general level, and it's also about assigning significance, or rather *resignifying* the use of the L1, and the use of code-switching as conventional classroom language use, toward unmarking the L1 and toward optimizing L2 use. Based on insights on group dynamics in the field of organizational psychology and educational psychology, and from Wenger's conceptualization of communities of practice, I suggest that it is not only possible and feasible to achieve this resignification, but it also may be crucial to the success of classroom L2 learning.

Developing group dynamics through co-construction of classroom conventions

Many scholars writing about groups and group dynamics agree that at the very least, whenever people get together for some common purpose they can be called a group, and the language class fits this definition. There are further characteristics we should consider, though, in our goal of constructing code choice norms. Dörnyei and Murphey (2003) identify the following characteristic features of a group:

(1) There is some interaction among group members.
(2) Group members perceive themselves as a distinct unit and demonstrate a level of commitment to it.
(3) Group members share some purpose or goal for being together.
(4) The group endures for a reasonable period of time (i.e. not only for minutes).
(5) The group has developed some sort of a salient 'internal structure', which includes:
the regulation of entry and departure into/from the group;
rules and standards of behaviours for members;
relatively stable interpersonal relationship patterns and an established status hierarchy;
some division of group roles.
(6) Finally, as a direct consequence of the above points, the group is held accountable for its members' actions. (Dörnyei & Murphey, 2003: 13)

For this discussion, points 5 and 6 are of particular interest. Dörnyei and Murphey point out that groups develop rules and standards of behaviors, stable interpersonal relationships and status hierarchies, division of group roles, and they hold each other accountable for group members' actions. With regard to code choice, the default condition that develops is often passed down from the institution, the curriculum or the instructor in the form of some explicit 'policy' for language use. The most common rule appears to be the 'no English' policy. Yet, recall that in an ecological perspective of language learning and teaching, what teachers do is provide affordances for learning and not learning itself (van Lier, 2004), what happens in a group is not the manifestation of rules or norms, but rather people's reactions to rules or norms (Wenger, 1998). Thus, we must question the logic of articulating such a rule in the first place. The formal stigmatization of L1 use by the teacher or the institution does not lead to the disappearance of L1 use, rather to learners' and teachers' reactions to the convention. The quotes in the epigraphs of Chapter 4 represent two students' reactions to the convention: one has bought into it wholesale; the other has openly rejected it.

Our job as language professionals, then, is not to establish the ground rules for code choice that learners would then 'follow', for in the classroom community of practice such conventions would be as problematic as the marked-L2 default condition. Instead, our job is to create affordances for the development of code choice conventions. What individuals do with those conventions is a secondary issue, and related to the nature and extent of the agreed-on norms. Code choice becomes about the *process* of code choice practices, rather than some target or end state, and this process is in the hands of all class members, instructor and students. Ultimately, it is engagement in the process that should also lead to greater opportunities and contexts for L2 use. At the very least, learners' sensitivity to and awareness of code choices will be heightened and sharpened.

In considering how best to provide effective affordances for the construction of multilingual norms, it should first be clear that there is conceivably a broad range of possibilities. Choices must be made based on the characteristics of a particular institution and its perceived needs, a particular group and its needs, and even based on what is known of individual students in the class. For example, if the instructor knows that all students in a given class are already bilingual in languages other than the L2 being learned, then presumably a different approach would be taken from a class in which it is known that all students are, say, monolingual English speakers on entering the class.

In light of the range of possibilities, I present just a few sample activities, based largely on my own experiences as a US university-level language teacher and language program director, and the constraints and structures in place in my institution. They are largely task based and learner centered in ways that accord with our curriculum in the UC Irvine German Department. In addition to creating affordances for the construction of code choice norms, the activities are also designed to foster learner and group autonomy.

A first step is to create conditions for students to examine and question conventions that exist in most language classes, or at least in the classes within learners' collective experience. Sample Activity 6 asks learners to do this in three stages. First, they discuss the characteristics of several common classroom conventions. Next, they select one of the conventions and decide how one or more group members might intentionally subvert or violate it. In a subsequent class session, this takes place, followed by a class discussion of the results of the whole 'experiment'.

Sample Activity 6

A class experiment: Open season on conventions! Part 1

> In a course I teach on social psychology, I asked students, if they felt comfortable doing so, to identify a social norm and break it, then report the results to the class. One student, wearing a strapless, red, sequined, floor-length evening dress, went to the (only) mall in town, and simply walked from one end to the other. Did I mention that the student was male? And quite hirsute (hairy). He was approached by security guards five times for simply walking the length of the mall. He had broken no rules, but people stopped and stared, and some called security officers! (Oyster, 2000: 28)

Social conventions, whether explicit or implicit, structure and guide our everyday lives. They have to do with the sorts of behaviors that are allowed or expected when people are together; we usually act in accord with social conventions, and most people feel more comfortable when others do the same. The anecdote above is a good example of a violation of expected appearance and behavior. In a shopping mall in this (presumably) small town, while it may not be illegal to cross-dress and parade through the mall, obviously it was considered socially unacceptable to many. Could you imagine other sorts of situations where this student's clothing might not have provoked this sort of response?

This activity is designed to help you begin the process of analyzing and 'constructing' how English and the foreign language are used in this class. To start, you'll be asked to think about – and then break – some language classroom conventions. They may relate to general behaviors, or to the ways language is used.

(A) Please get together with two other classmates and discuss the characteristics or nature of some or all of the following sorts of classroom conventions:
- 'turn-taking' (who gets to talk and when, or rather, when it's ok to interrupt someone and when it isn't);
- volume or tone of voice;
- body language (gestures or movements that usually accompany speaking);
- class seating arrangements (e.g. who gets to stand or sit at the 'front' of the room?);
- class role assignment (who gets to do or say what, and when);
- politeness behaviors toward the instructor and fellow students;
- range of possible classroom behaviors (the sorts of activities one is allowed or expected to do in the classroom, and the sorts that are not generally allowed);
- the ways a group discussion is carried out

Please keep the results of your discussion, at least for now, *confidential* within your group!

(B) Select one of the conventions you discussed (perhaps one that wasn't on the list) and decide how one or more of your group might subvert or violate it. Note: Please don't cross the line to anything that would intentionally embarrass or slight another person or that might be *illegal*! We're interested in breaking conventions, not laws, and we certainly don't want to be offensive or demeaning! Be prepared to carry out your secret plan in the next class hour.

(C) Follow-up discussion. When all groups have had a chance to carry out their violation of some identified classroom convention, some time should be set aside for the class to discuss as a group what happened, and how it was perceived by other class members. At this time, each group might also share the results of its discussion of conventions based on (A) above.

Sample Activity 7 is a continuation of Activity 6, except now the focus is exclusively on language conventions. Learners brainstorm and discuss the contexts in which English use would be acceptable and the contexts in which it would be unacceptable. They select one or more of these conventions and one person agrees to intentionally break it/them in a subsequent class hour. The other part of the activity asks learners to try out a form of dual code use common in immigrant situations, in part to determine whether this sort of dual code use is or should be acceptable in the language class. This is the first concrete step in having students decide what sorts of code-switching would be acceptable for their classroom group, and which would not. The follow-up discussion for this activity is crucial, because the insights (hopefully) gained should contribute to students' success with the next few activities.

Sample Activity 7
Class experiment: Open season on conventions! Part 2

In Part 1 of this activity, you discussed and analyzed various classroom conventions, both linguistic and non-linguistic. Then, you selected one convention and intentionally broke it! Hopefully, this was enjoyable, or at least useful as a learning experience.

In this second part of the activity, we'll narrow the focus on conventions to *code choice* conventions, which is when class members use English or the foreign language.

(A) **The language of conversation**: Assuming the overall goal in a foreign language class is to use the foreign language as much as possible (a reasonable assumption?), in what contexts would it be expected that English would be completely *un*acceptable? For example, is it acceptable to insert an English word into a foreign-language sentence when you can't think of the foreign-language word? In what contexts would it be completely *acceptable* to use some English? Together with one or two classmates, please make a list of these situations or contexts. As with Part 1, keep your discussion secret and make plans for one or more of your group to intentionally violate one or more of the conventions you have identified! This should take place during the next or some subsequent class hour.

(B) **The code choice structure of conversations**: You may have heard someone who grew up in an immigrant household say something like the following: 'My parents always spoke to me in Mandarin, but I always answered back in English'. Whether or not the parents in question liked this status quo, it was the code choice convention of the house. How do you think this sort of convention works in the foreign language class? Try it out! Together with a classmate, select one of the following language tasks:
- Make plans together for the weekend.
- Discuss your major course of study (and the reasons why you picked it).
- Discuss your reasons for studying this foreign language and/or what you plan to do with it in the future.
- Reach an agreement about the best time and place to study the foreign language most efficiently and effectively.
- Other.

The catch: one person should use English only and the other should use the foreign language only. This conversation can take place in front of the class if the group wishes to do it this way!

An Architecture of Classroom Code Choice 151

(C) After you have completed this activity, decide in your group whether this sort of dual code use is or should be acceptable in this language class. Why or why not? Be prepared to present the results of your discussion with the class.

(D) Follow-up discussion. (1) What did each group decide about the sort of dual code of (B) above? (2) When all groups have had a chance to carry out their violation of some identified code choice convention in (A), some time should be set aside for the class to discuss as a group what happened, and how it was perceived by other class members.

Once learners have begun to frame in earnest the class's approach to code choice, the real work of establishing formal code conventions can take place. Sample Activity 8 asks students as a class the sorts of contexts and situations in which speakers may or should switch to English, and those in which it absolutely would be expected that all class members use the L2. Next, they are asked to determine how a switch to English should be initiated, either in an open-ended way or by formal interlocutor sanction. Third, they are asked to decide if it would be acceptable to insert lexical items or phrases from the L1 into L2 sentences.

Sample Activity 8

Establishment of code choice conventions

In the activities you have done to date, you have spent time thinking about and analyzing the ways English and the foreign language can or should be used in the classroom. In this activity, you should plan – as a group – what the class's conventions for code choice should be, at least for the time being. You may use the following questions to guide you, or address additional questions you pose yourselves:

- When, or in what contexts, will it be acceptable to switch to English? These contexts might include carrying out textbook activities, giving or receiving instructions for activities, talking about grammar or vocabulary, discussing tests, quizzes or course procedures, discussing foreign-language culture, geography, etc.
- How should the switch to English be initiated, that is, will a person have to 'ask permission' to switch to English or should she/he just switch without announcing it?
- Will it be acceptable to 'insert' English words or phrases into a foreign-language conversation?
- When will it be absolutely expected that everyone in class uses the foreign language?

At this point, please don't worry about the 'consequences' of not adhering to one of the ground rules established in this activity. We'll take care of this issue in the next class activity!

Be prepared to write your conclusions on the board, an overhead transparency or other medium.

The issue of reinforcement or 'reward' for following agreed-on norms, and 'consequences' for violating them, is taken up in Sample Activity 9. This is, of course, a delicate issue, and the teacher's leadership will be important in avoiding the simple establishment of a 'language police' in the classroom. It should be stressed that the goal is to create conditions for learners to own their own discourse, to use English as they need (or want) it as a tool for facilitating meaningful communication, and for maximizing the amount of time they spend actually using the L2.

Sample Activity 9

Following and flouting conventions

In the activities you have done so far, you have thought about and analyzed the ways English and the foreign language can or should be used in the classroom, and you have planned the best 'code-switching conventions' for your particular class. In this activity, you'll decide – as a group – what should happen, *if anything*, if the instructor or fellow students choose to flout (i.e. openly defy) the conventions the class has decided on. What is the result if particular students remain true to the letter of these conventions? How can you prevent this from establishing a sort of 'language police', which may be counterproductive and ineffective?

To help you, the class should divide into groups of three or four students and carry out the following two tasks. In your discussion, remember that the overall goal of all this is to *maximize the amount of time that all class members spend using the foreign language*.

- After reviewing the specific ground rules for code-switching that have been established, prioritize them in order of 'importance' for helping class members use as much of the foreign language as possible. Assign a number from 1 (least important) to 5 (most important) to each one.
- Taking the rules from most to least important, discuss and decide what the 'consequences' should be for defying or ignoring the rules, if any. What is the 'reward' for following them? Enter the results of your discussion in the table. Afterward, be prepared to share the information in your table with the rest of the class.

Classroom code-switching convention	Rank: 1 = least important and 5 = most important	Result for following or flouting the convention

A final word about Sample Activities 6 through 9. As Chavez (2003) and Dailey-O'Cain and Liebscher (2009) warn, it may ultimately be impossible to affect exactly how code-switching happens in the 'real' interactions of the language classroom. Polio and Duff's (1994) study, to name just one example, showed that even teachers who think they are aware of how they use the L1, in fact are often not overtly aware of it. All that said, I underscore the awareness-raising function of these activities, of working toward at the very least marking the L1, of making the L1 a code that has many useful functions in the L2 learning process, but which should be made as 'foreign' as the L2 being learned. In essence, these activities can serve to 'other' the L1 toward bringing learners' development as bilinguals to the fore. In the following, I consider further ways to do this, to connect, at least pedagogically, L2 learners to wider bilingual or multilingual communities of practice.

Multilingual Content Instruction

In addition to critical discussion of code choice presented in the preceding sections, in order to develop as a classroom multilingual environment in ways that are both theoretically and politically sophisticated, class participants should also engage in what I have come to call multilingual content instruction. This means that students learn about and discuss speakers of the L2 who do not fit the profile of the monolingual native speaker, that is, the speaker represented in idealized form in most mainstream language textbooks. This project can, of course, take many forms and is dependent on several factors, such as the sociolinguistic and demographic circumstances of the language and its speakers in the world, the total number and geographic distribution of speakers, the number and type of different countries in which the language is used, the social status and prestige of its speakers in different communities, the relationship of speakers to other language groups, and so forth. So, for example, learners of Spanish are faced with a very different set of sociolinguistic and demographic issues than learners of, say, Navajo or Dutch or Polish.

In deciding how to approach the design of multilingual content instruction, the instructor should first ask what the goals of the instruction should be. In my own German program, the goal can be summarized in an activity I call 'Tearing down the German monolith', which is presented in Sample Activity 10. The goal of this partially web-based activity is to guide students in discovering that German, which is often represented in textbooks as a fairly monolithic, monocultural entity, is or has been spoken by diverse sorts of people both within Germany, Austria and Switzerland, as well as outside those countries, and that in many of these communities, multiple code use is or was the norm, rather than the exception. The aim is that the whole idea of using English and German in creative ways on an ongoing basis becomes 'normalized', that learners see themselves not only as the social equals of the multilingual speakers they learn about, but they also recognize how learners' own unique, intercultural position privileges them in ways that do not exist among monolingual German speakers (Kramsch, 1998).

Sample Activity 10

Tearing down the monolingual German monolith

(A) The class should divide into groups of three or four students each and discuss the following questions about 'American' languages and cultures:
  (1) How many languages do you think are spoken as people's primary language in the USA? Think about languages that have a longer history in the USA, those of large immigrant groups over the last few centuries, as well as those of more recent arrivals. Think about indigenous languages, or languages associated with particular religious groups. If you have the time, go to the US Census website and look up this information (http://www.census.gov; enter 'language use' in the search window to obtain the most recent reports).
  (2) What are the language experiences of the people in your discussion group? How many languages did each person use routinely while growing up? What languages does each person use now on a daily basis?

One person should take notes. Please be prepared to share the results of your discussion with the class.

(B) Collaborative web activity. With your group, investigate the following questions:
  (1) With regard to German, what languages other than German are spoken in Germany, Austria, Switzerland and Liechtenstein? What are the social or historical circumstances of those bilingual or multilingual groups? Tip: use search terms such as the following: *Türkisch-deutsch*; *Gastarbeiter*; *Migranten*; *Asylanten*; *Zweisprachige Sprachgemeinde*; or their English equivalents.
  (2) Are there bilingual or multilingual communities outside the country or countries in which German is a national language? What do you know about these? Tip: use search terms such as the following: South Tyrol (*Südtirol*); Germans in Australia, China, Russia, the USA, Namibia, New Guinea, etc.; Pennsylvania Dutch; colonial German; Rabaul Creole German; etc.

Homework: Go online and find at least one radio station in a German-speaking country that broadcasts primarily or partly in a language other than German. Listen to the station for long enough to make an assessment of whether and how the people engage in code-switching (listen for the German bits!). Take notes, write down examples and/or be prepared to present a segment of a broadcast to the class.

(C) Follow-up classroom discussion. With your instructor, discuss the results of all groups' findings. What have you learned that adds to or changes your perspectives or experience as learners of German? What is the most interesting insight that you personally have gained from these activities?

After particular instructional goals have been established, designing instruction becomes a matter of researching and selecting the speakers or groups the class should investigate. This could involve the study of a number of linguistic situations. For German, these could include:

- an immigrant or migrant group, such as the Turkish-German communities in Germany (history, literature, music, etc.);
- a borderland language contact situation, such as the German speakers in the South Tirol region of northern Italy;
- a (former) colonial language contact situation (in terms of history), such as the 'Unserdeutsch' speakers of New Guinea (see Volker, 1982);
- a speech island (socially insulated group of speakers), such as the Pennsylvania Dutch in North America.

Apart from investigating 'real' multilingual speech communities, multilingual content instruction could also involve the study of the works or biographies of authors, poets or singers that are inherently or intentionally multilingual. The novels of Rolando Hinojosa come to mind, in which both the narrative as well as the dialogue of the characters makes frequent and creative use of both Spanish and English (see Zilles, 2001). In French, the songs of Zachary Richard might be of interest, in which Cajun French and English lyrics are playfully interwoven.

Critical Reflection

The proposals for the particular manifestation of a multilingual approach presented in this chapter could occupy various amounts of class time, depending on the course goals, the instructor's or students' interests and motivations and so forth. No matter how little or how much time is devoted to exploring and constructing multilingual norms for the language class, however, of paramount importance is the collaborative, critical reflection about the class as a multilingual community of practice. This is important for several reasons. First, it serves to underscore the issue of learner autonomy. Learners, and perhaps also the instructors, are asked to self-assess and evaluate their level of success in creating a multilingual community of practice. Second, it keeps the question, Whose language is it, anyway? at the forefront of learners' consciousness, allowing learners' still limited L2 proficiency to nonetheless be validated on its own terms as developing bilingual knowledge. Third, it can contribute to raising awareness about other aspects of their language learning experience, such as the breadth and depth of their L2 vocabulary or grammar knowledge. Lastly, as an analytical process, critical reflection about these issues can help connect what goes on in the language class to other sorts of courses that learners take, in ways that go beyond the skills-acquisition focus of many CLT classes.

There are conceivably innumerable ways to help students reflect critically about the state of multilingual norms in their class, limited only by the course designer's or teacher's imagination. One example is presented in Sample Activity 11. The results of this discussion activity help shape, in turn, the approach the instructor takes in subsequent weeks toward renegotiating multilingual norms and designing multilingual content instruction.

Sample Activity 11
Explore your inner multilingual selves

For some time, we have been intentionally using English in our German class. Ostensibly, it is intended to *help* you acquire and use more German as a foreign language! The purpose of this brainstorming activity is to determine whether the class as a whole is generally using English in this way, or whether that language remains a disruptive factor in our German class.

(A) Please take a few moments to reflect on the following questions. You'll be asked to share these ideas later on.
   (1) What language do you believe 'dominates' the spoken communication in this classroom? What leads you to that conclusion? Write some brief notes.
   (2) What do you think is the 'unmarked' language for the following contexts? Recall that we defined 'unmarked' as the language that feels most natural or expected in a given situation. Please 'rank' each set of choices for each context, with 1 being the *most marked* and 3 being the most *un*marked.

____ German ____ English ____ Mixed German and English	'Partner or group work' (activities of all sorts that ask you to sit with one or more students and talk about something)
____ German ____ English ____ Mixed German and English	'Communicative tasks and activities' (activities that ask you to communicate with each other or the instructor to receive/provide information, express opinions, make plans, etc.)
____ German ____ English ____ Mixed German and English	'Grammar "drills"' (activities in which the main goal appears to be to manipulate particular grammar forms)
____ German ____ English ____ Mixed German and English	'Grammar instruction' (the instructor explains/ discusses grammar concepts to/with the class, and the class asks questions or makes comments)
____ German ____ English ____ Mixed German and English	'Cultural learning' (activities or discussions in which the main goal is to read, investigate or hear about literary texts or other texts dealing with German cultures or conventions)

_____ German _____ English _____ Mixed German and English	'Policies and procedures' (the instructor and/or students discuss course policies, upcoming events, tests, homework, etc.)
_____ German _____ English _____ Mixed German and English	'Small talk' (discussion with the instructor or other students during the class period that is not directly related to the course material)

Please tally the score for your choices for all seven items and enter them here:

_____ German
_____ English
_____ Mixed German and English

Now transfer these numbers to the table on the board, overhead transparency or other medium. Someone in the class should tally the entire class's results and calculate the means of each row to complete the following table:

Condition	Total class score	Class mean
Most *un*marked		
Next most *un*marked		
Most *marked*		

(3) Meet with one or two other students and discuss the following questions. You will be asked to share the results of your discussion with the class.
- Did the results for each person in the group match the class results? Briefly discuss why you think they are the same or different.
- What is/are the unmarked language(s) in our German class, based on the results of the survey?
- Are you as a group satisfied with this status quo, or would you like to see anything done differently, for example in any of the above-listed contexts? Discuss specific suggestions or questions.

(4) Group discussion. The class should discuss together the results of the smaller groups' discussions. The goal is to decide whether most students and the instructor are satisfied with the ways in which German, English or other languages are being used in this course. If some think things should be done differently, specific suggestions and examples should be offered and recorded.

Summary and Conclusion

In this chapter, the theoretical, conceptual and empirical discussions of the preceding chapters were connected to one manifestation of curricular architecture. Of course, numerous other sorts of manifestations of a multilingual approach would be possible, and I suggest that the proposals in this chapter exist at some mid-point between two conceivable extremes, a 'soft' and a 'hard' version of a multilingual approach. At the soft end, an instructor might simply call students' attention to the idea of dual code use and/or multilingual varieties of the L2, without further elaboration or alteration of the existing curriculum. At the hard end of this spectrum, one can imagine an entire language curriculum focusing not on monolingual, standard-language norms, rather on learners' 'fellow' bilinguals, a multilingual approach integrated fully into the language curriculum, a multilingual approach as *the* curriculum.

The comparatively moderate curricular proposals presented here, then, were designed to function as a component of the 'regular' business of the language class, essentially a supplementary set of units that run parallel and contribute to other sorts of activities. The agenda suggested by all of the example activities is, of course, that the success of the language curriculum overall is driven, in part, by the insights gained and norms developed as part of a multilingual approach.

The next issue in considering this model is curricular articulation, both horizontal and vertical. It is not sufficient to consider learner training, co-construction of norms, multilingual content instruction and critical reflection without also considering how these elements are to be understood and managed across multiple sections of the same course, and across language levels. This important topic will be taken up in Chapter 7.

Chapter 7
Getting from Marked to Unmarked and Back Again: Articulation of Multilingual Classroom Communities of Practice

> *We have been working at tidying up the cards to get them in order with a rubber band around them so that we could see how to take action. Now we would argue that the way to precipitate action is to do just the opposite: Snap off the rubber band, spread out the cards, and let the entropy flow.*
> (Scollon & Scollon, 2004: 151)

Principled Heterogeneity and Emerging Bilingualism

The goal of this chapter is to consider issues of horizontal and vertical articulation, topics whose main *raison d'être* is to tidy up our curricular cards. In this chapter, we examine how a multilingual approach could be articulated horizontally in multi-section language courses and vertically across instructional levels without undermining the heterogeneous and learner-empowering nature of the proposal overall. The inverse of this issue also holds important implications, namely, how does a multilingual approach contribute to the articulation of multi-section language programs? At the outset, I should establish my own understanding of these two dimensions of articulation.[1]

Horizontal articulation can be roughly defined as the objective to create and deliver similar (or identical) instruction across courses at the same level. Presumably, if one were to identify, through quantitative or qualitative study, particular trends in the establishment of code choice norms across multiple sections of the same course, then these trends might be generalized so that the most salient among them would become pre-established norms in all sections. Through such generalization, horizontal articulation would appear to have been successfully achieved. Although fairly straightforward and concrete at first glance, if one adopts an ecological perspective of language learning and teaching, then this definition of horizontal articulation is problematic. In fact, this approach to horizontal articulation represents an impediment to the development of viable classroom communities of practice in a multilingual approach. In this traditional understanding of the term, horizontal articulation follows from the institutional assumption that some sort of *homogeneity* exists among learners, instructors, curricula and institutions.

Yet, many of the scholars cited in this book have shown that classroom communication is always a complicated event, manageable primarily or only in the situated context of individual classes or classroom interactions (Dailey-O'Cain & Liebscher, 2009; Kumaravadivelu, 2003; Tudor, 2001; van Lier, 1996; Wenger, 1998). Under this approach to learning and teaching, any effort at horizontal articulation would not only be a futile endeavor, it would undermine the very goals of an ecological perspective. Still, for instructors and directors in multi-section language programs, disregarding the issue of horizontal articulation is not a reasonable option.

Toward a model of horizontal articulation that accommodates constructivist or ecological perspectives, I believe that some of the proposals made by Larsen-Freeman (2002) and Larsen-Freeman and Cameron (2008) are of help. Larsen-Freeman (2002) argues for adopting tenets of complexity theory in the second language acquisition (SLA) context. Larsen-Freeman (2002: 38–39) summarizes complexity theory for SLA scholars in the following way:

> Chaos/complexity science deals with complex, dynamic, nonlinear systems. It is the "science of process rather than state, of becoming rather than being" (Gleick 1987: 5). ...Unlike traditional scientific approaches that analyze systems into their components and study them individually, chaos/complexity theory (C/CT) considers the synthesis of emergent wholes from studying *the interactions* of the individual components. Outcomes arise that cannot be anticipated from an examination of the parts independently. Neither is it the case that there is a central executive responsible for managing the discrete parts. Rather, the agents/elements act, react to, and interact with their environment (i.e. the other actors/elements and any features of their environment) without any reference to global goals – *they are undertaking purely local transactions* [my emphasis]. The net result of these local transactions is a pattern that emerges at a global level. Thus, for example, the global pattern of a flock of birds emerges from the local behavior of the individual birds that comprise the flock.

Complexity theory, including Larsen-Freeman's proposals for adapting it, was, of course, conceptualized as a model of scientific inquiry, not of curriculum design or articulation. Yet, what is articulation but the desire to create patterns of instruction and learning behavior that are similar in different classes (horizontal articulation), or coordinated and coherent over time (vertical articulation)? Hence, while our goal is not to *study* parts or wholes per se, it is our goal to have some amount of influence on the ways these parts and wholes co-exist and develop. In this regard, the various constructivist approaches discussed earlier accord well with the observations of complexity theory: the complexity of classroom communication and L2 learning can be traced to learners' localized reactions to their environment, which is admittedly what makes the job of planning and carrying out instruction so difficult. In Wenger's (1998) terms, we can design learning situations, but we cannot design learners' reactions to them. The environment is comprised of a multitude of elements, such as the people in the room and their overt and tacit motivations and assumptions (is the class large or small, collectively motivated to learn L2, or are people tired, energized, amused?), the learning space itself (is it hot, cold, stuffy, comfortable?), the curriculum and its materials (do they facilitate verbal interaction, overt grammar learning, cultural insights?) and more. In terms of the Markedness Model and code choice practices, I also consider the relative social status of the languages of the classroom and the particular code that feels most 'natural' for different domains and contexts to be a crucial feature of the environment.

Bringing this around now to the issue of horizontal articulation, the multilingual approach proposed in this book represents an acknowledgment of the inherent complexity of the language classroom and can serve as a unifying factor in the face of messy reality, a means to promote learner (and instructor) autonomy under the umbrella of a principled, critical set of tenets and practices. The instructional proposals of Chapter 6 allow each section of a multi-section course to function as an independent 'community of practice' (Wenger, 1998), such that the language program director or the instructor acts as the architect of instruction and the learners themselves contribute to its design on an ongoing basis, at least in terms of code choice practices. All of this can be understood under the common pursuit of *principled heterogeneity* across language courses. Ultimately, it is the creation of conditions for learner critical reflection and control over code choice norms that help forge curricular bonds across sections of the same course.

For vertical articulation, the working assumption is that while important code choice work is done in any given language class, including an introductory course, learners develop as bilinguals across instructional levels, and the code choice practices of beginning learners will necessarily vary from the introductory through the intermediate and advanced levels; each level is nonetheless equally important to the learner's overall development. The task is deciding how to achieve a situation in which the L2 is generally, or always, unmarked, and in terms of complex human interactions, similar to those found in societal bilingual situations, in which speakers in interaction can deal with either the L1 or the L2 as marked or unmarked depending on any number of situated factors in the context of local interactions and features in the environment. Again, though we have designed numerous aspects of the curriculum to guide students through the investigation and discussion of parts of the whole, we proceed with the assumption of complexity, of dealing in a holistic manner with learners as developing bilinguals. To return to Larsen-Freeman's flock of birds metaphor, the job of the instructor is to keep an eye on whether the flock remains recognizable as a flock, and let the users of language in the classroom (which includes the instructor) deal with managing and reacting to situated actions and reactions as they unfold.

Figure 7.1 is a graphic representation of one sort of chronological progression from the default condition to a multilingual classroom community of practice (other versions would, of course, be conceivable). This is 'the flock', so to speak, the whole that the instructor can keep in mind as learners move through instructional levels. This chart also remains oriented to *process* over state, though states make up the milestones in the process; this is the reason I opted for a flow chart over other graphic choices. The timeframes associated with each stage would vary depending on the number of instructional hours, the characteristics of the particular language, the size and 'personality' of particular classes, and so forth and the process is, of course, assumed to span several academic terms. Thus, in an introductory language class such as that offered in the 10-week quarter in my institution, the group may only progress into Stage I, having succeeded in establishing some multilingual norms appropriate to that level and assigning a socially marked value to the L1. In Figure 7.1, marked is printed in quotes to indicate that at this stage (or perhaps at any stage) all class members agree that making the L1 socially marked is an artifice, a contrivance in service to the goal of helping the L2 become socially unmarked. The path to achieving Stage I is determined by learner training and co-construction of multilingual norms, as detailed in the last chapter.

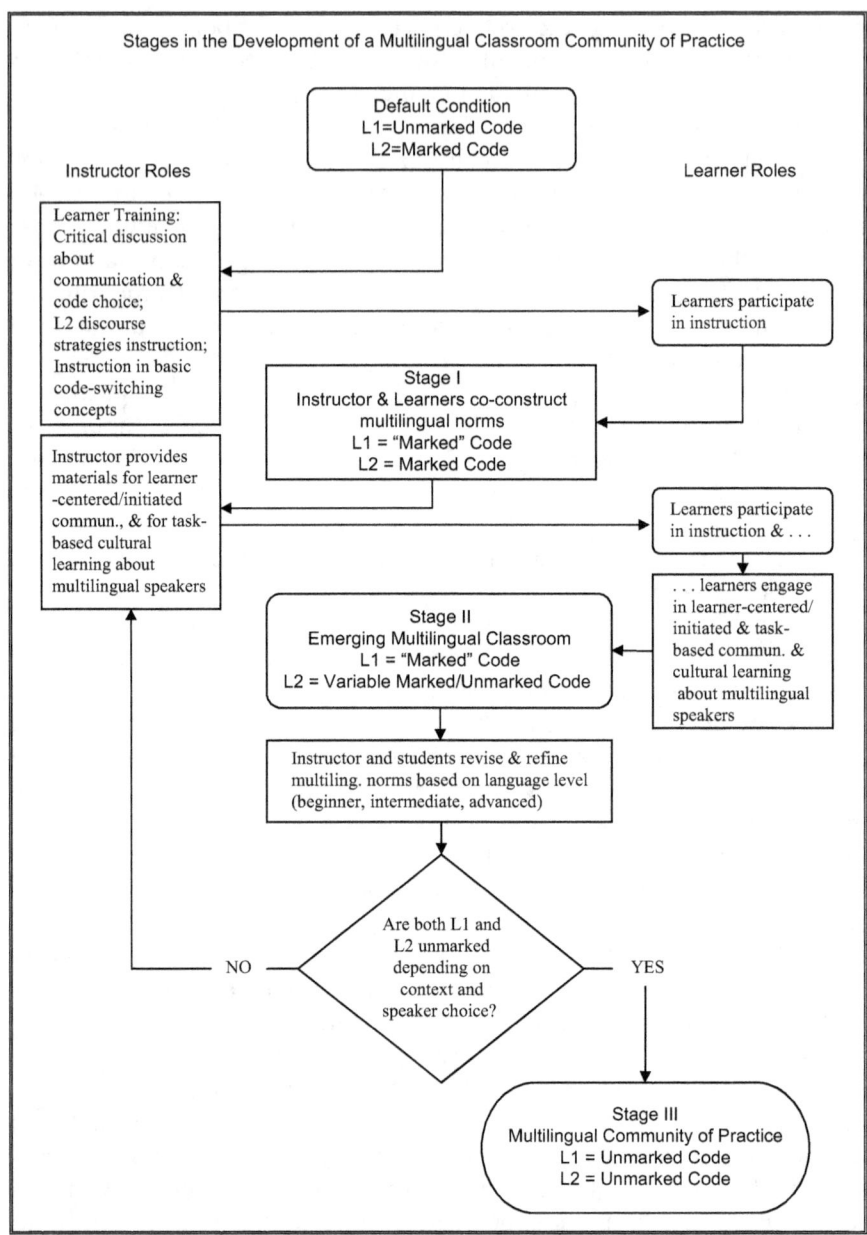

Figure 7.1 Stages in the development of a multilingual classroom community of practice

Stage I: Co-Construction of Multilingual Norms

When learners have participated in a sufficient amount of learner training and established at least some explicit conventions for dual code use, they should have succeeded, at the very least, in formally marking the L1 without stigmatizing its use. This means that they are critically aware of when and how they can or may use the L1, and thus are also aware of it when they flout one of the established ground rules for dual code use. In terms of the discourse of a given class hour, the L1 is socially marked, even though this marking is an intentional act on the part of most learners.

In moving toward Stage I, after a phase of learner training, learners decide when to speak what code and to whom. The sample activities in Chapter 6 are one means to helping learners achieve this. The fact that learners engage in the process of thinking about and monitoring code use in the classroom is crucial to marking the L1 without actually stigmatizing it (i.e. no one should act as the 'language police'), perhaps more crucial than any particular interactional patterns. Put another way, not only is learners' awareness of code use patterns raised, their sensitivity to the importance of different code choices in different contexts is heightened. As students move through subsequent instructional levels, the ground rules for language choice can and should be made more complex or domain-specific (Chavez, 2003). For example, in some courses, learners may agree to move explicit treatment of grammar – a context in which the L1 appears to be preferred as the unmarked code (Levine, 2003; Schultz et al., 2002) – into the L2.

Stage II: Emerging Multilingual Classroom

Establishing multilingual norms for the classroom is, by and large, the 'easy' part of working toward a multilingual classroom community of practice. That is the stage when code choice work is most probably 'fun' or game-like, and learners should be allowed and encouraged to regard this work as language play (see G. Cook, 2000; Crystal, 2001). During the 'normal' business of language classroom communication, which often follows its own rules and patterns as distinct from those outside the classroom, students should be allowed and encouraged to make use of the L1 to facilitate completion of tasks according to the norms they have established. All class members should keep in mind the central principle, that critical engagement of explicit, mutually agreed on code choice norms can facilitate optimal L2 use because the process of socially marking *but not stigmatizing* the L1 can actually minimize the absolute amount of time spent using L1, particularly in comparison with the default condition described in Chapter 5.

At this stage, dual code use/code-switching may still itself be a socially marked activity, even though time has been spent artificially 'marking' the L1. Activities such as Sample Activities 4 and 5 can be employed to help students scale this hurdle, and as they work toward or within Stage II, in which dual code use itself should become an unmarked condition regardless of the agreed-on conventions, not unlike dual code use as it takes place in societal bilingual situations. As students' active vocabulary expands and their L2 abilities develop, the domains and contexts in which the L1 is preferred will probably change, as well as the sorts of L1 uses that learners consider acceptable (see Dailey-O'Cain & Liebscher, 2009).

At the same time, some uses of the L1 may be common to all language levels, and teachers should be aware of this. For example, learners will code-switch in order to compensate for insufficient knowledge of the L2; this appears to occur right through the advanced levels. The key, as stressed thus far, is to keep that sort of switching in mind as 'acceptable' verbal behavior throughout. Zentella (1997) calls this sort of participant-related switching 'crutching' or switching that is not due to social motivations or markedness issues, but to a gap or momentary lapse in the speaker's linguistic knowledge. This sort of code-switching should still be seen as a *choice* against the backdrop of myriad contextual factors.

Two other common functions of code-switching that appear to manifest at all instructional levels, just as they do in almost all societal bilingual situations, have to do with the assertion of one's (presumably L1) linguistic identity and with obtaining or maintaining the floor in a conversation. In discursive terms, this is what S1 was accomplishing in Example 5.2.

These are two aspects of dual code use that tend to remain constant over time in the language classroom. What changes in code-switching behavior is the developing bilingual's *creative control* over the use of both languages in conversation. At the earlier instructional levels, *intersentential* switches will predominate; in later stages, as learners gain greater creative control over the L2, *intrasentential switches* of various sorts will become a common feature of learners' language (see Muysken, 1997). Here is another example of this common sort of code-switching, from the same intermediate-level German class as in Example 5.2.

Example 7.1

77 S4 wir haben (.) zwei: uh ausstellung ueber die deutsche technologie
we have (.) two uh exhibits about the german technologie

78 T uh huh

79 S4 **um together**

80 T yeah

81 S4 um ein ausstellung war ueber (.) uh die technology von **mechanical** (.) dinge
um one exhibit was about (.) uh the technology of mechanical (.) things

82 wie **cars** wir machen also und uh **what else** bombadiere und (xxx)?
like cars we're doing also and uh what else bombers and (xxx)?

Although far less frequent in their appearance in learner speech than lexical insertion, various sorts of code-mixing and code-blending (attaching L2 morphosyntax to an L1 word or phrase) will, nonetheless, probably occur more frequently at the intermediate or advanced levels, in part because of the creative control over German inflection necessary to assign tense, mood or aspect marking to an L1 item.

In addition to hammering out code-switching conventions, the flow chart in Figure 7.1 also indicates continued multilingual content instruction and critical reflection about code choice practices. With increasing proficiency, the L2 can become the unmarked code for this sort of activity. Critical reflection at this stage involves answering the crucial question: are both L1 and L2 unmarked codes depending on the choices of speakers in the interaction? A second question would be: does our classroom use of the L1 appear to help us to use the L2 more frequently, efficiently and in more contexts? Sample Activity 11 (Chapter 6) offers one possible way to get at these questions. If the answer is a strong *yes* to both, then the goal of a multilingual classroom community of practice can be considered successful at that point. If learners feel that the L1 is used frequently in situations in which they would rather see the L2 used, however, then the group may have more work to do. Of course, the point at which a class can consider itself to function in a truly multilingual way is necessarily variable, depending on the motivation and engagement of a particular group of learners, the characteristics of the L2 being learned, the number of instructional hours available and so forth (Levine, 2005).

Stage III: Multilingual Classroom Community of Practice

There is actually little we can say about Stage III here, except that it isn't some sort of code-choice nirvana to be aimed at. It is certainly something for teachers and students to be aware and proud of if achieved and recognized in the classroom community of practice, but it should also serve as the basis for continued reflection about classroom code choice norms, as well as the basis for more – and perhaps more sophisticated – investigation of their own and others' 'multilingual selves'. Put another way, the classroom community of practice may conduct itself more like a societal bilingual community, but this does not mean that it should rest on its laurels and cease reflecting critically on its own practices. For ultimately, it is *not* a societal bilingual situation, which goes through stages of stability and rapid or slow change due to intergenerational, intercultural, sociopolitical and other factors. In some ironic ways, the multilingual language classroom is a much more stable language situation than many conventional multilingual speech communities. While I would not risk prescribing what classroom activities at Stage III would look like, I suspect that in their ideal form, group activity would represent a harmonious synthesis of code choice investigations with other sorts of learning. For example, in reading and discussing an L2 novel, students could spend time analyzing and discussing the ways language varieties, whether of the L2 and other languages (e.g. standard language and dialect) are represented in the story.

Summary and Conclusion

In this chapter, I have addressed some issues of curricular articulation as they relate to developing a multilingual classroom community of practice, of marking the L1 in the early stages toward the goal of dynamic code choice practices as an integral part of what happens in the language classroom. I began by defining my understanding of horizontal articulation, which I reframed in complexity-theory terms as principled heterogeneity. The term vertical articulation was also defined, and I presented a three-stage progression, a way of dealing with articulation as process over state, and for allowing each classroom community of practice to approach multiple code use on its own terms, but informed by similar principles. The main purpose of this chapter was to show the importance, not just of what we do in the classroom, but of how we view what we do in a particular classroom in relation to other sections of the same class, and over time as learners develop as nascent bilinguals.

Note
1. This model of horizontal and vertical articulation of classroom code choice is derived largely from Levine (2005).

Epilogue: **Blessings of Babel**

The purpose of this book was to affect a rethinking about the role of code choice in the language classroom, both as a vehicle for facilitating maximal or optimal L2 use, as well as a means of rethinking other aspects of the curriculum and classroom practice. For example, my work on this topic has led me to rethink the ways we approach what is considered a more 'mainstream' aspect of language teaching and learning, namely, grammar (Levine, 2006), and the field is long overdue for curricular models of vocabulary teaching and learning based on ecological and sociocultural theory tenets. In a word, I hope the reader has gained some insights into the complexity of what happens in the language classroom through the ways that learners and teachers make use of their full linguistic repertoires, and that these insights serve as the basis for thinking about other pedagogical, linguistic, cultural, social, and political issues.

As is admittedly the case with many book projects, this one has taken more years than originally intended. In the preface, I described the evolution of my thinking about code choice from graduate school until the drafting of this book. In the intervening years since beginning the book, my thinking about language teaching and learning has not stood still. My perspectives have changed somewhat, and I have found my understanding of the language classroom as the site of multiple codes in dynamic interaction helpful. These perspectives range from concerns with the daily activities in the classroom, to the aims of what we do at the department and institutional level, to the highest level, that of national politics and policy. In the classroom, I have been greatly encouraged by what I see as a vigorous sort of idealism and intensity among many students; many appear to pursue learning a new language and culture so that they might ultimately help make the world a better place. This has surely always been the case for a vocal minority of students, but my own opposition to an extreme skills-based pedagogy is, in part, a response to what I perceive as many students' and teachers' increasing impatience with the often vacuous cultural content and orientation of CLT curricula. The multilingual approach to classroom communication proposed here will hopefully serve to accommodate what may be a sea change in the ways that many students and teachers think about learning, languages, cultures and connections among people.

My views on language education within the academy are not as bright-eyed, but even here there is hope. The economic crisis that has gripped many colleges and universities around the USA in recent years has in fact brought to light deep-seated and disturbing opinions about the place and value of language learning among even the most distinguished and erudite scholars and administrators. As questions of utility come to the fore, many language and literature programs have been cut or curtailed. Fortunately, the 2007 MLA report on language teaching and learning (MLA, 2007), and numerous public fora and scholarly responses to it, have helped to focus the debate on crucial issues of teaching, curriculum, articulation and, most importantly, the overall aims of foreign language learning at the university level. Those of us in fields concerned with foreign language teaching and learning in the academy must stake out a 'third place' of our own, a position that, hopefully, will thrive between the short-sighted, utilitarian stance spawned by budget cuts and the stubborn preoccupation with the lofty pursuit of humanistic inquiry without regard to institutional realities. Professors, language program directors, lecturers and graduate students need to come together in ways that have been difficult or impossible under institutional constraints to date, but which, ironically, the crisis in language education may now make possible. All these groups need to put the aims of language teaching and the well-being and learning of students at the center of all curricular and administrative reforms. It is hoped that this book will also provide some of the conceptual and curricular tools needed for this important project.

Regarding language education at the level of politics and policy, I share with many colleagues a deep concern for what has gone on at the national level in the USA, particularly with so-called 'critical' or 'strategic' languages; to my mind, this contrasts or even conflicts with the apparent idealism of today's generation of undergraduate students. In January 2006, President George W. Bush and Secretary of State, Condoleezza Rice announced that the US government would support, in large part through the National Security Language Initiative (NSLI), the learning of strategic or critical languages, which include primarily Arabic, Persian, Urdu and other languages considered important to national security (Graham, 2006). For the government, the motivation for learning these languages does not appear to be based on the development of the sort of intercultural communicative competence described in this book, or even on the MLA's sophisticated concept of translingual/transcultural competence (MLA, 2007), but rather on engaging in more effective intelligence gathering from speakers of particular languages, and on portraying the USA as somehow better informed and engaged than it is or is perceived to be. The latter motivation was tellingly reflected by President Bush in introducing the NSLI: 'When Americans learn to speak a language, learn to speak Arabic, those in the Arabic region will say, "Gosh, America's interested in us. They care enough to learn how we speak"' (Graham, 2006: A04). For President Bush, it was also 'a part of a strategic goal, and that is to protect this country in the short term and protect it in the long term by spreading freedom... We're facing an ideological struggle, and we're going to win' (Capriccioso & Epstein, 2006). Admittedly, politicians and policy makers have long placed a heavy emphasis on the study of languages deemed 'critical' in this sense (the study of German in the 20th century has certainly benefitted from this). In 1979, President Carter's Commission on Foreign Languages and International Studies (President's Commission, 1979) concluded that the USA was woefully behind the rest of the world in the learning of languages other than English. The ideas of the report also reached a wider audience through a monograph published by then-Congressman Paul Simon, entitled, *The Tongue-Tied American: Confronting the Foreign Language Crisis* (1980). As we know, however, despite remarkable progress in fields concerned with language education throughout the 1980s and 1990s, in the wake of the 11 September 2001 attacks on the USA, we have publicly 'realized' that many Americans remain ignorant, not just of the languages (grammar and vocabulary) of other peoples, but also of their cultures, of how those people *make meaning*. Thus, there has been an urgency at the national level to create bilinguals in so-called critical or strategic languages, which do not include the traditionally taught European languages, but rather the languages of those the US government regards as adversaries, enemies, potential enemies or otherwise crucial to national interests or security. In terms of the Tower of Babel story made reference to in this book, it is not clear whether this pursuit of (not necessarily mutual) intelligibility will ultimately be a curse or a blessing. What is clear is that US policy makers have approached the problem with questionable motives, questionable at least when viewed from the perspectives of language professionals seeking to make the world a better place through fostering mutual intelligibility and understanding toward, it is hoped, peaceful ends. It was thus encouraging when then-presidential candidate, Barack Obama, asserted in a 2008 debate with Senator Hillary Clinton that 'this world is becoming more interdependent and part of the process of America's continued leadership in the world is going to be our capacity to communicate across boundaries, across borders, and that's something frankly where we've fallen behind' (CNN, 2008). Candidate Obama also stressed on several occasions his belief that all Americans should be bilingual or multilingual. While these assertions alone did not represent a significant evolution beyond the national security concerns of the post-September 11 Bush years, and while President Obama's record of achievements as president has not yet lived up to the lofty goals asserted for language education in the USA, his views appear to come closer to what I have sought to show in this book, that becoming bilingual is about more than just acquiring skills; it is first and foremost about connecting to people. To become truly bilingual and bicultural, the learner must learn to use a creative repertoire of codes in order to function in the L2 society, not simply as a poor imitator of a native speaker, but as a legitimate peripheral participant, an outsider with a role and stake at both the conversational and discourse levels in the L2 culture. This is a tall order, and any learner will need years to attain a level of intercultural competence to function in many social and cultural settings. Still, in these pages I have tried to show that in our language classrooms there already exists the social, cultural and linguistic conditions needed to develop this sort of competence, and that we should not wait until learners are advanced speakers to approach code choice as a valuable resource. The proposed model is intended to help teachers and learners create and recognize affordances for meaningful communication and learning, for using their multiple codes from the very beginning of the introductory language class.

References

Adams, D. (1979) *The Hitchhiker's Guide to the Galaxy*. New York: Harmony Books.
American Council on the Teaching of Foreign Languages (2008) Position statement on use of the target language in the classroom. ON WWW at http://www.actfl.org.
Antón, M. and DiCamilla, F.J. (1999) Socio-cognitive functions of L1 collaborative interaction in the L2 classroom. *The Modern Language Journal* 83 (2), 233–247.
Atkinson, D. (2002) Toward a sociocognitive approach to second language acquisition. *The Modern Language Journal* 86 (4), 525–545.
Auer, P. (1984) *Bilingual Conversation*. Amsterdam: John Benjamins.
Auer, P. (1998) Introduction: Bilingual conversation revisited. In P. Auer (ed.) *Code-Switching in Conversation: Language, Interaction, and Identity* (pp. 1–24). London: Routledge.
Auer, P. (1999) From code-switching via language mixing to fused lects: Toward a dynamic typology of bilingual speech. *International Journal of Bilingualism* 3 (4), 309–332.
Bakhtin, M.M. (1981) *The Dialogic Imagination: Four Essays by M.M. Bakhtin* (C. Emerson and M. Holquist, trans.). Austin, TX: University of Texas Press.
Bakhtin, M.M. (1986) *Speech Genres and Other Late Essays* (V.W. McGee, trans.). Austin, TX: University of Texas Press.
Bakhtin, M.M. (1990) Marxism and the philosophy of language. In P. Bizzel and B. Herzberg (eds) *The Rhetorical Tradition: Readings from Classical Times to the Present* (pp. 928–944). Boston, MA: Bedford Books of St. Martins.
Barthes, R. (1972) *Mythologies* (A. Lavers, trans.). New York: Hill and Wang.
Belz, J.A. (2002) The myth of the deficient communicator. *Language Teaching Research* 6 (1), 59–82.
Belz, J.A. (2003) Identity, deficiency, and first language use in foreign language education. In C. Blyth (ed.) *The Sociolinguistics of Foreign-Language Classrooms: Contributions of the Native, the Near-Native, and the Non-Native Speaker* (pp. 209–248). Boston, MA: Heinle.
Birdsong, D. (1992) Ultimate attainment in second language acquisition. *Language* 68, 706–755.
Birdsong, D. (1999) *Second Language Acquisition and the Critical Period Hypothesis*. Mahwah, NJ: Lawrence Erlbaum Associates.
Block, D. (2002) 'McCommunication': A problem in the frame for SLA. In D. Block and D. Cameron (eds) *Globalization and Language Teaching* (pp. 117–133). London: Routledge.
Blommaert, J. (2005) *Discourse*. Cambridge: Cambridge University Press.
Bloomfield, L. (1942) *Outline Guide for the Practical Study of Foreign Languages*. Baltimore, MD: Linguistic Society of America.

Blyth, C. (1995) Redefining the boundaries of language use: The foreign language classroom as a multilingual speech community. In C. Kramsch (ed.) *Redefining the Boundaries of Language Study* (pp. 145–183). Boston, MA: Heinle.

Bourdieu, P. (1977) *Outline of a Theory of Practice* (R. Nice, trans.). Cambridge: Cambridge University Press.

Bourdieu, P. (1990) *The Logic of Practice* (R. Nice, trans.). Cambridge: Polity.

Bourdieu, P. (1991) *Language and Symbolic Power* (G. Raymond and M. Adamson, trans.). Cambridge, MA: Harvard University Press.

Breen, M.P. (1985) The social context of language learning—a neglected situation? *Studies in Second Language Acquisition* 7 (2), 135–158.

Breen, M.P. and Candlin, C. (1980) The essentials of a communicative curriculum in language teaching. *Applied Linguistics* 1 (2), 89–112.

Bronfenbrenner, U. (1979) *The Ecology of Human Development*. Cambridge, MA: Harvard University Press.

Butzkamm, W. (2003) We only learn language once. The role of the mother tongue in FL classrooms: Death of a dogma. *Language Learning Journal* 28 (1), 29–39.

Butzkamm, W. and Caldwell, J.A.W. (2009) *The Bilingual Reform: A Paradigm Shift in Foreign Language Teaching*. Tübingen, Germany: Narr.

Büttner, H. (1910) *Die Muttersprache im neusprachlichen Unterricht*. Marburg, Germany: Elwert.

Byram, M. (1997) *Teaching and Assessing Intercultural Communicative Competence*. Clevedon: Multilingual Matters.

Canagarajah, A.S. (2004) Subversive identities, pedagogical safe houses, and critical learning. In B. Norton and K. Toohey (eds), *Critical Pedagogies and Language Learning* (pp. 116–137). Cambridge: Cambridge University Press.

Capriccioso, R. and Epstein, D. (2006) Bush push on 'critical' foreign languages. *Inside Higher Ed*, Jan. 6. ON WWW at http://www.insidehighered.com.

Cashman, H.R. (2001) Doing being bilingual: Language maintenance, language shift, and conversational codeswitching in Southwest Detroit. Unpublished doctoral dissertation, The University of Michigan.

Chamot, A.U. (1994) A model for learning strategies instruction in the foreign language classroom. In J.E. Alatis (ed.) *Georgetown University Round Table on Languages and Linguistics 1994* (pp. 323–336). Washington, DC: Georgetown University Press.

Chamot, A.U. (2001) The role of learning strategies in second language acquisition. In M.P. Breen (ed.) *Learner Contributions to Language Learning* (pp. 25–43). Harlow: Longman.

Chavez, M. (2003) The diglossic foreign language classroom. In C. Blyth (ed.) *The Sociolinguistics of Foreign-Language Classrooms: Contributions of the Native, the Near-Native, and the Non-Native Speaker* (pp. 163–208). Boston, MA: Heinle.

Chomsky, N. (1965) *Aspects of the Theory of Syntax*. Cambridge, MA: MIT Press.

Chomsky, N. (1988) *Language and Problems of Knowledge: The Managua Lectures*. Cambridge, MA: MIT Press.

CNN Presidential Debate Transcript (2008) ON WWW at http://www.cnn.com/2008/POLITICS/02/21/debate.transcript/.

Cohen, A.D. (1998) *Strategies in Learning and Using a Second Language*. London: Longman.

Cook, G. (2000) *Language Play, Language Learning*. Oxford: Oxford University Press.

Cook, V.J. (1999) Going beyond the native speaker in language teaching. *TESOL Quarterly* 33 (2), 185–209.
Cook, V.J. (2001) Using the first language in the classroom. *Canadian Modern Language Review/La revue canadienne des langues vivantes* 57 (3), 402–423.
Coppieters, R. (1987) Competence differences between native and near-native speakers. *Language* 63 (3), 544–573.
Crocker, E. and Kramsch, C. (1990) *Reden, Mitreden, Dazwischenreden: Managing Conversations in German* (2nd edn). Boston, MA: Heinle & Heinle.
Crozet, C. and Liddicoat, A. (1999) The challenge of intercultural language teaching: Engaging with culture in the classroom. In J. Lo Bianco, C. Crozet and A. Liddicoat (eds) *Striving for the Third Place: Intercultural Competence through Language Education* (pp. 113–125). Melbourne: Language Australia.
Crystal, D. (2001) *Language Play*. Chicago, IL: University of Chicago Press.
Cummins, J. (2007) Rethinking monolingual instructional strategies in multilingual classrooms. *Canadian Journal of Applied Linguistics/La revue canadienne de linguistique appliquée* 10 (2), 221–240.
Dailey-O'Cain, J. and Liebscher, G. (2009) Teacher and student use of the first language in foreign language classroom interaction: Functions and applications. In M. Turnbull and J. Dailey-O'Cain (eds) *First Language Use in Second and Foreign Language Learning* (pp. 131–144). Bristol: Multilingual Matters.
de Bot, K., Lowie, W. and Verspoor, M. (2007) A dynamic systems theory approach to second language acquisition. *Bilingualism: Language and Cognition* 10 (1), 7–21.
de Guerrero, M.C.M. and Villamil, O.S. (2000) Activating the ZPD: Mutual scaffolding in L2 peer revision. *The Modern Language Journal* 84 (1), 51–68.
de la Campa, J.C. and Nassaji, H. (2009) The amount, purpose, and reasons for using L1 in L2 classrooms. *Foreign Language Annals* 42 (4), 742–759.
Derrida, J. (2002) *Acts of Religion*. New York: Routledge.
Dirim, İ. (2005) Gebrauch türkischer Routinen bei Hamburger Jugendlichen nicht-türkischer Herkunft. In V. Hinnenkamp and K. Meng (eds) *Sprachgrenzen überspringen. Sprachliche Hybridität und polykulturelles Selbstverständnis* (pp. 19–49). Tübingen: Narr.
Dirim, İ. and Auer, P. (2004) *Türkisch sprechen nicht nur die Türken: Über die Unschärfebeziehung zwischen Sprache und Ethnie in Deutschland*. Berlin: Walter de Gruyter.
Domasio, A. (1996) The somatic marker hypothesis and the possible functions of the prefrontal cortex. *Philosophical Transactions: Biological Sciences* 351 (1346), 1413–1420.
Dörnyei, Z. and Murphey, T. (2003) *Group Dynamics in the Language Classroom*. Cambridge: Cambridge University Press.
Drew, P. and Heritage, J. (1992) *Talk at Work: Interaction in Institutional Settings*. Cambridge: Cambridge University Press.
Duff, P. and Polio, C. (1990) How much foreign language is there in the foreign language classroom? *The Modern Language Journal* 74 (2), 154–166.
Dunn, W.E. and Lantolf, J.P. (1998) Vygotsky's zone of proximal development and Krashen's $i+1$: Incommensurable constructs; incommensurable theories. *Language Learning* 48 (3), 411–442.
Edmondson, W.J. (1985) Discourse worlds in the classroom and foreign language learning. *Studies in Second Language Acquisition* 7 (2), 159–168.

Edstrom, A. (2006) L1 use in the L2 classroom: One teacher's self-evaluation. *The Canadian Modern Language Review/La revue canadienne des langues vivantes* 63 (2), 275–292.

Elster, J. (1979) *Ulysses and the Sirens*. Cambridge: Cambridge University Press.

Ellwood, C. (2008) Questions of classroom identity: What can be learned from codeswitching in classroom peer group talk? *The Modern Language Journal* 92 (4), 538–557.

Firth, A. and Wagner, J. (1997) On discourse, communication, and (some) fundamental concepts in SLA research. *The Modern Language Journal* 81 (3), 285–300.

Ford, K. (2009) Principles and practices of L1/L2 use in the Japanese university EFL classroom. *JALT Journal* 31 (1), 63–80.

Foucault, M. (1980) *Power/Knowledge: Selected Interviews and Other Writings (1972–1977)*. New York: Pantheon.

Gardner-Chloros, P. (2009) *Code-Switching*. Cambridge: Cambridge University Press.

Gebhard, M. (2002/2004) Fast capitalism, school reform, and second language literacy practices. *The Canadian Modern Language Review/La revue canadienne des langues vivantes* 59 (1), 15–52. Reprinted in *The Modern Language Journal* 88 (2), 245–264, 2004.

Gee, J.P. (1992) *The Social Mind*. London: Bergin & Garvey.

Gee, J.P. (2005) *An Introduction to Discourse Analysis: Theory and Method* (2nd edn). New York: Routledge.

Geertz, C. (1973) *The Interpretation of Cultures*. New York: Basic Books.

Giles, H. and Smith, P. (1979) Accommodation theory: Optimal levels of convergence. In H. Giles and R. St. Clair (eds) *Language and Social Psychology* (pp. 45–65). Oxford: Blackwell.

Gleick, J. (1987) *Chaos: Making a New Science*. New York: Penguin Books.

Goffman, E. (1981) *Forms of Talk*. Philadelphia, PA: University of Pennsylvania Press.

Graham, B. (2006) Foreign-language learning promoted. *Washington Post*, January 6, A04.

Grennon Brooks, J. and Brooks, M.G. (1993) *In Search of Understanding. The Case for Constructivist Classrooms*. Alexandria, VI: Association for Supervision and Curriculum Development.

Gumperz, J.J. (1982) *Discourse Strategies*. Cambridge: Cambridge University Press.

Guthrie, E.M.L. (1984) Six cases in classroom communication: A study of teacher discourse in the foreign language classroom. In J.P. Lantolf and A. Labarca (eds) *Research in Second Language Learning: Focus on the Classroom* (pp. 173–194). Norwood, NJ: Ablex.

Halliday, M.A.K. (1978) *Language as Social Semiotic: The Social Interpretation of Language and Meaning*. Baltimore, MD: University Park Press.

Hancock, M. (1997) Behind classroom code switching: Layering and language choice in L2 learner interaction. *TESOL Quarterly* 31 (2), 217–235.

Haugen, E. (1972) *The Ecology of Language*. Stanford, CA: Stanford University Press.

Haugen, E. (1987) *Blessings of Babel: Bilingualism and Language Planning. Problems and Pleasures*. Berlin: Walter de Gruyter.

Heller, M. (1995) Code-switching and the politics of language. In L. Milroy and P. Muysken (eds) *One Speaker Two Languages: Cross-disciplinary Perspectives on Code-Switching* (pp. 158–174). Cambridge: Cambridge University Press.

Hersey, P. and Blanchard, K.H. (1982) *Management of Organizational Behavior: Utilizing Human Resources*. Englewood Cliffs, NJ: Prentice-Hall.

Horner, B. and Trimbur, J. (2002) English only and U.S. college composition. *College Composition and Communication* 53 (4), 594–630.

Hymes, D. (1972) On communicative competence. In J. Pride and J. Holmes (eds) *Sociolinguistics* (pp. 269–293). Harmondsworth: Penguin.

Johnson, K.E. (2009) *Second Language Teacher Education: A Sociocultural Perspective*. New York: Routledge.

Kasper, G. (1985) Repair in foreign language teaching. *Studies in Second Language Acquisition* 7 (2), 200–215.

Kaufman, D. and Grennon Brooks, J. (1996) Interdisciplinary collaboration in teacher education: A constructivist approach. *TESOL Quarterly* 30 (2), 231–251.

Kim, Y. and Petraki, E. (2009) Students' and teachers' use of and attitudes to L1 in the EFL classroom. *Asian EFL Journal* 11 (4), 58–89. On WWW at http://www.asian-efl-journal.com.

Kinginger, C. (2001) $i+1$ [does not equal] ZPD. *Foreign Language Annals* 34 (5), 417–425.

Kraemer, A. (2006) Teachers' use of English in communicative German language classrooms: A qualitative analysis. *Foreign Language Annals* 59 (3), 435–450.

Kramsch, C. (1993) *Context and Culture in Language Teaching*. Oxford: Oxford University Press.

Kramsch, C. (1997) The privilege of the nonnative speaker. *Publications of the Modern Language Association* 112 (3), 359–369.

Kramsch, C. (1998) The privilege of the intercultural speaker. In M. Byram and M. Fleming (eds) *Language Learning in Intercultural Perspective: Approaches through Drama and Ethnography* (pp. 16–31). Cambridge: Cambridge University Press.

Kramsch, C. (2002a) Introduction: "How can we tell the dancer from the dance?" In C. Kramsch (ed), *Language Acquisition and Language Socialization: Ecological Perspectives* (pp. 1–30). New York: Continuum.

Kramsch, C. (2002b) Language and culture: A social semiotic perspective. *ADFL Bulletin* 33 (2), 8–15.

Kramsch, C. (2006) From communicative competence to symbolic competence. *The Modern Language Journal* 90 (2), 249–252.

Kramsch, C. (2009) *The Multilingual Subject: What Foreign Language Learners Say about their Experience and Why it Matters*. Oxford: Oxford University Press.

Krashen, S. (1982) *Principles and Practice in Second Language Acquisition*. Oxford: Pergamon.

Krashen, S.D. and Terrell, T.D. (1983/2000) *The Natural Approach: Language Acquisition in the Classroom*. Essex: Longman.

Krause, C.A. (1916) *The Direct Method in Modern Languages*. New York: Charles Scribner's Sons.

Kumaravadivelu, B. (2003) *Beyond Methods: Macrostrategies for Language Teaching*. New Haven, CT: Yale University Press.

Kumaravadivelu, B. (2005) *Understanding Language Teaching: From Method to Post-Method*. Mahwah, NJ: Lawrence Erlbaum Associates.

Lantolf, J.P. (2000) Introducing sociocultural theory. In J.P. Lantolf (ed.) *Sociocultural Theory and Second Language Learning* (pp. 1–26.). Oxford: Oxford University Press.

Lantolf, J. and Appel, G. (eds) (1994) *Vygotskyan Approaches to Second Language Research*. Norwood, NJ: Ablex.

Lantolf, J.P. and Thorne, S.L. (2006) *Sociocultural Theory and the Genesis of Second Language Development*. Oxford: Oxford University Press.

Larsen-Freeman, D. (2002) A chaos/complexity theory perspective. In C. Kramsch (ed.) *Language Acquisition and Language Socialization: Ecological Perspectives* (pp. 33–46). London: Continuum.

Larsen-Freeman, D. (2003) *Teaching Language: From Grammar to Grammaring*. Boston, MA: Heinle.

Larsen-Freeman, D. and Cameron, L. (2008) *Complex Systems and Applied Linguistics*. Oxford: Oxford University Press.

Lave, J. and Wenger, E. (1991) *Situated Learning: Legitimate Peripheral Participation*. Cambridge: Cambridge University Press.

Leont'ev, A.N. (1978) *Activity, Consciousness and Personality*. Englewood Cliffs, NJ: Prentice Hall.

Le Page, R.B. and Tabouret-Keller, A. (1985) *Acts of Identity: Creole-based Approaches to Language and Ethnicity*. Cambridge: Cambridge University Press.

Levine, G.S. (2003) Student and instructor beliefs and attitudes about target language use, first language use, and anxiety: Report of a questionnaire study. *The Modern Language Journal* 87 (3), 343–64.

Levine, G.S. (2005) Articulation of code-choice practices in the foreign language classroom. In C. Barrett and K. Paesani (eds) *Language Program Articulation: Theoretical and Practical Foundations*. Boston, MA: Heinle.

Levine, G.S. (2006) Problematizing the teaching and learning of grammar in the intermediate German classroom: A sociocultural approach. *Die Unterrichtspraxis/Teaching German* 39 (2), 1–13.

Levine, G.S. (2009) Building meaning through code choice in L2 learner interaction: A D/discourse analysis and proposals for curriculum design and teaching. In M. Turnbull and J. Dailey-O'Cain (eds) *First Language Use in Second-Language Learning and Teaching* (pp. 145–162). Bristol: Multilingual Matters.

Levine, G.S., Eppelsheimer, N., Kuzay, F., Moti, S. and Wilby, J. (2004) Global simulation at the intersection of theory and practice in the intermediate-level German class. *Die Unterrichtspraxis/Teaching German* 37 (2), 99–116.

Liddicoat, A. (2003) Teaching languages for intercultural communication. *UC Consortium for Language Learning and Teaching Newsletter* 3 (1), 9–11 (transcript of symposium presentation). On WWW at http://uccllt.ucdavis.edu.

Liebscher, G. and Dailey-O'Cain, J. (2004) Learner code-switching in the content-based foreign language classroom. *Canadian Modern Language Review/La revue canadienne des langues vivantes* 60 (4), 501–25. Reprinted in *The Modern Language Journal* 89 (2), 234–47, 2005.

Littlewood, W. and Yu, B. (2009) First language and target language in the foreign language classroom. *Language Teaching* doi: 10.1017, 1–14. On WWW at http://journals.cambridge.org/action/displayAbstract?fromPage=online&aid=6821596.

Li Wei (1998) The 'why' and 'how' questions in the analysis of conversational code-switching. In P. Auer (ed) *Code-Switching in Conversation: Language, Interaction, and Identity* (pp. 156–76). London: Routledge.

Li Wei (2000) Dimensions of bilingualism. In Li Wei (ed) *The Bilingualism Reader* (pp. 3–25). London: Routledge.
Li Wei (2005) 'How can you tell?' Towards a common sense explanation of conversational code-switching. *Journal of Pragmatics* 37 (3), 375–389.
Lucas, T. and Katz, A. (1994) Reframing the debate: The roles of native languages in English-only programs for language minority students. *TESOL Quarterly* 28 (3), 537–561.
Macaro, E. (2001) Analyzing student teachers' code-switching in foreign language classrooms: Theories and decision making. *The Modern Language Journal* 85 (4), 531–548.
Macaro, E. (2009) Teacher use of code-switching in the L2 classroom: Exploring 'optimal' use. In M. Turnbull and J. Dailey-O'Cain (eds) *First Language Use in Second and Foreign Language Learning* (pp. 35–49). Bristol: Multilingual Matters.
Meeuwis, M. and Blommaert, J. (1994) The 'markedness model' and the absence of society: Remarks on code-switching. *Multilingua* 13 (4), 387–423.
Muysken, P. (1997) Code-switching processes: Alternation, insertion, congruent lexicalization. In M. Pütz (ed.) *Language Choices: Conditions, Constraints, and Consequences* (pp. 361–380). Amsterdam: John Benjamins.
Myers-Scotton, C. (1983) The negotiation of identities in conversation: A theory of markedness and code choice. *Journal of the Sociology of Language* 44, 115–136.
Myers-Scotton, C. (1993) *Social Motivations for Codeswitching: Evidence from Africa*. Oxford: Clarendon.
Myers-Scotton, C. (1997) *Duelling Languages: Grammatical Structure in Codeswitching* (Rev. edn). Oxford: Oxford University Press.
Myers-Scotton, C. (2002) Frequency and intentionality in (un)marked choices in codeswitching: 'This is a 24-hour country'. *The International Journal of Bilingualism* 6 (2), 205–219.
Myers-Scotton, C. and Bolonyai, A. (2001) Calculating speakers: Codeswitching in a rational choice model. *Language in Society* 30 (1), 1–28.
Nzwanga, M.A. (2000) A study of French-English codeswitching in a foreign language college teaching environment. Unpublished doctoral dissertation, The Ohio State University.
Ohta, A.S. (2000) Rethinking interaction in SLA: Developmentally appropriate assistance in the zone of proximal development and the acquisition of L2 grammar. In J.P. Lantolf (ed.) *Sociocultural Theory and Second Language Learning* (pp. 51–78). Oxford: Oxford University Press.
Olshtain, E. and Celce-Murcia, M. (2003) Discourse analysis and language teaching. In D. Schiffrin, D. Tannen and H. Hamilton (eds) *The Handbook of Discourse Analysis* (pp. 707–724). Oxford: Blackwell.
Ortega, L. (2010) The bilingual turn in SLA. Plenary address at the American Association for Applied Linguistics conference, Atlanta, GA.
Oyster, C. (2000) *Groups: A User's Guide*. Boston, MA: McGraw-Hill.
Pennycook, A. (2001) *Critical Applied Linguistics: A Critical Introduction*. Mahwah, NJ: Lawrence Erlbaum.
Phipps, A. and Gonzalez, M. (2005) *Modern Languages: Learning and Teaching in an Intercultural Field*. London: Sage.

Polio, C.G. and Duff, P.A. (1994) Teachers' language use in university foreign language classrooms: A qualitative analysis of English and target language alternation. *The Modern Language Journal* 78 (3), 313–326.
Poplack, S. (1980) "Sometimes I'll start a sentence in Spanish y termino en español": Toward a typology of code-switching. *Linguistics* 18 (7/8), 581–618.
President's Commission on Foreign Languages and International Studies (1979) *Strength through Wisdom: A Critique of U.S. Capability.* Washington, DC: U.S. Government Printing Office.
Rampton, B. (1995) *Crossing: Language and Ethnicity among Adolescents.* New York: Longman.
Reagan, T.G. and Osborn, T.A. (2002) *The Foreign Language Educator in Society: Toward a Critical Pedagogy.* Mahwah, NJ: Lawrence Erlbaum Associates.
Richards, J.C. and Rodgers, T.S. (2001) *Approaches and Methods in Language Teaching* (2nd edn). Cambridge: Cambridge University Press.
Robbins, T. (1980) *Still Life with Woodpecker.* New York: Bantam.
Romaine, S. (1989) *Bilingualism.* Oxford: Blackwell.
Sankoff, D. and Poplack, S. (1981) A formal grammar for code-switching. *Papers in Linguistics* 14 (1–4), 3–46.
Savignon, S. (2002) *Interpreting Communicative Language Teaching: Contexts and Concerns in Teacher Education.* New Haven, CT: Yale University Press.
Saville-Troike, M. (2003) *The Ethnography of Communication: An Introduction.* Oxford: Blackwell.
Schulz, R. (2006) Reevaluating communicative competence as a major goal in postsecondary language requirement courses. *The Modern Language Journal* 90 (2), 252–255.
Schultz, J.M., Di Carlo, A., Frame, L., Kern, R., Kerr, H., Little, L., Mchombo, S., Richards, K. and You, C. (2002) The use of L1 in the foreign language classroom at UC Berkeley. *Language Teaching at Berkeley: Newsletter of the Berkeley Language Center* 17 (2), 1–4.
Scollon, R. (2001) *Mediated Discourse: The Nexus of Practice.* London: Routledge.
Scollon, R. and Scollon, S.W. (2003) *Discourses in Place: Language in the Material World.* London: Routledge.
Scollon, R. and Scollon, S.W. (2004) *Nexus Analysis: Discourse and the Emerging Internet.* London: Routledge.
Seedhouse, P. (2004) *The Interactional Architecture of the Second Language Classroom: A Conversational Analytic Perspective.* Oxford: Blackwell.
Simon, P. (1980) *The Tongue-Tied American: Confronting the Foreign Language Crisis.* New York: Continuum.
Spada, N. and Fröhlich, M. (1995) *COLT Observation Scheme: Communicative Orientation of Language Teaching Coding Conventions and Applications.* National Center for Language Teaching and Research.
Stetsenko, A. and Arievitch, I. (1997) Constructing and deconstructing the self: Comparing post-Vygotskyan and discourse-based versions of social constructivism. *Mind, Culture, and Activity, An International Journal* 4 (3), 159–172.
Swain, M. and Lapkin, S. (1998) Interaction and second language learning: Two adolescent French immersion students working together. *The Modern Language Journal* 82 (3), 320–337.
Swain, M. and Lapkin, S. (2000) Task-based second language learning: The uses of the first language. *Language Teaching Research* 4 (3), 251–274.

Tharp, R.G. and Gallimore, R. (1991) *The Instructional Conversation: Teaching and Learning in Social Activity.* Santa Cruz, CA: National Center for Research on Cultural Diversity and Second Language Learning.

Thompson, G.L. (2006) Teacher and student first language and target language use in the foreign language classroom: A qualitative and quantitative study of language choice. Unpublished doctoral dissertation, University of Arizona.

Tudor, I. (1995) *Learner-Centredness as Language Education.* Cambridge: Cambridge University Press.

Tudor, I. (2001) *The Dynamics of the Language Classroom.* Cambridge: Cambridge University Press.

Turnbull, M. and Arnett, A. (2002) Teachers' uses of the target and first languages in second and foreign language classrooms. *Annual Review of Applied Linguistics* 22, 204–218.

Turnbull, M. and Dailey-O'Cain, J. (2009) Introduction. In M. Turnbull and J. Dailey-O'Cain (eds) *First Language Use in Second and Foreign Language Learning* (pp. 1–14). Bristol: Multilingual Matters.

Valdman, A. (1989) The problem of the target model in proficiency-oriented foreign language instruction. *Applied Language Learning* 1 (1), 33–51.

van Lier, L. (1988) *The Classroom and the Language Learner.* London: Longman.

van Lier, L. (1994). Educational linguistics: Field and project. In J. Alatis (Ed.), *Georgetown University Round Table on Languages and Linguistics 1994* (pp. 199–209). Washington, D.C.: Georgetown University Press.

van Lier, L. (1995) *Introducing Language Awareness.* London: Penguin.

van Lier, L. (1996) *Interaction in the Language Curriculum: Awareness, Autonomy, and Authenticity.* London: Longman.

van Lier, L. (2004) *The Ecology and Semiotics of Language Learning: A Sociocultural Perspective.* Boston, MA: Kluwer.

VanPatten, B. (1995) *Input Processing.* Clevedon: Multilingual Matters.

Volker, C.A. (1982) An Introduction to Rabaul Creole German (Unserdeutsch). Unpublished master's thesis, University of Queensland.

Vygotsky, L.S. (1978) *Mind in Society: The Development of Higher Psychological Processes.* Cambridge, MA: Harvard University Press.

Walsh, S. (2006) *Investigating Classroom Discourse.* London: Routledge.

Weinreich, M. (1945) Der yivo un di problemen fun undzer tsayt. *YIVO–Bleter* 25 (1), 13.

Wenger, E. (1998) *Communities of Practice.* Cambridge: Cambridge University Press.

Wing, B.H. (1980) The languages of the foreign language classroom: A study of teacher use of the native and target languages for linguistics and communicative functions. Unpublished doctoral dissertation, The Ohio State University.

Young, R.F. (2009) *Discursive Practice in Language Learning and Teaching.* Malden, MA: Wiley-Blackwell.

Zentella, A.C. (1997) *Growing up Bilingual: Puerto Rican Children in New York.* Oxford: Blackwell.

Zilles, K. (2001) *Rolando Hinojosa: A Reader's Guide.* Albuquerque, NM: University of New Mexico Press.

Index

ACTFL, see American Council on the Teaching of Foreign Languages
activity theory, 41
acts of identity, 26
Adams, D., 47-48
affordances for learning, xii, xv, 4, 8, 16, 25, 32, 42-44, 102, 126, 147, 172
– definition of, 32
Afghan, 143
American Council on the Teaching of Foreign Languages (ACTFL), 14
Antón, M., 5, 79-80, 83, 100-101, 137
anxiety, 76, 79
Appel, G., 4
Arabic, 170-171
Arievitch, I., 24
Arnett, A., 101
articulation, xv, 159, 160-164, 168, 170
– horizontal, definition of, 160
– vertical, definition of, 162-163
Atkinson, D., 71
Auer, P., 12, 15, 49, 51, 53-56, 60, 82, 103, 155
Australia, 155
Austria, 154-155

Bakhtin, M.M., 21, 25, 27, 39, 63
Barthes, R., 3, 17, 121
behaviorism, 71
Belz, J.A., 5, 12, 16, 101
bilingual vs. multilingual, 18
bilingualism, xv, 14, 18, 102
– societal, definition of, 18
Birdsong, D., 22, 126
Blanchard, K.H., 128
Block, D., 58-59, 143
Blommaert, J., 48, 51, 54, 62-63
Bloomfield, L., 71
Blyth, C., 4-5, 71, 101
Bolonyai, A., 55-56
Bourdieu, P., 41, 60, 62-63, 102, 104, 121
Breen, M.P., 4, 9
Bronfenbrenner, U., 22, 30
Brooks, M.G., 130
Bush, G.W., 170-172

Büttner, H., 71, 101
Butzkamm, W., 4, 71-72
Byram, M., 18, 36-38, 41, 45

Cajun French, 156
Caldwell, J.A.W., 71-72
Cameron, L., 8, 30, 34, 161
Canagarajah, A.S., 81
Candlin, C., 9
Cantonese, 53-54
Capriccioso, R., 171
Cashman, H.R., 36, 54
Catalan, 58-61, 142-143
Celce-Murcia, M., 64
Chamot, A.U., 58, 131
Chavez, M., 5, 14, 145, 153, 165
chaos/complexity theory, 8, 30, 161
China, 155
Chinese, 49, 54, 69-70, 140, 150
Chomsky, N., 102
chunks (of language), 137
classical languages, 11-12, 20
Clinton, H., 171
CLT, see communicative language teaching
code vs. language, 48-49
code-switching, xiv-xv, 9, 49-64, 65-66, 74, 81-82, 103-104, 120, 139, 141, 145-146, 152-153, 164, 166
– conversation-analytic approaches to, 53-54, 57, 82, 104
– crutching, 166
– definitions of, 49-51
– discourse-analytical approaches to, xiv, 51, 55, 57, 61-64, 66, 104, 120
– discourse-related, 82
– interactional approach to, xiv, 49, 53-56, 61, 65, 103
– intersentential, 166
– intrasentential, 74, 145, 166
– Markedness Model of, xiv, 51-56, 103, 139, 162
– and opportunity sets, 56-57, 60
– participant-related, 166
– Rational Choice Model of, xiv, 51, 54-61, 64-65

Index

- and rights and obligations sets (RO), 52, 54
- and somatic markers, 57
cognitive science, 6, 22
Cohen, A.D., 58
communicative competence, 6, 9, 36-37
communicative language teaching (CLT), xi, 7, 9, 14, 17, 21, 37, 70-71, 74, 79, 97, 99-100, 107, 120-121, 156, 169
community of practice, xii, xv, 8, 17, 24, 36, 40-43, 66, 83, 125, 128-129, 132, 144, 147, 156, 162-165, 167-168
- definition of, 41-42
complexity theory, *see* chaos/complexity theory
composition, pedagogy of, 10-11
connectionism, 25-26, 45-46
conversation analytic approaches to code-switching, *see* code-switching
Cook, G., 12, 165
Cook, V.J., 4-5, 14, 71, 75, 101
Coppieters, R., 126
creole, 18, 155
Creole German, *see* Rabaul Creole German
critical languages, 171
critical pedagogy, 128
critical reflection, xv, 8, 16, 61, 70, 100, 129-130, 132, 156-159, 162, 167-168
Crocker, E., 137
Crozet, C., 36-37, 45, 101, 139
Crystal, D., 12, 165
Cummins, J., 12, 18, 23
curricular architecture, xii, xv, 8, 21, 32, 43, 46, 66, 98, 100, 103, 125-130, 145, 159
- description of, 125-130

Dailey-O'Cain, J., 5, 15, 72, 82-83, 101n, 103, 145, 153, 161, 166
de Bot, K., 30, 34
de Guerrero, M.C.M., 24-25
de la Campa, J.C., 72
Derrida, J., 20
DiCamilla, F.J., 5, 79-80, 83, 100-101, 137
diglossia, 14, 145
direct method, 71
Dirim, İ, 12, 142, 144
discourse analysis, xv, 9, 61-64, 65, 74, 102ff
- building tasks, 64, 105-107, 118, 120-121
- 'big D' and 'little d' discourses, 63, 104
Domasio, A., 57
Dörnyei, Z., 35, 69, 128, 130-131, 146
Drew, P., 105
Duff, P.A., 73-75, 77, 101, 103, 153
Dunn, W.E., 61

Dutch, 154
dynamic systems theory, *see* chaos/complexity theory

ecological linguistics, *see* ecological perspective
ecological perspective, xii, xiv-xv, 7-8, 21-23, 26-36, 43-45, 47, 51, 61, 104, 125, 147, 160-161, 169
Edmondson, W.J., 5
Edstrom, A., 72
Elster, J., 56
Epstein, D., 171
exclusive L2 use, xi, xii, 14, 17, 72, 75, 83

Ferguson, C., 14
Firth, A., 4
Fishman, J., 14
Ford, K., 72
fossilized errors, 15-16
Foucault, M., 40
French, 20, 37, 72-74, 77, 80, 87-98, 101, 126, 156
Fröhlich, M., 85

Gallimore, R., 24
gambits, 137
Gardner-Chloros, P., 15
Gebhard, M., 119
Gee, J.P., xv, 8-9, 26, 46, 57, 60, 63-64, 85, 102, 104-107, 110-111, 114, 118, 121
Geertz, C., xv, 7
Genesis, Book of, 19
German, xi, 12, 30-31, 48-49, 76, 82, 86, 98, 101, 106, 107-121, 122, 126, 135-136, 139-144, 152, 154-155, 157-158, 165, 167, 171
- UC Irvine Department of, 86, 141, 148
Germany, 12, 136, 154-155
Giles, H., 15
Gleick, J., 161
Gonzalez, M., 102
Graham, B., 170-171
grammar translation method, 71
Greek, 11
Grennon Brooks, J., 130
Gumperz, J.J., 49, 62
Guthrie, E.M.L., 16, 73, 77, 97, 101

habitus, 63, 121
Halliday, M.A.K., 27, 36
Hancock, M., 87, 101
Haugen, E., 22, 27, 45, 48
Heller, M., 62

Heritage, J., 105
Hersey, P., 128
Hinojosa, R., 156
horizontal articulation, *see* articulation
Horner, B., 10-12, 127
Hymes, D., 9, 51, 71, 145

i + 1, 46
ICC, *see* intercultural communicative competence
innatist models, 21-23
intercultural communicative competence (ICC), 6, 18, 36-40, 42, 61, 170
interlanguage, 44
Iran, *see* Persian
Italy, 155

Japanese, 37, 126
Johnson, K.E., 9

Kasper, G., 110
Katz, A., 15
Kaufman, D., 130
Kim, Y., 72
Kinginger, C., 45
Kraemer, A., 72
Kramsch, C., 3, 5, 6, 8, 9, 13-14, 16, 27, 36, 39, 101, 112, 137, 139, 154
Krashen, S., xi, 45, 71
Krause, C.A., 71
Kumaravadivelu, B., 4, 7, 161

language play, 12, 165
Lantolf, J.P., 4, 9, 26, 27, 45
Lapkin, S., 24-25, 79-80, 83, 97, 100-101, 110, 113, 137
Larsen-Freeman, D., 7-8, 30, 34, 102, 161, 163
Latin, 11-12, 20
Lave, J., 40-42, 61
leadership styles, 128-129
Le Page, R.B., 15, 26, 46
learner training, 128-132, 134, 138-139, 144, 159, 163-165
legitimate peripheral participation, 24, 172
Leont'ev, A.N., 42
Levine, G.S., 5, 23, 45, 75-77, 97, 101, 104, 115, 122, 165, 167-169
Li Wei, 15, 49, 51, 53-56, 60, 104, 139
Libyan, 143
Liddicoat, A., 36-37, 39, 45, 101, 112, 139
Liebscher, G., 5, 15, 72, 82-83, 101, 103, 145, 153, 161, 166
Liechtenstein, 155

Littlewood, W., 72, 101
Lowie, W., 30
Lucas, T., 15

Macaro, E., xiv, 5, 14, 18, 74-75, 77, 80, 101
Macedonian, 142
Mandarin, *see* Chinese
Markedness Model, *see* code-switching
Meeuwis, M., 51, 54
meta-communication, 80, 112, 137
MLA Ad Hoc Committee report, 38, 170, 171
monolingualism, 3-6, 10-15, 18-19, 34, 70, 127, 159
Murphey, T., 35, 69, 128, 130-131, 146
Muysken, P., 166
Myers-Scotton, C., xiv, 15, 49, 51-58, 60-62, 65, 103, 105, 139

Namibia, 155
Nassaji, H., 72
native speaker, xiv, 3, 10, 13-16, 21, 39, 153, 172
National Security Language Initiative, 170-171
Navajo, 154
New Guinea, 155
NSLI, *see* National Security Language Initiative
Nzwanga, M.A., 74, 77, 101

Obama, B., 171-172
observational chart metholodogy, 71, 75, 85-87, 89
Ohta, A.S., 24, 25
Olshtain, E., 64
opportunity sets, *see* code-switching
optimal L2 use, xiv, 6-8, 18, 70, 125, 127, 132, 137, 165, 169
Ortega, L., 12, 14, 23
Osborn, T.A., 4, 127-128, 130
Oyster, C., 148

parameter setting, 21, 22
Pennsylvania Dutch, 155
Persian, 141-142
Petraki, E., 72
Phipps, A., 102
pidgin languages, 18, 39
pidginization, 10, 15-16
Polio, C.G., 73-75, 77, 101, 103, 153
Polish, 154
Poplack, S., 49
President's Commission on Languages and International Studies, 171

principled heterogeneity, xv, 127-128, 160, 162, 168
– definition of, 127-128
prolepsis, 24, 32-33, 44
– definition of, 32-33
psycholinguistic approaches, 6, 22-23

Rabaul Creole German, 155
Rampton, B., 62, 81
Rational Choice Model, *see* code-switching
Reagan, T.G., 4, 127-128, 130
Rice, C., 170
Richard, Z., 156
Richards, J.C., 4
rights and obligations sets, *see* code-switching
Robbins, T., v, 20
Rodgers, T.S., 4
Romaine, S., 14

Savignon, S., 4
Saville-Troike, M., 85
scaffolding, *see* sociocultural theory
Schultz, J.M., 165
Schulz, R., 4
Scollon, R., 30, 36, 62-63, 66, 106, 160
Scollon, S.W., 30, 62, 160
SCT, *see* sociocultural theory
Seedhouse, P., 110
Simon, P., 12, 171
Smith, P., 15
social semiotic perspective, xiv, 28, 36
sociocognitive perspective, 25-26
sociocultural theory (SCT), xii-xiv, 9, 23-27, 40, 47, 63, 83, 169
– scaffolding, 15, 24-25, 80, 83, 110-111, 113, 115, 136
– tenets of, 24-25
– Zone of Proximal Development (ZPD), 24-25, 32, 44, 45
    definition of, 24
sociolinguistics, 15, 85
somatic markers, *see* code-switching
South Tirol, 155
Spada, N., 85
Spain, 58, 142
Spanish, 15, 18, 52-54, 58-61, 69, 72, 76, 80, 84, 87-98, 101, 105, 126, 140, 142-143, 154, 156
speech economies, 62
speech genres, 39, 63
Stetsenko, A., 24
strategic languages, 171
strategies instruction, xi, 16, 58, 131-132,
    134, 136-138, 164
Swain, M., 24-25, 79-80, 83, 97, 100-101, 110, 113, 137
Switzerland, 154-155
symbolic capital, 62
symbolic power, 60

Tabouret-Keller, A., 15, 26, 46
Terrell, T.D., xi, 71
Tharp, R.G., 24
third place, 36-41, 43, 45, 139-140, 170
– definition of, 39
Thompson, G.L., 72
Thorne, S.L., 9, 26
Tower of Babel, 19-22, 45, 171
transcription conventions, 66, 122
translation, 20, 39, 71
translingual/transcultural competence, 38-39, 61, 171
Trimbur, J., 10-12, 127
Tudor, I., 4, 10, 14, 33-36, 46, 128, 131-132, 161
Turkish, 141-142, 144, 155
Turnbull, M., 5, 71, 101

Unserdeutsch, *see* Rabaul Creole German
Urdu, 170

Valdman, A., 12, 15
van Lier, L., 4-5, 8-9, 21-22, 26-30, 32-34, 43-44, 48, 65, 97, 100, 110, 125, 147, 161
Verspoor, M., 30
vertical articulation, *see* articulation
Villamil, O.S., 24-25
Volker, C.A., 155
Vygotsky, L.S., 23-25, 27, 32, 36, 44, 70, 80, 110, 131

Wagner, J., 4
Walsh, S., 104-105, 110
Weinreich, M., 48, 66
Wenger, E., 5, 40-43, 46, 61, 125, 146-147, 161-162
Wing, B.H., 72-75, 77-79, 85, 101

Yiddish, 66
Young, R.F., 64, 104-105
Yu, B., 72, 101

Zentella, A.C., 15, 52, 54, 166
Zilles, K., 156
Zone of Proximal Development (ZPD), *see* sociocultural theory
ZPD, *see* sociocultural theory

For Product Safety Concerns and Information please contact our EU Authorised Representative:

Easy Access System Europe

Mustamäe tee 50

10621 Tallinn

Estonia

gpsr.requests@easproject.com